Yoga and Meditational Psychotherapy

Yoga and Meditational Psychotherapy

N.K. Singh

GLOBAL VISION PUBLISHING HOUSE
20, Ansari Road, Daryaganj, New Delhi-110002 (INDIA)

GLOBAL VISION PUBLISHING HOUSE
F-4, 1st Floor, 'Hari Sadan' 20, Ansari Road,
Daryaganj, New Delhi-110002 (INDIA)
Tel.: 23261581, 23276291, 43037885 Mob: 9810644769
Email: nsingh_2004@vsnl.net, info@globalvisionpub.com
Website: www.globalvisionpub.com

Yoga and Meditational Psychotherapy

First Edition 2012

ISBN: 978-81-8220-482-9

PRINTED IN INDIA

Published by Dr. N.K. Singh for Global Vision Publishing House, New Delhi-2 and *Printed at* Balaji Offset, Naveen Shahdara, Delhi-32.

Preface

The combination of yoga through physical exercise and meditation with breath awareness is a wonderful way to connect with the divine on all levels of human existence. Psychotherapy is based on the holistic view of body, mind and spirit. The attitude of the therapist is one of cooperation with the client. Together they set out on the journey to explore and understand where the symptoms or issues that the client brings to the sessions originate and what the person needs to regain his or her balance. The therapist takes sides with the healthy core and supports the person in his or her ability to connect with that core and listen to its messages.

The present book *Yoga and Meditational Psychotherapy* is a compilation of twenty one important research papers contributed by eminent scholars. This book is divided into three parts. First part includes twelve papers which deal with psycho-physiological parameters of yoga therapy. The main thrust of these papers are yoga psychotherapy and transcendental meditation; effect of yoga practice on personality and behaviour; yogic practices on psycho-physiological parameters; emotional and spiritual intelligence on psychological well being; impact of yoga therapy in management of anxiety, stress and negative mood regulation; impact of yogasanas on the mentally challenged; effects of meditation on HIV positive patients; the physiological impact of yogic package in diabetes mellitus patients; reducing anxiety through yogic practices; and the Samkhya, Yogic and Gita models of stress and coping.

Second part covers five papers which emphasises promotion, practice and research of yoga and health. These papers explain yoga and its relation with health; how combination of modern medicine and yoga can provide holistic health science; mental health management in yoga-sutra; efficacy of yoga in harmonious development of physical and psychological aspect of personality; and research in yoga as a holistic model of health.

Four papers have been included in third part which explains meditation psychotherapy and psychological wellbeing. These papers examine concepts, effects and uses of meditation psychotherapy; positive approach to psychological well-being in vipassana meditation; effect of vipassana meditation on good quality of life; and the effectiveness of occupational stress management through meditation.

I hope, this book will be one of the monumental works in theory, research and practices in yoga and meditational psychotherapy. I am thankful to all the contributors for their support.

About the Contributors

Abha Singh, Sr. Lecturer and Head of the Department, Department of Psychology, P.P.N. College, Kanpur-208001, U.P.

Amulya Khurana, Indian Institute of Technology, New Delhi-110016.

Anup Sud, Professor and Head, Department of Psychology, H.P.U. Shimla.

Awadhesh Upadhyay, Associate Professor in Department of Psychology, Udai Pratap Autonomous College, Varanasi.

B.S.S Mandal, Research Scholar, Andhra University, Visakhapatnam.

Bishamber Singh, Yoga Instructor, Department of Physical Education, Punjabi University, Patiala-147002.

C.B. Dwivedi, Professor, Department of Psychology, Banaras Hindu University, Varanasi.

Chandra Shekhar, Assistant Professor, P.G. Deptt. of Psychology, University of Jammu, Jammu (J&K).

Charu Sharma, Lecturer, Department of Human Consciousness & Yogic Science, Dev Sanskriti Vishwavidyalaya, Shantikunj, Gayatrikunj, Haridwar- 249411.

D.K. Diwan, Director, Sharvan Centre For Rehabilitation of Mentally Challenged Adult Persons And Institution of Special Education and Research, Rohtak.

D.V. Vonu Gopal, Research Scholar, Andhra University, Visakhapatnam.

Ganesh Shankar, Department of Human Consciousness and Yogic Science, University of Sagar, Sagar-470003 (M.P.).

K. Parimala, Research Scholar, Andhra University, Visakhapatnam.

K.M. Tripathi, P.G. in Clinical psychology, Dy. Director (Yoga) in Yoga Centre of the University.

Latha, Research Scientist "B", Department of Psychology, University of Madras (TN).

M.A. Bhardwaj, Department of Psychology L.V.H. College, Nasik.(Maharastra)

M.G. Sharma, Assistant Profesor of psychology, in Sri. Agrasen Kanya P.G. College and Hon. Director, S.I. Mental and Physical Health Society (SIMPHS) Varanasi.

Meenakshi Sharma, Reader and Head, Department of Psychology, G.N.D. University, Amritsar.

Mukesh Kumar, Special Educator, Sharvan Centre for Rehabilitation of Mentally Challenged Adult Persons and Institution of Special Education and Research, Rohtak.

O.P. Sharma, Assistant Professor, Department of Psychology, University of Rajasthan, Jaipur-04.

P. Sharma, Lecturer, L-7-D, University Campus, University of Rajasthan, Jaipur.

Prem Verma, Professor and Ex Head, Department of Psychology, Punjab University, Chandigarh.

R.K. Mishra, Yoga Centre, Department of Physical Education, University of Rajasthan, Jaipur-4 (Rajsthan).

Rita Bhalla, Reader, Department of Yoga, H.P.U., Shimla (H.P.).

Ritu Modi, Lecturer, Department of Psychology, P.P.N. College, Kanpur-208001, U.P.

S.K. Srivastava, Department of Psychology, Gurukul Kangri University, Haridwar, 12-A, Gangotri Street, Vishnu Garden, P.O.: Gurukul Kangri, Haridwar-249404.

Safia Akhtar, Research scholar, Deptt. of Psychology, University of Rajasthan, Jaipur. E-mail: akhtar.safia@gmail.com

Sunil Sharma, Research Scholar, Deptt. of Psychology, Gurukul Kangri University, Haridwar.

Sunita Gupta, Reader and Head, Department of Psychology, G.N.D. University, Amritsar.

Sunita Malhotra, Professor of Psychology, M.D. University, Rohtak.

Surendra Kumar Sia, Lecturer, Department of Psychology, Punjabi University, Patiala – 147002.

Sweta Maheshwari, Deptt. of Psychology, Gurukul Kangri Vishvavidayalay, Haridwar.

Uma Mittal, Assistant Professor, Deptt. of Psychology, University of Rajasthan, Jaipur. E-mail: mittaluma14@gmail.com

Zinnia Sethi, Research Scholar, Department of Psychology, Himanchal Pradesh University, Shimla (H.P.)

Contents

Part—III

Meditation Psychotherapy and Psychological Wellbeing

1

Introduction

Psychotherapy and Yoga practice share many of the same aims, such as promoting health and creating cognitive, behavioural, and emotional change. To meet these aims, they each promote introspection, self-awareness, self-acceptance, and connection. However, there are important differences in the two approaches, the most fundamental of which is the framework each uses to understand well-being and suffering.

Because the frameworks for psychotherapy and Yoga are different, the emphases, techniques, and practices also differ. The convergence of many of the aims and outcomes—most notably the promotion of health—is, therefore, quite remarkable. This article focuses on how psychotherapy and Yoga each facilitate (1) selfawareness and introspection, (2) behavioural change, (3) cognitive change and self-acceptance, and (4) connection.

Assumptions of Each Framework

Psychotherapy focuses on promoting health, relieving symptoms and difficulties, and increasing self-understanding. A 'Side effect' of therapy may include greater connection to self, others, and nature. In contrast, Yoga practice promotes the experience of union and the realization of universal, non-dualistic consciousness (*Samadhi*). 'Side effects' of the practice include healthy change and the experience of bliss (*ananda*).

Western psychological theory proposes that our troubles stem from a combination of genetic predispositions, life experience, stress, and cognitive and behavioural habits. In contrast, Yoga philosophy proposes that our difficulties are rooted in separation (which causes dissatisfaction and suffering), ignorance of our true nature, and our false identification with what we experience.

Self-awareness and Introspection

Psychotherapy

Psychotherapy develops introspection and self-awareness through the process of reflecting on, verbally identifying, and exploring one's feelings, thoughts, and behaviour. Psychotherapy may focus on a client's present feeling/thoughts (*e.g.*, 'What are you feeling now?'), and ways in which awareness appears to be limited or restricted. Therapy may encourage a client to reflect on what is healthy, on the client's goals, and on what impedes healthy choices and behaviours. It is assumed that such enhanced awareness will lead to healthy self-integration and change.

Yoga

Each of the eight limbs of Yoga leads to enhanced awareness. Through the *yamas* (restraints promoting ethical behaviour) and *niyamas* (observances of healthy attitudes), practitioners have the opportunity to reflect on their intentions, choices, actions, and greater purpose. The integration of *asana* (postures), *pranayama* (breathing practices), and *dharana* (concentration) enhances awareness of body, breath, mind, and their connections, The development of one-pointed focus through *pratyahara* (sense withdrawal) and *dharana* flows into *dhyana* (meditation). Through practices such as *asana* and meditation, Yoga teaches practitioners to be present to immediate experience. *Dhyana,* in turn, leads to the experience of higher states of consciousness and to the experience and to the experience of 'witness consciousness'. Ultimately, practitioners experience universal awareness, in which the distinction between subject and object (or knower and known) dissolves.

Are there limits to awareness

Like modern Western research psychologists, Yoga practitioners recognize that the ordinary (*i.e.*, untrained) mind is unable to accurately study itself. The untrained mind remains too much a part of what is being studied; it is swayed, overwhelmed, or caught up in its own thoughts. According to Yoga practitioners, however, meditation techniques gradually extend the mind's capacity for observing itself objectively, overcoming the limitations of untrained introspection.

As we have seen, psychotherapeutic practices count on introspection and self-reflection to develop awareness and promote health change. On the other hand, Western psychology postulates that there will always exist an indeterminate amount of unconscious material unavailable for introspection, making it difficult—if not impossible—for human beings to achieve a consciousness of the self. A frequent criticism of Western perspectives by Yoga practitioners is that Western psychology has limited its exploration and theorizing about levels of consciousness to a limited range of 'I-ness' (*ahankara*), referring only to personal identity and failing to involve transcendence of the ego.

In contrast, practitioners of Yoga believe that Yoga deals with levels of consciousness beyond the ego level, outlining a path for further development. Transcending 'average' awareness is, thus, an important goal in Yoga practice. To the extent that Western-based psychotherapy encourages self-actualization and the exploration of one's potential (most often seen in existential, humanistic, and transpersonal theories), such goals may also be promoted in psychotherapeutic treatment.

Such approaches may consider a client's search for meaning and purpose in the midst of apparent meaninglessness, isolation, helplessness, and hopelessness. They may recognize and acknowledge the varied levels of human experience, including the spiritual level and our connection to that which is beyond the individual self. Such therapeutic approaches may also take into account the context and relativity of experience, the integration of body-mind, the difficulties that arise when there are discrepancies between clients' ideal and true selves, and the healing experience of union of different aspects of self and consciousness.

Behavioural Change

Psychotherapy

Behavioural change is one of the central goals of psychotherapy. Many clients seek therapy in order to change behaviours that are not working for them. When a client is engaged in life-threatening self-injurious behaviour, treatment must initially focus on decreasing the behaviour and promoting safety. When a client is not a danger to self or others, therapy will, at some point, help the client to examine why he or she behaves in unhealthy or unsatisfying ways.

Behaviour theory specializes in explaining how both problematic behaviours and new healthy behaviours are learned and maintained. Therapy may involve reflection on the origins, meaning, or function of a behaviour, and the thoughts, emotions, and environmental factors that contribute to the behaviour.

Certain psychotherapeutic methods emphasize skills-building, such as communication skills, social skills, and parenting skills. Other orientations encourage 'experiments'—getting clients to try different things, particularly when what they have been doing has not been working or has stopped working. Psychotherapists have also appreciated the therapeutic benefits of relaxation for bahaviour change, developing techniques such as progressive relaxation, autogenic training, and biofeedback.

Yoga

Yoga psychology also recognizes that positive or negative habits. be they mental, physical, or energetic, are learned over time. For example, Yoga philosophy includes discussion of *samskaras* (impressions derived from past experiences in previous incarnations and/or in this lifetime that influence future responses and behaviour). Yoga uses the tools of *asana*, *pranayama*, and meditation to reshape habits of the body and mind. Such reshaping may occur via practices that target the physical body, releasing tension and calming the body, through breathing and concentration practices that affect body and mind, and through practices that increase focus and promote meditation (*e.g.*, *mantra* repetition, visualization, mindfulness).

Behaviour change is also encouraged through the *yamas* (restraints), which promote a commitment to ethical behaviour (*e.g.*, refraining from lying, stealing, violence towards self or others) and moderation (*e.g.*, eating until you are satisfied, eating in a way that is healthy for one's body), and through *karma* Yoga, which encourages service to others.

Cognitive Change and Self-acceptance

Psychotherapy

Many psychotherapeutic approaches focus on creating cognitive change—in other words, helping people think differently. This includes how clients think about themselves. Some approaches actively challenge 'faulty' cognitions through 'cognitive restructuring', or through problem-solving or coping skills training. Some types of therapy may focus on unresolved issues, including automatic ways of negatively perceiving, interpreting, or reacting to events.

Therapy may also highlight the emotional impact of one's thought patterns. Clients may be encouraged to see how a pattern of thinking developed and became generalized as a response to a given situation or as a creative adaptation to a past situation. This cognitive pattern from the past, although adaptive or necessary for the client's survival at the time, may be problematic or maladaptive in current environments. Therapy, through cognitive change, seeks to alter these patterns of thinking to allow clients to experience, react to, and adjust to present circumstances.

The psychotherapeutic relationship, via the acceptance and understanding of the therapist, also becomes a model for self-understanding and kindness towards oneself. The therapist, through empathy, othen aims to create a safe 'holding environment', in which clients can work on their issues, develop insight, and promote change while remaining compassionate towards themselves.

Yoga

Yoga instructors also aim to create environments in which practitioners can compassionately and non-judgmentally observe thoughts and emotions that surface during the practice. While Yoga and meditation can be seen as more passive or organic—perhaps less forceful—ways to support cognitive change than certain psychotherapeutic techniques, both psychotherapy and Yoga encourage self-reflection, self-acceptance, and transformation.

Yoga is based on a number of principles that support self acceptance. For example, Yoga philosophy maintains that we are just right as we are, and that we have forgotten this over time. While promoting the experience of union as our natural state, Yoga helps practitioners question fals, illusory identifications with our perceptions, beliefs, and patterns.

Yoga also helps practitioners learn to be present to and cope with anxiety, tension, anger, negative memories, and conflicts. The practices of *asana,pranayama*, concentration, and meditation often assist practitioners in becoming aware of distractions, strengthening focus and mental clarity, and, ultimately, reducing distractions. Through the *niyamas* (observances), Yoga helps practitioners cultivate and strengthen other healthy attitudes such as mindfulness, generosity, equanimity, simplicity, calm, and joy.

There is also a Yogic assumption that we are different from our thoughts. The mind is filled with continually changing thoughts, images, internal commentary, and fantasies. Yogis believe that it is possible to observe thoughts, if one cultivates the ability to disidentify from them. Although practitioners often initially experience their identity as a stream of thoughts, emotions, and urges, one eventually witnesses the stream of consciousness. Such observation of and separation from the cognitive process naturally leads to cognitive transformation.

Integrating Approaches to Cognitive Change

The combination of Yoga and psychotherapeutic practices may be particularly potent for clients who have more difficulty expressing themselves—and healing—through talk therapy. We are beings with bodies and experiences that are sometimes difficult to describe through language. Emotions and sensations may also be embodied in physical experiences. Clients may be blocked or struggling with powerful physical reactions and memories, such as those evoked by trauma, eating disorders, anxiety, or medical concerns. Physical, Yoga-based work may assist specific therapeutic goals, such as helping clients feel more comfortable in and accepting of their bodies, as well as helping clients who have problematic reactions to their bodies and bodily functions.

Connection

Psychotherapy

The various psychotherapeutic orientations place different degrees of emphasis and importance on connection. At some level, however, all psychotherapies recognize connection and the role this plays in treatment.

All psychotherapeutic orientations acknowledge that we are social, that wc arc affcctcd by our environment and culture, and that we affect and are affected by others. All psychotherapies also recognize the central importance of the client-therapist relationship and its effect on treatment. In fact, the therapeutic relationship has been identified as a key, perhaps the key, factor in healing. Therapists are trained to consider the interpersonal dynamics of therapy. For example, therapists are often aware of the effect of their 'expert' role and knowledge on clients. Furthermore, most modern psychotherapeutic approaches acknowledge the link between mind and body, as well as the connection between thoughts, emotions, and behaviour.

Yoga

Yoga, as a practice and experience of union, can be seen as a philosophy and practice of connection, as an individual develops a sense of internal relatedness and relationship to other people, other beings, the environment, and the universe. An individual develops a sense of connection to him- or herself through Yoga, becoming aware of the links between mind, body, breath, feelings, memories, experiences, health, and states of consciousness. In observing these internal connections one develops greater understanding of the self, others, and relationships. Yoga not only promotes the experience that all beings all interrelated, but the ultimate experience of direct realization of the Self, the reunion of the individual self (*jiva*) with the Absolute or pure consciousness (*Brahman*). Yoga refers to 'any method by which an individual human being is brought into union with God, with reality, with the ground of being, or with source." The techniques of Yoga aim to uncover and highlight these connections.

Psychotherapy and Yoga practice can be seen as complementary practices. Because both promote introspection and self-awareness in different ways, the combination of both practices may enhance inner work. Both practices attempt to resolve splits (*e.g.*, the mind-body split) in order to promote a healthy, integrated self. As we have seen above, both approaches also promote behavioural, cognitive, and emotional change. Both aim to help clients more clearly experience the present. Yoga and psychotherapy both focus on promoting a sense and experience of connection.

However, the differences between Yoga and psychotherapy also suggest that each approach has distinct assets and limitations. Psychotherapy, for example, tends to encompass a more historical focus, using the past to reflect on the present, whereas Yoga tends to focus more on the here-and-now of immediate experience. In certain cases, psychotherapy may advance cognitive change more quickly than Yoga through its direct challenge to long-standing, automatic, or unchallenged patterns of thinking.

On the other hand, reflection on the past may, from a Yogic perspective, be viewed as leading to continued misidentification with *samskaras* and illusions if it mistakenly encourages dwelling on the past rather than more clearly seeing and experiencing reality. Furthermore, one could argue that Yoga places greater emphasis than many psychotherapeutic orientations on both intrapsychic connection and universal connection, and less emphasis on interpersonal connection and improving contact between people.

Yoga practice is not a substitute for professional psychological or psychiatric care, which may first be needed to stabilize and alleviate some clients' distress or self-destructive patterns. Nonetheless, given the complementary and distinct benefits of each approach, an integrated therapy, adapted to an individual's needs, has the potential to be uniquely effective. For some individuals, Yoga practices may enhance the benefits of traditional psychological interventions. Others may find that psychotherapy deepens the Yoga practice, promoting greater insight and integration.

REFERENCES

Cope, S. (1999). *Yoga and the Quest for the True Self.* New York: Bantam Books. p. 311.

Rama, S., Ballentine, R., & Ajaya, S. (1976). *Yoga and Psychotherapy: The Evolution of Consciousness.* Honesdale, PA: Himalayan International Institute of Yoga Science and Philosophy.

Sivananda Yoga Center. (2000). *The Sivananda Companion to Yoga.* New York: Fireside.

Winnicott, D. (1960). The theory of the parent-child relationship. *International Journal of Psychoanalysis, 41*, 585-595.

●●●

Part—I
Yoga Psychotherapy: Psychophysiological Parameters

- Yoga Psychotherapy Around the World
- Effect of Yoga Practice on Personality, Emotional and Behavioural Problems
- Effect of Yogic Practices on Psychological and Physiological Parameters
- Effect of Emotional and Spiritual Intelligence on Psychological Well-being in Long Term Yoga Practitioners
- Efficacy of Yoga Therapy for the Management of Anxiety, Stress, Negative Mood Regulation and Self-Esteem of Female Adolescents
- Impact of Yogasana on the Mentally Challenged: An Observation
- Psycho-physiological Responsiveness to Meditation in HIV Positive Patients
- Effect of Yogic Package on the Patients of Diabetes Mellitus
- Yoga and Psychophysiological Disorders
- Reducing Anxiety through Yogic Practices
- The Samkhya, Yogic and Gita Models of Stress and Coping

2

Yoga Psychotherapy Around the World

Ganesh Shankar

Throughout Yoga's long history, there have been many misconceptions which shrouded it in mystery until proper scientific research began in the beginning of 20th century. In India, people became aware of the need to revive old traditions and sciences which might otherwise die out and scientific research into Yoga was one of the areas which generated a lot of interest. Many western scholars too realized the utility of Yoga and made efforts to study its significance from scientific point of view. They made some longitudinal studies in this area and their research findings are available to us for further work in this area (Kuvalyananda, 1925, 1928; Behanan, K.T., 1937; Bagchi, B.K.& Wenger, M.A. 1957; Hirai. T, 1960; de Vries, H.A. 1961; Giri, C, 1966; Wallace, R.K. 1970; Joseph C and et al, 1987; Meti, B.L. and et al, 1989; Joseph, S and et al, 1993; Meti, B.L. 1995). Swami Kuvalyananda reported sub-atmospheric pressure in the various internal cavities during Uddian Bandha and its extension of Nauli. He also took X rays to demonstrate the movements of the diaphragm during Uddiyana Bandha. A pupil of his, Behanana, undertook further research leading to a doctoral thesis of Yale University in 1937. He estimated the oxygen consumption during Pranayama practice and reported an increase during Ujjai, Bhastrika and Kapapbhati. He also brought different types of Pranayama on to kymographic record. The ability of Yogis to voluntarily stop the beating of the heart was considered-a fascinating feat, and aroused the interest of scientists in India and elsewhere.

In 1936 an article by the French cardiologist, Brosse, reported studies on subjects of both Hatha and Raj Yoga, the former showing the more significant results. Bagchi and Wenger (1957) studied practitioners of RajYoga in India. They found a lower respiratory rate and raised G.S.R (Galvanic Skin Resistance) with no consistent alterations in heart rate or blood pressure during meditation. During Meditation, the EEG showed an increase in alpha wave amplitude and activity and in some of the Yogis there was a loss of the alpha blocking response to all external stimuli. Around 1960, Maharishi Mahesh Yogi introduced Transcendental Meditation to the world. This technique is neither a religion nor a way of life. It is a natural effortless technique, which aims at improving all aspects of life.

Adapted from ancient Indian technique, it gained in popularity and has spread all over the world. In 1968, R.K.Wallace undertook an investigation of physiological effects of TM, for his doctoral thesis, entitled, "The physiological effects of TM: A proposed fourth major state of consciousness". In this as well as in later studies by him (Wallace et al,1971) the practice of TM was found to be associated with changes in the EEG. In some of the subjects during Meditation, there was an increase in alpha wave amplitude, associated with a slowing of the frequency. In some cases, there were brief periods of about 2.5. seconds during which theta waves predominated. There was also an increase in GSR, decrease in heart rate, decrease in oxygen consumption and carbondioxide elimination, along with a reduction in both rate and volume of respiration. Blood lactate levels were also reduced after Meditation. This led to TM being called a "Wakeful Hypometabolic State". The changes were interpreted a signs of a functional trophotropic state, chiefly mediated by increased parasympathetic and decreased sympathetic discharge, rather like other assimilatory processes such as sleep and digestion. Kasamatsu (1973) categorised the EEG changes in Zen meditation as four stages. The first is the appearance of alpha rhythm in spite of the eyes being open. In the second stage, there is an increase in amplitude of persistent alpha frequency and finally, in the fourth stage the appearance of rhythmic theta train was observed. During the last 3-6 decades, the Hatha Yogic practices have been evaluated for their efficacy in the management of diabetes and found useful (Udupa & Singh, 1972; Malkote, 1973; Sahay, 1986; Gore, 1988).

One may wonder how Yoga can effect all these responses. The practice of Asanas may send a volley of nerve impulses from muscles and joints, spine and other receptors located on the surface as well as inside the viscera. It can influence the haemodynamic mechanism improving blood circulation to vital organs like brain, heart, lungs, liver, kidney, pancreas etc. it may also act through the neuro-endocrine axis. Scientists like Anand, B.K. (1961) strongly feel that Yogic practices may modulate the cerebral corticolimbic system of the brain and strengthen the inhibitory components of the nervous system. More documentary evidences are required to consolidate these claims and assumptions. Whatever be the mechanism involved, it is established beyond doubt that regular practice of Yoga certainly has many beneficial effects on the human physiology, biochemistry and psychology.

It is true that Yoga is ancient. Infact, its origin is shrouded in antiquity. No one really knows when Yoga was first developed or who gave it to man. There are many historical conjectures which even suggest that the Gods themselves taught Yoga to man. The fact is that Yogic practices were unknown even in the Vedic times, and references to Yoga abound in the Vedas, in particular the Rig - Veda, and in the Upanishads and Bhagawad Gita. That they only prove how ancient Yoga is and consequently how much they evolved it, is the growth of Indian culture. Indian Rishis of old, recognised the unalterable fact of life, namely that man is not a mere body, not a mere mind, but a bodymind complex in which one reacts on the other end in which one can not be separated from each other. No modern educationist or thinker could possibly disagree with such a comprehensive view of man. Yoga even emphasizes that mind influences the body more than the body influences the mind. The knowledge of Yogic practices was handed down through the ages from generation to generation by word of mouth and by example through unbroken chain of devoted Guru- Chela relationship untill around 200 years before the Christian era or over 2000 years age, Patanjali, the founder of what is known as classic Yoga or Patanjala Yoga first systematised and codified the then existing knowledge of Yoga into 194 aphorism or sayings and gave it to the world the Yoga sutras. The Yoga system of Patanjali which is also known as Raj Yoga, is a world view, a way of life and a set of practices for regulation of mind to achieve the highest goal of Yoga *i.e.* Kaivalya. The celebrated text, Yoga sutra of Patanjali virtually presents a psychological system. Gardner Murphy once remarked that the systematic development of Yoga by Patanjali "constitute one of the great psychological achievements of all times"(Murphy & Murphy,1968).

Patanjali has prescribed an eight fold path for achieving the goal of Kaivalya. Ashtanga Yoga involves: Yama (restraints), Niyama (discipline), Asana (body attitude/postures), Pranayama (breath regulation), Pratyhara (detachment of sensory activity from the external objects), Dharana (concentration), Dhyana (Yogic Meditation) and Samadhi (spiritual absorption). Patanjali describes the first five limbs as the external form of Yoga and that they are preparatory, the last three as internal and essential aspects. The foundations of Yoga practice lie in Abhyasa (practice) and Vairagya (detachment). The Yamas are : Ahimsa (non-injury), Satya (non-lying), Asteya (non-stealing), Brahamacharya (sexual abstinence) Aparigraha (non-posession). The Niyamas are : sauch (cleanliness), Santosh (contentment), Tapas (asceticism), Swadhyaya (self study) and Ishwarpranidhan (devotion to God). Asana is a body posture that is stable and comfortable. Patanjali devotes only one verse to it. The important point about asana is that it gives the body stability reducing physical effort to a minimum which may be distraction to meditation. Pranayama is a discipline of respiration. Patanjali devotes only three verses to it. It is the arrest of the movement of inhalation and exhalation which is practised after mastering the asana. Pratyahara, the withdrawl senses from external objects is the final stage of the external Yoga. The core of Yoga practice lies in Dharana (concentration), Dhyana (Yogic meditation) and Samadhi (absorption). Concentration involves attention to a single object or place, external or internal, like a lamp, the space between the eye brows, the tip of the nose or thought (like God or mantra). The continuous concentration is called Ekagrata (on a single point). When the mind flows towards the object of concentration uninterruptedly and effortlessly, it is the stage of meditation when it happens for a prolonged period of time, it leads to Samadhi. Samadhi is a state of absorption in which the subject/object distinction is lost. The state of Samadhi is believed to be characterised by the comprehension of the true nature of reality which ultimately emancipates the individual. A variety of stages in Samadhi have been described by Patanjali. In modern times, the meditative practices like Trancendental Meditation (T.M. of Mahesh Yogi, 1963), Benson,s technique (Benson,1975) and Carrington,s clininically standardized Meditation (Carrignton, 1977) among others are based on the system of Patanjali.

Hatha Yoga

Techniques of Yoga have been practised for thousands of years mainly for the sake of the final goal of liberation from the cycle of rebirths and the pain associated with it. These techniques were intended to influence the mind more than the body. With the Hathayogis who flourished in comparatively later times in the history of Yoga (may be about the 15th century A.D.), there was greater emphasis on the body. Their ultimate aim was also the same namely, attainment of the state of Samadhi. But their means were more suited to the abilities of the common man. Gorksha Shataka of Gorakhnath (Briggs, 1973) of 10th century A.D.; Gherands Samhita of 12th century (Vasu, 1974), Hatha Yoga Pradipika of Swatmarama (Brahmanda, 1989) of 15th century are three important texts of Hatha Yoga school. Hatha Yoga as a holistic system does not consists of mere Kriyas, Asanas, Pranayamas, Bandhas, Mudras and Meditation etc. but lays great stress on control of diet social attitude and personal habits so as to bring about beneficial changes in the whole of the metabolic process. It is truly a integrated approach, treating man as a whole (Kuvalyananda & Vinekar, 1971).

Asana

These are certain special pattern of postures that stabilizes the mind and body. Their aim is to establish proper rhythm in the neromuscular tonic impulses and to improve the general tone of the muscles. Asana, as a preventive medicine can be used for avoiding the causation of postural deformities like cervical spondylosis (by Bhujanga/ Dhanura/Matsya/ Ustrasana etc.), lordosis (Hala/ Pawanmukta/ Paschimottan asana etc.). Asanas can be used for release of physical stress resulted from day-today negative emotions of behavioural pattern. This will help to avoid psychosomatic or psychological disorders like hypertension, gastric acidity, depression neurosis etc. The regular correct practice of Asanas also help to prevent constipation, arthritis, asthma, diabetes, obesity etc.

Pranayama

These are practices to control respiratory impulses which form one of the main channels of the flow of the autonomic nerve currents. Pranayama have important role in prevention of the diseases. The various diseases caused by disturbed homeostatic state of autonomic nervous system like obesity, hypertension, hyperthyirodism, diabetes, gastric acidity etc. can be prevented by Nadishodhan Pranayama, Bhastrika Pranayama etc. The imbalaced state of Doshas caused Suryabhedan and Bhastrika Pranayamas. The intensity of psychosomatic ailments can be prevented by restoring the normal rhythmic breathing.

Bandhas and Mudras

In these practices one tries to consciously control certain semi-voluntary and involuntary muscles in the body. These influence the activity of the autonomic nervous system which functions as a whole. These tone up the internal organs, decongest them and stimulate their healthy functioning.

Shatakarma

These are purificatory processes usually classified into six divisions, each of which consists of many sub-sections. They bring in control over the autonomic nervous system. Neti is an important means to develop resistance against environmental offending factors like temperature, dust, pollen grains, humidity and other particles to prevent the respiratory disorder, for example, the Neti in the evening by the labourer working at flour mills, cotton textiles mills mines, dusty roads, harvesting rains in the fields, libraries etc. can wash out the inhaled particles and thereby preventing their decay and decomposition in nasal passage and Pharynz for viral and bacterial infection. The use of neti helps also in development of resistance against seasonal change by using water of different temperature in Neti lota during the period of change of season as it would increase the adaptability of inner lining of nasal passage for vaso-constriction and dilution in response to temperature variation of environment. Similarly, one can prevent digestive disorders by the use of Shankhprakhshalana at time of start of new season, Basti once in a month, daily practice of Nauli etc. in case of dyspepsia, the Vaman Dhouti/Vyaghra Dhoti will be useful to prevent intensity of digestive disorder. The regular practice of Tratak and Kapalbhati can be used to prevent the eye and respiratory disorders respectively.

Meditation

It involves mental practice from initial withdrawal of the senses to the complete oblivion of the external environment. There are innumerable states and practices which could be included under this head. Meditation is a great tranquilliser. The regular practice of meditation by any of the various techniques, the inherent defence mechanism to fight with external physical, mental, emotional and environmental factors for causation of diseases can be developed. The meditation provides physical and mental resting pause to restore and revitalize the bodily organs for their normal functioning. Meditation practices have been widely used to counteract the day-today stress and strains of modern life. Therefore, the Meditation can be used for prevention of psychological and psychosomatic disorders like depression anxiety, neurosis, hypertension, asthma, arthritis, angina etc.

Swara Yogic and Dietary Norms

Various norms of SwaraYoga and Yoga dietetics also helps in prevention of diseases. Some important norms are :

- The moderation of diet, intake of meal during Surya Swara, observance of sequence while taking food; viz. Sweet articles taken firstly, sour and saline in middle and pungent and astringent lastly; helps in digestion avoids causation of digestive disorder. Taking water after ½ to ¾ hrs of meals, avoiding sweet dishes at the end of meals, taking hot potency articles during Chandra Swara and cold potency articles in Surya Swara also prevents the causation of disease in respect of digestive disorders, respiratory disorders etc.
- Sleeping by keeping the head in geographical south direction and lying on left side of the body helps to maintain health and prevents the causation of cardiovascular ailments especially.
- Taking bath during the Surya Swara also prevents the causation of common colds, digestive disorders arthritis etc. Avoidig the intake of betel during Surya Swara prevents the diseases of bile's and pitta Doshas like hypertension, acidity etc.

Indian tradition, Scientific research and clinical experience all point out that Yoga practices are probably the most important and effective self-help tools available to man. It appears that the Indian practitioners of psychotherapy, who have been looking for a conceptual framework and a set of procedures which are not alien but intimate to the Indian mind would definitely find an alternative in Yoga. The importance of Yoga is coming into light in the west in the comparative analysis of different systems by psychologists to find out meaningful answers to some problems of life. We seem to be very close to a behaviour technology and self reliance in the domain of Yoga. The main principle of Yoga therapy is that it seems to establish the homeostasis in the organism as a whole. As yet, however, it has not been established exactly how this is accomplished. But when proper investigation along scientific lines has been set up in several places throughout the world, Yoga therapy will be properly recognized as a valid form of treatment. The doors of Yoga therapy have already been knocked and opened up. Only earnest research and therapeutic pursuits by scientists and clinicians may perfect the ages old Yoga and make it more and more refined and suitable to people all over the world.

REFERENCES

Ajaya, Swami (1984). *Psychotherapy East & West: A unifying paradigm*, Honesdale: Himalayan International Institute of Yoga, Science and Philosophy.

Akhilanad, S. (1952). *Mental health and Hindu psychology*, London:George Allen & Unwin.

Ananda, B.K. and Chinna, G.S. (1961). Investigations on Yogies claiming to stop their heart beats. *Ind. J. Med. Res.*, 49.1. Jan. 82-94.

Bagchi, B.K. (1936). Mental hygiene and Hindu doctrine of relaxation. *Mental Hygiene*, 20, 424-440.

Bagchi, B.K. and Wnger, M.A. (1957). Electrophysiological correlates of some yogic exercises. *Electroencephaclin Neurophysol.*, 7, 132-149.

Behanan, K.T. (1937). *Yoga: A scientific evaluation*, Dover Publications New York.

Benson, H. (1975). *The relaxation response*, New York. Mc.Millian

Bhaba, Brahmananda (Tr.) (1989). *HathaYogapradipika*. Sacred Books of Hinds, Bombay.

Briggs, G.W. (ed. & Tr.) (1973). *Gorakhnath and the Kanphata Yogis*, Motilal Banarsidas, Delhi.

Carrington, P. (1977). *Freedom in meditation*. Doubleday, Garden city, New York.

Coster, G. (1934). *Yoga and western psychology: A comparison*; Oxford University Press, London.

Dasgupta, S.(1975). *A histroy of Indian philosophy*. Vol.2.Delhi: Motilal Banarsidas.

De Vries, Herbert (1961). Prevention muscular distress after exercise. *Research Qr.*, 32:32; 177-185.

Deatherage, G. (1975). Clinical use of mindfulness meditation technique in shor term psychotherapy. *Journal of Transpersonal psychology*, 7, 133-143.

Eagan, G. (1982). *The skilled helper*. Monterey:Brooks/cole Publishing Company.

Eliade, M. (1969). *Yoga: Immortality and freedom*. Princeton: Princeton University Press.

Engler, J. (1984). Therapeutic aims in psychotherapy and meditation:Developmental stages in the representation of self. *Journal of Transpersonal Psychology*, 16, 25-61.

Frankl, V.E. (1975). *The unconscious god: Psychotherapy and theology*. New York :Simon & Schuster

Freud, S. (1961). *The future of an illusion*. New York: Double day.

Garbe, R. (Ed. & Tr.) (1985). *Samkhya-pravachna sutra*, Cambridge, Harvard.

Giri, C. (1966). Yoga and physical fitness with special reference to atheletes. *IATHPER Qr. Jour.*, 2:6.

Goleman, D. (1971). Meditation as meta therapy: Hypothesis towards a proposed 5th state of consciousness, *Journal of Transpersonal Psychology*", 31, 1-26.

Gore, M.M. (1987). *Anatomy and physiology of yogic practices*, Kanchan Prakashan, Kaivalyadhama, Lonavla, India.

Harver, R. J. (1976). Behaviour therapy and Yoga. In Swami Ajay (Ed.), *Psychology East and West* (pp.50-75). Honesdale: The Himalayan International Institute of Yoga Science and Philosophy.

Harver, R.J. (1980). Behavioural principles cast in the non reductionastic context of classical Yoga psychology. Paper presented at the Annual convention of the American Psychological Association, Montreal, Canada.

Hirai, T. (1960). Electroencephalographic study on Zen meditation. *Folia Psychatr Neurol*, Japan, 62: 76-105.

Horney, K. (1937). *Neurotic personality of our times*, Norton, New York.

Joseph C, Shankar, Ram, A. Kulkarni, D.D. Ramchandra T. (1987). Post meditational effects of brankmkumari (BK) and transcendental meditation ™ on computer averaged event related evoked potential components recorded in the P 300 congnitive paradigm. *Ind. J. Physiol. Pharmac.*, Vol. 31; 5 pp 49.

Joseph, S, Sridharan, K., Patil, S.K.B., Kumar, M.L, Selwamurthy, W.Joseph, N.T. and Nayen, H.S. (1981). Study of some physioligical and biochemical parameters in subjects undergoing yogic training. *Ind. Jour. Of Med. Res.*, 14: 120-124.

Kasamatsu, A and Hirai T. (1960). "An electroencephalographic study on zen meditation : In Altered states of consciousness. Tart, C. (Ed.) John Wiley and sons, New York.

Krishna Rao P.V. (1995). Yoga : its scientific and applied aspect. *Jour. of Indian Psychology*, 13:2; 1-11.

Kuppuswamy, B. (1985). *Elements of ancient Indian psychology*. New Delhi:Vani Educational Books.

Kuvalyananda, Swami and Vinekar, S.L. (1963). Yogic Therapy. Central Health Education Bureau, Ministry of Health, Govt. of India, New Delhi.

Melkote, G.S. (1973). Concise report of work done at Yoga research Institute, Hyderabad, Presented at first scientific seminar, CCRIMH, New Delhi.

Meti, B.L. (1995). Sleep pattern abnormality in dysthnic syndrome. Abstract, ANCIPS, Patana, 36.

Murphy, G. & Murphy, L.B. (Eds.) (1968). *Asian Psychology*, Basic Books, New York.

Nuernberber P. (1976). Yoga encounter groups. In Swami Ajay (Ed.), *Psychology East and West*. (pp.75-102). Honesdale : The Himalalyan International Institute of Yoga Science and Philosophy

Nurenberger, P. (1986). Mind meditation and emotion, In Ballentine, R.M. (ed), *The theory and practice of meditation* (pp 67-89) honesdale, Pennsylvania: Himalyan International Institute.

Ram, Swami, Ballentine, R & Ajay, Swami (1976). *Yoga and psychotherapy: The evolution of consciousness*. Honesdale: The Himalyan International Institute of Yoga and philosophy.

Sahay, B.K.Sitaram Raju et al (1986). Glucose and Insulin levels in obese non-diabetics. *JAPI* Vol.34:6.

Satyananda, D. (1972). Dynamic psychology of the Gita of Hinduism. New Delhi: Oxford & I B H.

Singh, H.G. (1977). Psychotherapy in India. Agra: National psychological corporation.

Tart,C.T.& Deikman, A.J. (1991). Mindfulness, spiritual seeking and psychotherapy. *Journal of Transpersonal Psychology*, 23 (1), 29-52.

Vasu, Sris, Chandra (Tr.) (1914). *Gheranda- Samhita*, Allahabad, Sacred Books of Hindus.

Vaughan, F.(1991). Spiritual issues in psychotherapy. *Journal of Transpersonal Psychology*, 23 (23), 105-121.

Vijaylakshi, S, Vindhya Sudhakar, U. & Kalpana Rao, V. (1986). Role of a conselor in the Indian context. *Journal of Indian Psychology*, 5, 76-82.

Wallace, K.W and H. Benson (1972). The physiology of meditation. *Scientific American*, 226, 846.

Wallace, R.K. (1970). Physiological effects of transcendental meditation, *Science*, 167, 1751.

Werner, K. (1977). *Yoga and Indian philosophy*. Delhi: Motilal Banarsidass

Woods, J.H. (Ed & Tr.) (1924). *The Yoga system of Patanjali*, Harvard Cambridge.

Yogi Mahesh (1963). *Transcendental meditation*, New American library, New York.

●●●

3

Effect of Yoga Practice on Personality, Emotional and Behavioural Problems

D.V. Venu Gopal, B.S.S. Mandal and K. Parimala

The present study investigates the effect of yoga practice on personality dimensions and mental health problems. For this purpose, a group of yoga practitioners (n=51, male=33, mean age=29.16 years) was compared with a group of non-practitioners (n=54, male=29, mean age=36.59 years) on measures of personality and mental health problems. Vedic personality Inventory (VPI), developed by Wolf (1998), was used to measure personality in terms of Sattva, Rajas and Tamas and Adult self Report (ASR), a behavioural check list developed by Achenbach & Rescorla (2003) was used to measure mental health problems in the sample. Results indicated that compared to non-practitioners yoga practitioners were significantly high on *sattva* aspect of personality and low on *rajas* and *tamas* aspects of personality. Further, yoga practitioners were found to be significantly low on six out of eight emotional and behavioural problems measured by the ASR.. They are Anxious/ Depressed, Somatic, Aggressive, Attention, Rule-breaking and Intrusive behaviours. It was also found that sattva guna was negatively related to emotional and behavioural problems while *rajas* and *tamas* were positively related to. The findings of this study indicate the role of yoga in nurturing sattva aspect of personality which can be a resilient factor against psychological problems.

The present age is an age of swift change in every aspect of life. There occurred tremendous changes in science in the last 100 years which made life rather complex and challenging. It necessitates the need to learn to adapt to these changes in order to have a productive and satisfying life. Often these changes are so demanding that individuals fail to adapt and become vulnerable to psychological distress. This is the case even with those who are perceived as better adjusted. It seems that we need to have a kind of life support system in our daily lives which will better protect us from the negative emotional effects of life's unprecedented challenges. Western psychotherapeutic system, as it is still struggling to find its place in India, may not cater to this need effectively. Moreover, there has been an increased skepticism regarding the applicability of western approaches for understanding the psychology of indigenous people (Gergen, Gulerce, Lock & Misra, 1996). It is often argued that psychological data and theories emanated from developed western countries have little or no relevance to the conditions of developing countries.

This need to study the psychology of the native people from their own cultural perspective stimulated the Indian scholars to look back into their cultural roots and they have found a rich fountain of knowledge available to study human psychology in the form of ancient Indian literature (the *Vedas* and the *Bhagavat Gita, Yoga Sutras* etc). In this context, Yoga, an ancient life style system, seem to be the most promising approach to promote mental health among the common people. With its religio-philosophical richness it can be readily accepted by the common folk.

Yoga is both philosophy and practice. It provides a conceptual outlook towards life. On one hand it views life essentially as suffering and, on the other hand, it provides a set of practices which help the individual to overcome this suffering in life. Yoga, an ancient holistic life style system has attracted the attention of researchers as early as 1930s. Pioneering studies on yoga were carried out by Behanan and Brosse (Rao, 1995). This was followed by an upsurge in research on the influence of yoga and meditation practices on various cognitive and physiological variables. For example, Sridevi, Sitamma & Rao (1998) studied the effect of yoga training on school students' cognitive abilities. They found that fluid intelligence, abstract thinking and memory were increased after yoga practice. Padmasri & Telles (2007) found that yogic breathing would significantly reduce the frontalis muscle contraction.

Effect of yoga on emotional functioning is of special interest to researchers as there is an attempt to develop yoga system as an indigenous psychotherapeutic system. A number of studies have emerged to suggest the positive effects of yogic practices on psychological/emotional functioning (Narayana & Gopal, 2008; Basyal, 2002; Bhushan, 20007). In a study, Ahmad, Ahmad & Sumboo (1988) compared meditators with non meditators and found that meditators showed better adjustment and personality integration. Triveni and Aminabhavi (1999) found that yoga practitioners as compared to non-practitioners showed significantly lower levels of neuroticism, depression and anxiety. Sudha, Jyotsna, Sumita & Nalini (2006) found that yoga practitioners compared to their non practitioner counterparts showed significant decrease in psychological distress.

Triguna Theory of Personality

The philosophy of yoga postulates that human personality is a dynamic interaction of the three *gunas* (qualities), namely *Sattva, Rajas* and *Tamas*. Predominance of a particular *guna* determines the individual's personality characteristics. Thus, personality is classified as *sattvic, rajasic* and *tamasic*. When *sattva* is predominant the intellect works steadily. *The Bhagavat Gita* gives a detailed description of *sattvic* personality. It includes characteristics such as fearlessness, purity of heart, control over senses, truthfulness, absence of anger, renunciation, peacefulness, compassion towards other beings and absence of fickleness. A person with *sattvic* nature remains at peace. Persons with the predominance of *rajas* act with great effort to satisfy their desires. They are described as being sensuous, thirsty, little interest in spiritual pursuit, hatred, jealous, imitative, passionate, anxious, industrious etc. When *tamas* predominates, the individual becomes ignorant, lethargic and delusional. *Tamasics* are described as destructive, drowsy, angry, fearful, slothful etc. In an ideal state, rajas and *tamas* operate at optimal subordinate levels to *sattva* because in day to day life one cannot totally be devoid of them.

Trigunas and Psychological Problems

As the three *gunas* account for a wide range of characteristics and behaviours, they are also account for the rise of psychological problems. Caraka and Suœruta, two ancient Indian scholars, opined that *tamasic,* followed by *rajasic*, personality is predisposed to psychological maladies while *sattvic*, being pure, is free from these problems.

Though the ancient texts describe the relation of *trigunas* with psychological problems, only a few studies have examined this relationship. Mohan and Sandhu (1988) reported a positive correlation between *tamas* and psychoticism and a negative correlation between *sattva* and psychoticism and neuroticism. More recently Das & Gopal (in press) studied the relationship between *trigunas* and emotional and behavioural problems. They found that *sattva* was negatively correlated with emotional and behavioural problems while *rajas* and *tamas* were positively associated, with *tamas* having stronger correlations.

Though yoga is getting increased attention from the researchers there are not many studies on the influence of yoga on *trigunas* and the relation between *trigunas* and mental health problems. In this context, the present study investigates the effect of yoga practice on personality transformation and psychological problems.

Objectives

1. To study the effect of yoga practice on personality transformation.
2. To study the effect of yoga practice on emotional and behavioural problems.
3. To examine the relation between *trigunas* and psychological problems.

METHOD

Participants

The study was carried out on two independent samples. The yoga group consists of 51 yoga practitioners (male = 29 and female = 25) with a mean age of 36.59 years (SD= 13.52). These practitioners were selected from various yoga-teaching institutes in Visakhapatnam city. Their length of experience in yoga ranged from 3 months to 2 years. The control group with 54 subjects (male = 33 and female = 18) were selected from the general population. The mean age of the control group is 29.16 years (SD= 9.20).

Yoga group had yoga sessions for one hour either in the morning or in the evening. The yoga program primarily consists of *asnas* (physical postures), *Pranayama* (breathing exercises), *kriyas* (cleansing procedures), *mudras* (gestures or attitudes) and relaxation procedures.

Measures

Vedic Personality Inventory (VPI), developed by Wolf (1999) was used to measure *trigunas* in the sample. It consists of 57 items that measure *sattva*, *rajas* and *tamas* dimensions of personality. As it is in English, it was translated into Telugu by a group of five scholars independently. Their work was pooled and consensus among the translators was obtained with regard to the final version. Originally, VPI is a 7-point scale ranging from "very strongly disagree' to 'very strongly agree". However, as the participants had difficulty in understanding the meaning of the fine differences in the scale points it was changed into a 5-point scale ranging from "strongly disagree" to "strongly agree". Chronbach alphas for *sattva*, *rajas* and *tamas* on the present data are .81, .82 and .89 respectively against the originally reported values of .93, .94 and .93.

Emotional and behavioural problems were measured by the *Adult Self Report (ASR),* a 126-item checklist, developed by Achenbach & Rescorla (2003). The ASR gives scores on eight syndrome scales, namely- Anxious/Depressed, Withdrawn, Somatic problems, Thought problems, Attention problems, Aggressive behaviour, Rule-Breaking behaviour and Intrusive behaviours. Test-retest reliability of the syndrome scales ranges from .83 to .94 and the internal consistency reliability co-efficient ranges from .51 to .97. For the present study, Telugu version of the Adult Self Report was used (Gopal, 2010).

RESULTS AND DISCUSSION

Table 1

Yoga Practice and Emotional and Behavioural Problems

Emotional/Behavioural Problems	*Groups*	*Mean*	*S.D*	*T*
Anxious/Depressed (a)	Yoga (51)	7.01	6.48	2.50**
	Non-yoga (54)	10.25	6.74	
Withdrawn/Depressed (a)	Yoga (51)	4.46	3.05	2.50
	Non-yoga (54)	5.15	3.78	
Somatic Complaints (a)	Yoga (51)	1.92	2.15	2.23*
	Non-yoga (54)	3.09	3.14	
Thought Problems	Yoga (51)	3.57	2.94	.46
	Non-yoga (54)	3.84	3.02	
Attention Problems	Yoga (51)	7.16	5.35	2.12*
	Non-yoga (54)	9.41	5.39	
Rule Breaking Behaviour (b)	Yoga (51)	3.47	3.43	3.54**
	Non-yoga (54)	5.98	3.77	
Aggressive Behaviour (b)	Yoga (51)	6.33	4.79	2.66**
	Non-yoga (54)	8.70	4.19	
Intrusive Behaviour (b)	Yoga (51)	2.46	2.22	1.98*
	Non-yoga (54)	3.30	2.08	

Note: *pd £ 0.05, ** pd £ 0.01, (a) = emotional problems, (b) = behavioural problems

Table-1 shows the mean differences between yoga and non-yoga groups on emotional and behavioural problems. T-test results indicate significant differences between the two groups on six out of eight problem scales. The two groups had significant mean differences on emotional problems such as anxious/depressed and somatic complaints and behavioural problems such as rule breaking behaviour, aggressive behaviour and intrusive behaviour. They also had significant mean differences on attention problems. Descriptive statistics show that yoga group obtained low scores on all these problem scales compared to non-yoga group. It means that non-yoga group was more anxious/depressed, experiencing more somatic and attention problems, more aggressive and intrusive and tend be more rule-breaking.

The above results are in line with both the theoretical postulations and with the previous research. Traditionally, yoga is viewed as a method to overcome suffering. Research in general found that practicing yoga postures, *pranayama* and meditation significantly reduces emotional problems such as psychological distress, anxiety and depression. Practice of yoga methods controls the excessive activity of sympathetic activity and endocrinal activity and thereby establishes stability in the person (Deatherage, 1975; Ajaya, 1984; Engler, 1984). Yoga practices also reduce behavioural problems such as aggression and rule-breaking behaviours. When the mind becomes calm and non-reactive the individual has time to think of and to decide the appropriate course of action. Deshpande, Nagendra & Raghuram (2008) reported that eight week intervention of yoga module significantly decreased verbal aggressiveness in a group of 1228 adults.

Table 2

Yoga Practice and Trigunas

Guna	*Groups*	*Mean*	*S.D*	*T*
Sattva	Yoga (51)	54.07	10.89	.434**
	Non-yoga (54)	48.31	9.33	
Rajas	Yoga (51)	42.29	12.38	.708**
	Non-yoga (54)	49.84	11.38	
Tamas	Yoga (51)	35.96	12.74	.411**
	Non-yoga (54)	43.21	13.34	

*pd £ 0.05, ** pd £ 0.01

Table-2 shows the t-test results of the mean differences between yoga and non-yoga groups on *Trigunas.* Significant mean differences (pd"0.01) were found between yoga and non-yoga groups on all the three *gunas- sattva, rajas* and *tamas*. An examination of the mean scores shows that yoga group obtained higher score on *sattva* and lower scores on *rajas* and *tamas* indicating that yoga group was high on *sattva guna* while control group was high on rajas and *tamas gunas.*

As *sattva* is described as a desirable quality and yoga methods are said to emancipate suffering it is logical to postulate that yoga practice should result in increase in *sattva* aspect of personality and decrease in *rajas* and *tamas* aspects of personality. The above findings clearly confirm this. In a recent study Deshpande, Nagendra & Raghuram (2009) found that eight week practice of yoga increased *sattva* aspect of personality.

Table 3

Partial Correlations between Trigunas and Emotional and Behavioural Problems

Guna *Attention*	*Anxious/* *Aggressive* *Depressed*	*Withdrawn* *Rule-* *breaking*	*Somatic* *Intrusive*	*Thought*
Sattva -.41**	-.36** -.44**	-.17 -.32**	-.23* -.27**	-.12
Rajas .36**	.35** .36**	.17 .50**	.06 .26**	.23*
Tamas .45**	.43** .41**	.26** .55**	.14 .24**	.28**

*pd £ 0.05, ** pd £ 0.01

Table-3 shows the correlations between the three *gunas* and emotional and behavioural problems by partialling out the possible covariance of experimental conditions (yoga and non-yoga). *Sattva guna* was found to have negative correlations with all the problems. It has significant negative correlations with anxious/depressed, somatic and attention problems, aggressive, rule-breaking and intrusive behaviours. *Rajas* and *tamas* have positive correlations with all the problem scales. *Rajas* was found to have significant positive correlations with anxious/depressed, thought and attention problems, aggressive, rule-breaking and intrusive behaviours. Similarly, *tamas* was found to have significant positive correlations with anxious/depressed, withdrawn, thought and attention problems, aggressive, rule-breaking and intrusive behaviours.

These findings are in line with scriptural descriptions and also with the limited previous research in this aspect. Caraka and Suœruta, two ancient Indian scholars opined that *tamasic,* followed by *rajasic*, personality is predisposed to psychological maladies while *sattvic*, being pure, is free from these problems. Das & Gopal (in press) also reported similar findings. They reported significant negative correlations between *sattva* and emotional and behavioural problems and significant positive correlations in the case of *rajas* and *tamas* with these problems. The present results further support these findings.

From the above findings it can be concluded that: practice of yoga increases *sattva* aspect of personality and, thus, can be a resilient factor against psychological maladies; and *sattva* aspect of personality is negatively related to mental health problems while rajas and *tamas* are positively related to.

REFERENCES

Achenbach, T.M. and Rescorla, L.A. (2003). *Manual for the ASEBA Adult Forms and Profiles*. Burlington, VT: University of Vermont, Research Center for Children, Youth, & Families.

Ahmad, S., Ahmad, H. & Sumboo, S.S. (1988). Personality study of individuals regularly practising T.M. technique. *Journal of Personality and Clinical Studies*, 4, 89-92.

Ajaya, S. (1984). *Psychotherapy East and West: A Unifying Paradigm.* Pennsylvania: Himalyan Institute.

Basyal, S.P. (2002). *The effect of pranayama on depression.* (Typescript). Bihar Yoga Bharti: Munger.

Bhushan, S. (2007). Qualitative transformation in personality: A function of yoga nidra. *Journal of Indian Psychology*, 25, 6-15.

Das, G.M.A & Gopal, D.V.V. (in press). Trigunas and Psychological Problems. *Journal of Indian Psychology.*

Deatherage, G. (1975). Clinical use of mindfulness meditation technique in short term psychotherapy. *Journal of Transpersonal Psychology*, 7, 133-143.

Deshpande, Nagendra & Raghuram (2008). A randomized control trial of the effect of yoga on verbal aggressiveness in normal healthy volunteers. *International Journal of Yoga,* 1 (2), 76-82.

Deshpande, Nagendra & Raghuram (2009). A randomized control trial of the effect of yoga on Gunas (personality) and Self-esteem in normal healthy volunteers. *International Journal of Yoga,* 2 (1), 13-21

Engler, J. (1984). Therapeutic aims in psychotherapy and meditation: Developmental stages in the representation of self. *Journal of Transpersonal Psychology,* 16, 25-61.

Gergen, K.J., Gulerce, A., Lock, A & Misra, G. (1996). Psychological Science in Cultural Context. *American Psychologist,* 51(5), 496-503.

Mohan, V & Sandhu, S. (1988). Samkhyan tri-guna and Eysenck's Dimensions of Personality. *The Vedic Path,* 23-38.

Narayana, N.V.V.S & Gopal, D.V.V. (2008). Effect of yoga on women's psychological well-being. *Journal of Indian Psychology,* 26 (1&2), 39-46.

Padmasri & Telles (2007). Frontalis EMG changes during yoga relaxation based on initial levels. *Journal of Indian Psychology,* 25 (1&2), 16-23.

Rao, P.V.K. (1995). Yoga: Its Scientific and applied Aspects. *Journal of Indian Psychology,* 13(2), 1-12.

Sinha, D. (1994). Indigenous Psychology: Need and Potentiality. *Journal of Indian Psychology,* 12(1&2), 1-7.

Sitamma, M., Sridevi, K & Krishna Rao, K. (1995). Three Gunas and cognitive characteristics; A study of field dependence – independence and perceptual acuity. *Journal of Indian Psychology,* 13 (2), 13-20.

Sridevi, Sitamma & Rao (1998). Yoga Training and Cognitive Task Performance. *Journal of Indian Psychology,* 16 (2), 34-40.

Triveni, S. & Aminabhavi, V. (1999). Impact of yoga practices on neuroticism, anxiety and depression. *Praachi Journal of Psycho-Cultural Dimension,* 15, 83-85.

Wolf, D.B. (1998). The Vedic Personality Inventory: A study of the gunas. *Journal of Indian Psychology,* 16 (1), 26-43.

●●●

4

Effect of Yogic Practices on Psychological and Physiological Parameters

Awadhesh Upadhyay and M.G. Sharma

The first pioneering attempt along the scientific lines to study the psychological and physiological effects of yogic practices was made by Kuvalayannanda (1924), his study occupy a very important and unique position among the scientific works in yoga done so for in the field. Later, other workers like there, Brosse (1964), Bagchi and Wenger (1959), Anand, Chhina, and Singh (1961), studied electrical activity of the brain during yogic meditation. ANS activity among practioners was studied by Winger and Bagahi (1961). Attempts to study individual yogic practices have been done by Kuvalayananda and Karamabelker (1956, 1957), Bhole and Karmbelker (1971), Rao (1968), Gharote (1971), Wallace (1970), Sharma and Sharma (2009) and Sharma and Sharma (2009). Theoretical aspect of yogic exercises has been very brought forward by Kuvalayananda and Vivekar (1963), Datey, Deshmuk Dalvi and Vivekar (1969), Tulpule, Shah, Shah and Maveligala (1973), Bhole and Karam Belkar (1972) and Gharote (1973). In spite of these attempts to study different yogic exercise individually and their utility in the treatment of certain disorder, limited research has been carried out to study the effect of the selected routine of yogic exercises on the important of physical fitness.

Several types of yogic exercises are known and each has its advantages and disadvantage. For example, wrestlers and boxers are seen with massive bodies requiring very large quantity of food and yet having a short span of life. On the other hand there are persons leading a less stressful and regulated life maintaining themselves on a very small quantity of food for a longer span of life.

Effect of short term yogic training on mental health have been studied by Pratap (1968), Kocher and Pratap (1971), Kocher and Pratap (1972), Palsane and Kocher (1973) and they reported favourable results. Karambelkar, Bhole and Gharote (1970), studies uropepsin secretion and found yogic exercises reducing uropepsin secretion as a result of three weeks training. Bhole, Karambelkar and Gharote (1969) disclosed that short-term yogic training improved vital capacity. Gharote (1970) reported significant increase in the strength and endurance of the abdominal muscles of the females as a result of yogic training for three weeks. In another study of Gharote (1962) evaluated psycho-physiological effects of selected yogic exercises using Wenger's Autonomic Balance Test Battery and McCurdy-Larson Organic Efficiency Test and observed significant shifting of autonomic balance score towards increased parasympathetic functions and encouraging trends in the cardio respiratory efficiency.

There are some other studies of yogic practices on mental health have been studied by Pratap (1968), Kocher and Pratap (1971), Kocher and Pratap (1972), Palsane and Kocher (1973) and they reported favourable results. Karambelkar, Bhole and Gharote (1970), studies uropepsin secretion and found yogic exercises reducing uropepsin secretion as a result of three weeks training. Bhole, Karambelkar and Gharote (1969) disclosed that short term yogic training improved vital capacity. Gharote (1970) reported significant increase in the strength and endurance of the abdominal muscles of the females as a result of yogic training for three weeks. In another study of Gharote (1962) evaluated psycho-physiological effects of selected yogic exercises using Wenger's Autonomic Balance Test Battery and McCurdy-Larson Organic

Efficiency Test and observed significant shifting of autonomic balance score towards increased parasympathetic functions and encouraging trends in the cardio respiratory efficiency.

The aim of this research was to assess the status of mental and physical fitness of the school going boys and to analyse the effects of longs term yogic training programe of six months on their mental and physical fitness.

METHODOLOGY

Sample

Four-hundred students of class IX and class X were selected for this study out of these 40 pre-stage and 40 post stage yogic practices subjects were consisted. These groups were matched on the variable of age range 14 to 17 years with a mean age of 14.50 years. All the subjects attending a centre S.I. Mental and Physical Health Society (SIMPHS), Varanasi. Yoga and meditation was provided by a group of there experts clinical psychologist and yoga therapist including researcher of this study for about six months they did yoga in a particular time and place for 30 to 40 minutes/ day. After yogic practices they were requested to attend the centre and complete the test and requested to cooperate in data collection.

RESULTS AND DISCUSSION

Comparison of mean scores of pre stage and post stage yogic practices on psychological and physiological parameters and its seven variables, viz., anxiety, immediate memory, respiration rate, pulse rate, blood pressure (high and low), and breath holding time would be available in Tables no. 1 and 2. Scores obtained of anxiety and immediate memory on psychological parameters were analysed using't' test of significance. Results of such an analysis are presented in the table which is given on next page.

It is obvious from the above table that post stage yogic practices subjects had lower mean scores of anxiety variable on psychological parameters (M = 45.07, SD = 3.05) than that of the pre-stage yogic practices (M = 64.26, SD = 4.03) and this difference was significance at or beyond .01 level of confidence (t = 24.29, df = 78 and P = <.01).

TABLE 1

Variables	*N*	*Pre-stage of yogic practices subjects*		*Post-stage of yogic practices subjects*		*'t'value*
		M	*SD*	*M*	*SD*	
Anxiety	40	64.26	4.03	45.07	3.05	24.29**
Immediate Memory	40	4.08	2.39	6.81	1.96	5.80**

** Significant on .01 level of confidence

A glance from the table that the two groups, viz., pre-stage and post-stage yogic practices subjects of immediate memory variable on psychological parameters did differ significant the obtained't' value of 5.80 with 78 df was significant at .01 level of confidence. The mean scores of pre and post-stage of immediate memory on psychological parameters were 4.08 and 6.81 with 2.39 SDs and 1.96 SDs respectively.

On the basis of the findings that post stage yogic practices subjects were found to have significantly lower on anxiety variable on psychological parameters as compared to the pre-stage subjects of yogic practices. So it clarifies that post stage subjects had low range of anxiety in comparison to the pre-stage subjects. Sharma and Sharma (2008) disclosed in a study that after meditation pathological gamblers had improved their mental health. In other study of Sharma and Sharma (2008) also found that vipasana meditation is more effective techniques for reducing their anxiety of the pathological gamblers.

Post-stage yogic practices subjects were found to have significantly higher on immediate memory span of psychological parameters as compared to the pre-stage subjects. It would be clear that post-stage of yogic practices subjects had better immediate memory span as compared to the pre-stage subjects. It effect was due to yogic exercises. Comparison of pre stage and post stage of respiration rate, pulse rate, blood pressure (high and low) and breath holding time on physiological parameter is presented in the following Table 2.

A perusal of Table 2 revealed that pre-stage of yoga practices subjects had higher mean value on respiration rate/minute (M =

21.09, SD = 2.03) than the post-stage subjects of yoga practices (M = 18.69, SD = 1.69). This difference was significant at .01 level of confidence (t = 5.71, df = 78 and P<.01). It clarifies that post-stage subject of yoga practices had controlled their respiration rate/minute in comparison to the pre-stage subjects of yoga practices.

TABLE 2

Variable		*Pre-stage of yoga practices*		*Post-stage of yoga practices*		*'t' value*
	N.	*M*	*SD*	*M*	*SD*	
Respiration Rate/minute	40	21.09	2.03	18.69	1.69	5.7**
Pulse rate/minute	40	78.39	2.31	62.37	2.17	32.1**
Blood pressure (high)	40	124.09	8.78	110.6	7.23	7.49**
Blood pressure (low)	40	68.30	7.97	83.8	7.18	9.11**
Breath holding time/second	40	83.7	5.79	80.01	5.01	3.04**

** Significant on .01 level of confidence

The table revealed that the two groups, viz., pre-stage and post-stage of yoga practices on physiological parameter did differ significantly on pulse rate / minute. The obtained't' value of 32.1 with 78 df was significant at .01 level of confidence. The mean value of post-stage yoga practices subjects was 78.39 with 2.31 SDs and 62.37 with 2.17 SDs of the post-stage yoga practice subjects. It is clear from the findings that after yoga practice subjects had reduced their pulse rate / minute.

Table 2 showed that the two groups, viz., pre-stage and post of yoga practices subjects did differ significantly on high blood pressure. The obtained't' value of 7.49 with 78 df was significant at .01 level of confidence. The post stage yoga practices subjects had obtained the mean scores of 110.6 with 7.23 SDs, whereas pre-stage yoga practices subjects had obtained the mean scores of 124.09 with 8.78 SDs. It would be clear that post stage yoga practices subjects had controlled their blood pressure after the practices of yogic exercises.

It is apparent from the Table 2 that the two groups' viz. pre stage and post stage yoga practices subjects did differ significantly on their mean scores of low blood pressure. The obtained't' value of 9.11 with 78 df was significant at .01 level of confidence. The post stage yoga practices subjects had obtained the mean scores of 83.8 with 7.18 SDs, whereas pre stage yoga practices subjects had obtained the mean scores of 68.30 with 7.97 SDs. It would be clear that post stage yoga practices subjects had increased their blood pressure/minute after the yoga practices.

It would be clear from the table 2 that two groups, viz., pre-stage and post-stage subjects of yoga practices did differ significantly on their mean scores of breath holding time in second. The obtained't' value of 3.04 with 78 df was significant at or beyond .01 level of confidence. The mean scores of the post-stage yoga practices were 80.01 with 5.01 SDs and it was 83.7 with 5.79 SDs of the pre-stage yoga practices subjects. Joshi (2003) revealed in his study that a combination of bio feedback and yogic practices and relaxation techniques has been found to lower blood pressure and reduce the need for high blood pressure medication in people suffering from it.

It is observed from the following finding of the study that post stage subjects of yoga practices had controlled their breath holding time in per second as compared to the pre stage subjects of yoga practices. This effect was only due to yoga exercise. In a study of Joshi (2003) also disclosed that patients whose practices yoga have a better change of gaining the ability to control their breathing problems with the help of breathing controlled exercises. It is possible to central an attack of severe shortness of breath without having to seek medical assistance, various studies have confirmed the beneficial effect of yoga for patients with respiratory problems.

It would be appear that characteristics of pre-stage subjects of yogic practices is associated with anxiety whereas characteristics of post-stage yogic practices subjects is associated with immediate memory span. The research did also showed that the post-stage subjects of yogic practices had controlled in respiration, pulse rate, blood pressure (high and low) and breath holding time as compared to the pre-stage yogic practices subjects.

REFERENCES

Anand, B.K., Chhina, G.S. and Singh, B. (1961). Some aspects of electro encephalographic studies in yogic. Electro enceph. *Clinic Neurophysiology, 134*, 452-456.

Bagchi, B.K., Wenger, M.A. (1959). Electrophysiological Correlates of some yogic exercises. In EEG. *Clinical Neurophysiology and Epilepsy.*

Bhole, M.V. and Karambelkar, P.V. (1971). Pressure changes in internal cavities during Uddiyana and Nauli, *Yoga-Mimamsa,* 13(4), 19-25.

Bhole, M.V. and Karambelkar, P.V. (1972). Yoga practices in relation to therapeutics. *Seminar of the 24th Annual Conference Indian Psychiatric Society.* 39-43.

Bhole, M.V., Karambelkar, P.V. and Gharte, M.L. (1970). Effect of yogic practices on Vital capacity. *Indian Journal of Chest Disease, 12*(1), 1-14.

Brosse, T. (1964). Contribution to the experimental study of Altruism. In P.A. Sorokin (Ed.), *Forms and Techniques Altruistic and Spiritual Growth,* Boston : The Beacon Press, 189-282.

Datey, K.K., Deshmukh, S.N., Dalvi, C.P. and Vinekar (1969). Shavasan. A yogic exercise in the management of hypertension. *Angiology, 20,* 325-333.

Gharote, M.L. (1962). A study of psychophysiological effects of short term yogic exercises on the adolescents high school boys – A research report submitted to Govt. of India. Ministry of Education, 55 pp. (Unpublished).

Gharote, M.L. (1970). Effect of yogic exercises on the strength and endurance of the abdominal muscles of the females. *Vyayam Vidnyan, 4*(1), 11-13.

Gharote, M.L. (1971). Effect of air-swallowing on the gastric acidity – A pilot study. *Yoga-Mimamsa, 14*(1), 7-10.

Gharote, M.L. (1973). Effect of yogic training on physical fitness. *Yoga-Mimamsa, 15*(3), 31-35.

Karambelkar, P.V., Bhole, M.V. and Gharote, M.L. (1969). Muscle activity in some asanas. *Yoga-Mimamsa, 12*(1), 1-13.

Kocher, H.C., and Pratap, V. (1971). A free association study before and after yogic practices. *Yoga-Mimamsa, 14*(1), 14-56.

Kocher, H.C. and Pratap, V. (1972). Anxiety level and yogic practices. *Yoga Mimams, 15*(1), 11-15.

Kuvalayananda,S. and Karambelkar, P.V. (1956). Experiments on Pranayam-Bhastrika Pranayam. *Yoga Mimamsa, 6*, 203-208.

Kuvalayananda, S. and Karambelkar, P.V. (1957). A studies in internal and external pressure changes in Madhya (central), Dakshina (Right) and Vama (Left) Naulies. *Yoga Mimamsa*, 6, 273-296.

Kuvalayananda, S. Vivekar, S.L. (1963). *Yogic therapy its basic principles and method*, New Delhi, Central Heath Education Bureau. 96 pp.

Kuvalayananda, S. (1924). X-ray experiments on Uddiyona. *Yoga Mimamsa, 1*:15-24.

Palsane, M.N. and Kocher, H.C. (1973). The effect of short term yogic training programme on immediate memory of school boys. *Research Bulletin*, 3(1), 33-43.

Pratap, V. (1968). Steadiness in normals before and after yogic practices *– An Exploratory Study Yoga – Mimamsa,* 11(2). 1-13.

Rao, S. (1968). Respiratory responses to head stand posture. *Journal of Applied Physiology, 24*, 697-699.

Sharma, M.G. and Sharma, V. (2009). Pathological gamblers with psychotherapy and meditation compared on the MHQ. *Journal of Indian Psychology*.

Tulpule, T.H.S., Shah. J., Shah, H.M. and Mavelivala (1973). Yogic exercises in the management of Ischemic Heart Diseases. *Indian Heart Journal. 23(4),* 259-264.

Wallace, R.K. (1970). Physiological effects of transactional meditation. *Science, 167*: 1751-1754.

Wenger, M.A. and Bagehi, B.K. (1961). Studies of autonomic functions in practioners of yoga in India. *Behavioural Science, 6*, 312-323.

●●●

5

Effect of Emotional and Spiritual Intelligence on Psychological Well-being in Long Term Yoga Practitioners

Uma Mittal and Safia Akhtar

In the world where most people are failing to live up to some standard of behaviour that has been judged good or desirable, there is a need for looking forward, to the importance of spiritual and emotional factors in attainment of well being and to transform ourselves and others, heal relationships, cope with grief. Golman (1996) said that EQ gives empathy, motivation, compassion and an ability to respond skillfully to pleasure and pain on the other hand. Zohar and Marshal (2000) stated that SQ focuses on control over sense organs, soul consciousness, humility love, relaxation, selflessness, contentment, detachment, cheerfulness, tranquility, and equanimity of mind which guarantees well being. There are paucity of researches establishing these attributes as constructs of happiness, therefore the present study has been undertaken to see the impact of emotional intelligence and spiritual intelligence on psychological well being among yoga practitioners.2*2 factorial design was used by dividing the sample into two groups (high and low) on the basis of median scores on EI and SI. Sample comprised of 300 participants who were practicing yoga, since last one year, aged 35 to 75 years, selected from major yoga centers of Jaipur city. Tools used were satisfaction with life scale (Deiner et al., 1985), 8 SQ (Cattell et al.,1986),Wong and law emotional intelligence scale(Wong & Law,2002) and spiritual intelligence scale developed by Helliwell (2001).Findings revealed that persons high on emotional and spiritual intelligence are more satisfied in comparison to the other three groups. But at the same time the presence of either high EI or high SI can foster life satisfaction and freedom from anxiety, stress and depression. Further this study stressed the need for developing these attributes for leading life of values and virtues. It further highlighted that enhancing positive emotions and developing positive potentials are key to happiness in this highly complex world.

The concept of psychological well being is related to people's feeling about everyday life activities. (Bradburn, 1969; Warr & Wall,1975; Campbell,1976). Psychological or subjective well being may be defined as one's evaluations of his or her life (Diener, et al.,2003). These evaluations can be either cognitive or affective (Andrews & Whitney, 1976). The cognitive part, an information-based appraisal of one's life, is when a person gives conscious evaluative judgments about one's satisfaction with life as a whole. The affective part is a hedonic evaluation guided by emotions and feelings such as the frequency with which people experience pleasant/ unpleasant moods in reaction to their lives. Although these components are separable, they often interrelate, suggesting the existence of a higher order construct of subjective well being (Kozma, 1996). Ryff (1995) believed that well being can be described by a number of components- self-acceptance, personal growth, purpose in life, environmental mastery, autonomy, positive relations with others. A few other terms like subjective well-being, quality of life, mental health and life satisfaction have been used as synonyms of psychological well-being (PWB). According to Ryff and Keys (1995), self acceptance is the major component of psychological well being.

Researches revealed that meaning in life is highly correlated with psychological well being (Rathi & Rastogi, 2007; Debats, et. al. 1995; Shek, 1992; Zika & Chamberlain, 1987; Recker, et. al.

1987). Also individuals who are extroverted (Lucas, et al., 1998) and optimistic (Taylor & Armor, 1996) and posses a stronger sense of coherence.(Nilsson, et. al. 2009) reported higher levels of well being. Some studies have suggested that well being results from achieving a goal (Diener, 1984; Scitovsky, 1976; Wilson, 1960).Achievement goal striving was accompanied by high positive affected (Job et al., 2009).Work, family, marriage, leisure, health and finances have also been found to be correlated with well being. More recent researches have been found that individuals who are married are happier than those who are single, divorced or widowed (Diener et al., 1999; Diener, et al., 2000). A study by Anthony and Marika (1990) showed that gaining employment produces an improvement in psychological well-being in school leavers; unemployment does not have the opposite effect.

With regards to emotional intelligence (EI), when people evaluate their psychological wellbeing, the ratio of their pleasant to unpleasant emotions over time plays pivotal role. Emotions can be central to well-being because these effects are related to person's evaluation of life. Sreehari (2006) found that there is a positive relationship between EI and spiritual well being. Further he also found these factors are of crucial importance in medical care for enhancing better outcomes in patients with illness. Mathur (2006) highlighted that women executives with high E.Q. disclosed significantly more overall satisfaction and self esteem than those who were low in E.Q. Similarly subjects who scored high on EI and have internal locus of control scored significantly high life satisfaction (Kulshrestha & Sen, 2006). In another study positive association between EI and PWB components: self-esteem, life satisfaction, and self-acceptance have been reported. The study indicated that employees who experience a psychological state of well-being may function better than employees who experience emotional deficit (Carmeli, et al., 2009). High trait EI adolescents seem to be less vulnerable to psychological disorders compared to their low trait EI peers (Mavroveli, et al., 2007). Dulewicz, et al. (2007) reported significant correlations between EI and measures of well being. Landa et al.

(2006) found strong correlation between life satisfaction and EI. Social support may not always be necessary for SWB (Gallagher & Vella-Brodrick, 2008).

Further researches reported strong correlation between EI and stress, anxiety and depression (Kumar & Rooprai, 2009; Fernandez, et al., 2006). Further self-reported EI was negatively related to levels of depression and anxiety. Downey (2008) on the other hand found that EI does not prevent people from experiencing sadness, anger nor are they immune to life's disappointments and frustrations. EI was found to be highly related to social interaction anxiety. (Summerfeldt, et al., 2005).

Spirituality is an important part of the lives of many individuals (Seybold & Hill, 2001). The relationship between spirituality and psychological functioning has been found to exist across ethnic groups and cultures, and in studies that have measured religiosity in various ways (Seybold & Hill, 2001). Religiosity also accounted for variance in well being (Ellison, 1991). Significant correlations were found between measures of religiosity and psychological well-being. Findings suggested that frequency of personal prayer is the dominant factor in the relationship between religiosity and psychological well-being. (Maltby, et al., 1999).

Research has shown that spirituality and religion may actually enhance mental health in many cases. Spirituality has been shown to be associated with several positive psychological outcomes including subjective well-being (Witter, et. al. 1985), self-esteem (Falbo & Shepperd, 1986), physical health (Gottlieb & Green, 1984) and marital satisfaction (Glenn & Weaver, 1978). Lack of spirituality has been associated with several negative behavioural and psychological outcomes including depression (Wright, et. al. 1993), substance abuse (Zimmerman & Maton, 1992), and suicide and anxiety (Gartner, et al. 1991;Baker & Gorsuch, 1982;Sturgeon & Hamley, 1979). Frankl (1984) recognized that the personal belief that one's life fulfills some higher purpose and serves some higher power is of enormous psychogenic value, "There is nothing in the world, I venture to say, and that would so effectively help one to survive even the worst conditions as the knowledge that there is a meaning in one's life." Frankl believed this psychotherapeutic value held true for not only adults but also adolescents (Dienelt, 1984). Spirituality or religious beliefs can cultivate a belief in adolescents that their life has meaning, and that they have some control over their fate. Spirituality can also contribute to the adoption of a positive cognitive appraisal of negative life events (Martin & Carlson, 1988; Maton, 1989). Religion or spirituality can provide an "overarching interpretive scheme" (Peterson & Roy, 1985) that allows an individual to perceive his or her individual circumstances against a larger cohesive backdrop of order and normality. In a study on African American females, it was observed that higher level of religiosity was associated with higher self esteem and better psychological functioning (Ball, et al., 2003).

Several studies support a positive effect of spirituality on physical and psychological health (Matthews, et al., 1994; Maltby, et al., 1999; Clark, et. al. 1999). Gartner (1996) found positive relationship between spirituality and marital satisfaction, and general psychological functioning. He found negative correlations with drug and alcohol use, delinquency, criminal behaviour and suicide. Researchers found that spirituality had a direct beneficial effect on negative affect, and that it buffered the detrimental effects of stress on negative affect and physical adjustment (Kim & Seidlitz, 2002). Unterrainer,et al.(2010) observed evidence that Religious/Spiritual Well-Being is substantially correlated with different aspects of Psychological Well-Being and personality (*e.g.*, Extraversion, Neuroticism, and Openness). Spiritual intelligence is necessary for discernment in making spiritual choices that contribute to psychological well-being and overall healthy human development (Vaughan, 2002). Adams, et al. (2000) study revealed that the effect of life purpose on perceived wellness was mediated by optimism and sense of coherence, which had independent effects on perceived wellness beyond that of life purpose. The findings suggested that an optimistic outlook and sense of coherence must be present for life purpose to enhance a sense of overall well-being.

Researchers have studied the relationship between spirituality and anxiety in several different populations, with the notable exception of adolescents. Kaczorowski (1989) investigated this relationship in adults who had been diagnosed with cancer using the Spiritual Well-Being Scale and found inverse relationship between spiritual well-being and state-trait anxiety. Sturgeon and Hamley (1979) examined the relationship between anxiety and intrinsic (genuine and committed) religious orientation and extrinsic (when religion is used superficially for personal gain) religious orientation and found that the intrinsically oriented sample was less anxious on trait anxiety than the extrinsically oriented sample, but no differences were found on state anxiety. Using the same instruments, Baker and Gorsuch (1982) had nearly identical results; intrinsic religious orientation was negatively correlated with trait anxiety and extrinsic religious orientation was positively correlated with trait anxiety.

The review highlighted the important components, correlates of psychological wellbeing and their relationship with EI and SI, there is paucity of researches studying their joint effect of EI and SI on psychological wellbeing. India is a religious state therefore spirituality occupies an important position here.

Therefore the present investigation has being undertaken to study the independent and joint impact of EI and SI on psychological wellbeing of long term yoga practitioners. Following hypotheses were framed.

1. There will be a differential impact of emotional intelligence and spiritual intelligence on various measures of psychological well being (life satisfaction, anxiety, stress and depression).
2. Emotional Intelligence and Spiritual Intelligence will jointly influence the various measures of psychological well being.

MATERIALS AND METHOD

Design

2*2 factorial design was used by dividing the sample into two groups (high and low) on the basis of median scores on EI and SI.

Participants

The total sample comprised of 300 participants with the age range from 35 to 75years.. The sample was taken from major yoga centers of Jaipur city.

Tools

Following tools were used in the study:

1. ***Psychological well being-*** psychological well being was assessed by measuring life satisfaction, anxiety, stress and depression.
   - 1.1 **8SQ** – This is an 8 dimensional mood state questionnaire prepared by Cattell et al. (1986) comprising of 96 items. But for the present study only 3 components (anxiety, stress and depression) were considered. Each component comprised of 12 items.
   - 1.2 ***Life satisfaction*** – This dimension of PWB was measured by satisfaction with life scale (Diener, Emmons, Larsen & Griffin,1985). It is a five item measure designed to assess individual's global judgment of life satisfaction. Subjects respond using a 7 point likert scale, scores ranged from 5 to 35 and are interpreted in terms of absolute life satisfaction. Scoring criteria was more the score – more the satisfaction, with below 19 scores represent dissatisfaction and above 26 represent satisfaction.
2. ***Emotional intelligence*** – Emotional intelligence was assessed by Wong and Law emotional intelligence scale (2002).It was designed to measure global emotional intelligence of an individual in respect of 4 dimensions that are self awareness, others awareness, self motivation, self control. It is a 16 item scale. Responses on 5 point likert scale are summed up.
3. ***Spiritual intelligence*** – To assess the spiritual intelligence level of the individual, spiritual intelligence self test,

developed by Helliwell (2001) was used. This scale comprised of 31 items, it is a 5 point likert scale where scores can range from 0 to155 with neutral response ranging from 115 to 129.

RESULTS

TABLE 1

Mean F-ratio and significance level for life satisfaction scores with regards to EI and SI. (N=300)

Factors	*Groups/Mean scores on life satisfaction*	*F*	*Significance level*
Emotional Intelligence	Low EI = 18.72 High EI – 28.78	98.22	.00
Spiritual Intelligence	Low SI – 21.80 High SI – 25.70	14.80	.00
Interaction Effect EI * SI	Low EI * low SI – 15.08 Low EI * high SI – 22.37 High EI * low SI – 28.52 High EI * high SI – 29.03	11.15	.00

For life satisfaction results revealed that there were positive significant main effects of EI (F = 98.225; <.01) SI (F= 14.800; < .01) and interaction effect of EI and SI (F = 11.153; < .001).The mean value on life satisfaction for low EI group is lower than high EI group as depicted in table 1. Similarly the mean value on life satisfaction for low SI group is lower than high SI group.

Table 2 presents the significance level and main effects of EI and SI for anxiety. EI (F = 13.51; <.00) SI (F = 5.84 ;< .01) were found significant whereas the interaction effect of EI and SI on anxiety was not found significant. The mean value for low EI group represents the high anxiety as compared to high EI group. SI group also depicted similar results with low SI group scoring high on anxiety than high SI group.

TABLE 2

Mean F-ratio and significance level for anxiety scores with regards to EI and SI. (N=300)

Factors	*Groups/Mean scores on anxiety*	*F*	*Significance level*
Emotional Intelligence	Low EI – 1.90 High EI – 1.27	13.51	.00
Spiritual Intelligence	Low SI – 1.80 High SI – 1.38	5.84	.01
Interaction Effect EI * SI	Low EI * low SI – 2.23 Low EI * high SI – 1.77 High EI * low SI – 1.55 High EI * high SI – 0.98	0.81	.36

Above table shows the significance level and main effects of EI and SI on stress. EI (F = 8.27; <.00) SI (F = 10.22; < .00) were significant whereas the interaction effect of EI and SI on stress was not found significant. The mean value for low EI group depicts more stress level as compared to high EI group. Similarly high mean value for stress is also associated with low SI.

TABLE 3

Mean F-ratio and significance level for stress scores with regards to EI and SI. (N=300)

Factors	*Groups/Mean scores on stress*	*F*	*Significance level*
Emotional Intelligence	Low EI – 1.82 High EI – 1.33	8.27	.00
Spiritual Intelligence	Low SI – 1.84 High SI - 1.31	10.22	.00
Interaction Effect EI * SI	Low EI * low SI – 2.07 Low EI * high SI – 1.57 High EI * low SI – 1.62 High EI * high SI – 1.05	.04	.83

Table 4 represents the significance level and main effects of EI and SI for depression. EI (F= 11.71; <.00) is significant, whereas SI (F = 1.60; > .01) and interaction effect for EI and SI on anxiety were not found significant. The mean value for low EI represents the high depressive state as compared to high EI value.

TABLE 4

Mean F-ratio and significance level for depression scores with regards to EI and SI. (N=300)

Factors	*Mean scores on depression*	*F*	*Significance level*
Emotional Intelligence	Low EI – 1.82 High EI – 1.25	11.71	.00
Spiritual Intelligence	Low SI - 1.64 High SI – 1.43	1.60	.20
Interaction Effect EI * SI	Low EI * low SI – 1.90 Low EI * high SI – 1.73 High EI * low SI – 1.38 High EI * high SI – 1.13	.07	.79

TABLE 5

Tukey Post Hoc on life satisfaction with consideration of EI and SI

Group (I)	*Group (J)*	*Mean*	*Std. Difference (I-J)*	*Sig. Error*
LOW EI * LOW SI	HIGH EI * LOW SI	-7.07	1.309	.00
	LOW EI * HIGHSI	-13.26	1.182	.00
	HIGH EI *HIGH SI	-13.95	1.234	.00
HIGH EI * LOW SI	LOW EI * LOW SI	7.07	1.159	.00
	LOW EI *HIGH SI	-6.19	0.535	.00
	HIGH EI * HIGH SI	-6.88	0.556	.00
LOW EI * HIGH SI	LOW EI * LOW SI	13.26	0.524	.00
	HIGH EI * LOW SI	6.19	0.665	.00
	HIGH EI * HIGH SI	-.69	0.627	.96
HIGH EI * HIGH SI	LOW EI * LOW SI	13.95		.00
	HIGH EI * LOW SI	6.88		.00
	LOW EI *HIGH SI	.69		.96

The above table depicted following results:

LOW EI * LOW SI

(a) The mean differences are greater for all the other three groups in comparison to LOW EI* LOW SI group and are significant at .00 levels. This suggests that the persons low on EI and SI both are low on life satisfaction too.

HIGH EI * LOW SI

The mean differences are greater for the groups LOW EI *HIGH SI and HIGH EI * HIGH SI than this group and are found to be significant at .00 levels. This finding suggests that persons high on spiritual intelligence are more satisfied in comparison to persons low on spiritual intelligence and high or low on emotional intelligence.

LOW EI * HIGH SI

The mean differences are greater for this group than the group HIGH EI *LOW SI and is found to be significant at .00 levels. This finding suggests that persons high on spiritual intelligence are more satisfied in comparison to persons low on spiritual intelligence and high or low on emotional intelligence.

HIGH EI * HIGH SI

The mean differences are lower for all the other three groups in comparison to HIGH EI * HIGH SI group and are significant at .00 levels. This suggests that the persons high on emotional and spiritual intelligence both are more satisfied than persons low or high on emotional intelligence and low on spiritual intelligence.

DISCUSSION

In the present investigation effects of EI and SI on psychological wellbeing were analyzed for life satisfaction, anxiety, stress and depression specifically in the sample of yoga practitioners. The results of the investigation revealed significant impact of the two factors on psychological wellbeing of yoga practitioners.

The first hypotheses which stated that emotional intelligence and spiritual intelligence will independently influence life satisfaction, anxiety, stress, depression has been proved.

Results (table 1) revealed that main effects of EI and SI have been found significant for life satisfaction. Further the interaction effects are also significant. Person low on EI as well as on SI is also low on life satisfaction. This shows that EI and SI are important constructs which can determine the life satisfaction of an individual. These finding are similar with the findings of other researchers (Slaski & Cartwright, 2003; Ozer & Benet-Martínez, 2005; Zohar & Marshall, 2000). The results also specify that a person may be satisfied with high level of either EI or SI.

With regards to anxiety too, significant main effects emerged for EI and SI. Findings revealed that EI and SI both are detrimental for anxiety. Other researches also (Summerfeldt, et al., 2005) supported that anxiety is negatively related to emotional intelligence. As shown in result table 2 that lower the mean value of EI more the anxiety, similarly low SI leads to high anxiety level. This shows that a person with high EI or SI will be less anxious. Frankl (1984) recognized that the personal belief that one's life fulfils some higher purpose and serves some higher power is of enormous psychogenic value. Spirituality can also contribute to the adoption of a positive cognitive appraisal of negative life events (Martin & Carlson, 1988). Similarly it can be said that 'emotional intelligence,' is the ability to restrain negative feelings such as anger, self-doubt, stress, anxiety and instead focus on positive ones such as confidence, empathy and congeniality. So one should emphasize on developing emotional intelligent to overcome stress and anxiety at workplace and to get success in life.

Table 3 depicts that EI and SI both significantly effect stress. The mean value of stress is greater in high EI group as compared to low EI group. This supports the idea that EI helps us to cope with stressful situations. Matthews et al.(2006), in their study confirmed that low EI was related to worry states and avoidance coping. Montes-Berges et al.(2007) study with nursing students have shown that emotional intelligence is a skill that minimizes the negative stress consequences. Similarly spiritual intelligence mean on stress is found greater in low SI group as compared to high SI group. This shows that low SI people are high on stress whereas people high on spiritual intelligence have high tolerance level of stress.

With regards to depression - result table 4 revealed that the f value for EI group is significant but it was found non significant for SI group. It further shows that high EI has less mean value for depression as compared to low EI. This proves that people with low emotional intelligence tend to be more depressed whereas person with high emotional intelligence manage the situation and overcome easily with depressive states. Downey (2008) also indicated that in a clinical sample, severity of depression was related to the ability to manage and control emotions.

The second hypothesis stated that emotional intelligence and spiritual intelligence will jointly influence the various measures of psychological well being, and the results herein support this for life satisfaction. Results revealed that person low on EI; high on SI were more satisfied as compared to other groups. The mean values shows that if a person is high on either EI or SI he will have better life satisfaction. Thus it is not necessary for an individual to be high on both constructs for satisfaction. Further post hoc test for life satisfaction scores revealed that persons high on spiritual as well as emotional intelligence are most satisfied than the other three groups.

As stated by Zohar & Marshal (2000) EQ is essential for success in life whereas SQ is useful for meaningful life, if a person is high on EQ he tends to think about the situation and then behave appropriately within it. Or if a person is high on SQ, his spiritual intelligence level allows him to alter the situation or to walk out from there. So it can be said that EI works within boundaries, allows the situation to guide the individual. Whereas spiritual intelligence works with the boundaries of the situation and allows the person to guide and lead the situation. The interaction effect of EI and SI was not found significant on anxiety stress and depression variables.

In sum the results of this study suggest that (a) people who are high on emotional intelligence and those who are high on spiritual intelligence tend to be more satisfied in all aspects of life, (b) this study also shows that for life satisfaction the presence of both constructs is not necessary. A person may be satisfied with either higher level of emotional intelligence or higher level of spiritual intelligence, (c) results also revealed conclusive statement that if a person is high on both emotional intelligence and spiritual intelligent he/she will be most satisfied with life.

As psychological wellbeing is an important construct for life and health it cannot be ignored. Chida (2008) studied that positive psychological well-being was associated with reduced mortality. Higher levels of psychological well-being were associated with better cognitive function. (Llewellyn et al., 2008).Thus more researches are needed to explore the construct in detail.

Human beings in their continual endeavor to know more and accomplish greater feats are more prone to stresses of life. Since modern life in all its luxuriousness creates a smothering cloud in which it is difficult to have a clear view of our deepest sense for establishing bonds and uncluttered values, these two factor (EI &SI) rather qualities can help, create a sense of meaning and purpose in life. As rightly said EI is essential for success in life and SI is necessary for meaning in life, therefore there seems to be an essential need to inculcate these qualities, for promoting psychological wellbeing in individuals. It is highly suggested that positive potentials and positive emotions should be fostered and life of values and virtues must be developed. As they are key to happiness in this highly complex world.

REFERENCES

Adams, T.B., Bezner, J.R., Drabbs, M.E., Zambarano, R.J., & Steinhardt, M.A.(2000). Conceptualization and measurement of the spiritual and psychological dimensions of wellness in a college population. *Journal of American College Health*, 48(4), 165-173.

Andrews, F.M., & Whitney, S.B. (1976). *Social indicator of well being: Americans perception of life quality*. New York: Plenum press.

Baker, M., & Gorsuch, R. (1982).Trait anxiety and intrinsic-extrinsic religiousness. *Journal for the Scientific Study of Religion*, 21, 119-122.

Ball, J., Armistied, L., & Austin, B.(2003).The relationship between religiosity and adjustment among African- American, female, urban adolescents, 26(4), 431-446.

Bradburn, N. (1969). *The structure of psychological well being.* Chicago: Aldine.

Campbell, A. (1976). Subjective measures of well-being. *Am. Psychology, 31*(2), 117-124.

Carmeli, A., Yitzhak-Halevy, M., & Weisberg, J. (2009). The relationship between emotional intelligence and psychological wellbeing. *Journal of Managerial Psychology,* 24(1), 66 -78.

Chida, Y. (2008). Positive Psychological Well-Being and Mortality: A Quantitative Review of Prospective Observational Studies. *Psychosomatic Medicine,* 70, 741-756.

Clark, K. M.; Friedman, H. S., & Martin, L. R.(1999). A longitudinal study of religiosity and mortality risk. *Journal of Health Psychology,* 4 (3), 381–391.

Debats, D., Drost, J., & Prartho, P. (1995). Experiences of meaning in life: a combined qualitative and quantitative approach. *British Journal of Psychology,* 86, 359-375.

Dienelt, Karl. (1984). The Quest for Meaning among Today's Youth. *International Forum for Logotherapy,* 7, 89-95.

Diener, E. (1984). Subjective Well Being. *Psychological Bulletin,* 95(3), 542-575.

Diener, E., Emmons, R., Larson, R., & Griffin, S.(1985). The satisfaction with life scale. *Journal of Personality Assessment,* 49(1), 71-75.

Diener, E., Gohm, C., Suh, E. & Oishi, S. (2000). Similarity of the relations between marital status and subjective well being across cultures. *Journal of Cross Cultural Psychology,* 31(4), 419-436.

Diener, E., Oishi, S., & Lucas, R. E.(2003).Personality, culture, and subjective well-being. *Annual Review of Psychology,* 54, 403-425.

Diener, E., Suh, E., Lucas, R., & Smith, H. (1999). Subjective well being: Three decades of progress. *Psychological Bulletin,* 125 (2), 276-302.

Downey, L.A., Johnston, P.J., Hansen, K., Schembri, R., Stough, C., Tuckwell, V. & Schweitzer, I. (2008).The relationship between emotional intelligence and depression in a clinical sample.*The European Journal of Psychiatry, 22*(2).

Dulewicz, Victor; & Higgs, Malcolm.(2007).Relationships between Psychological Well-Being, Emotional Intelligence and Personality. Retrieved from http://www.henleymc.ac.uk/elibrary/hwpr02.nsf/number/HWP0717

Ellison, C.G.(1991).Religious Involvement and Subjective Well Being. *Journal of Health and Social Behavior*, 32, 80-99

Falbo, T. & Shcppcrd, J. A. (1986). Self-righteousness: Cognitive, power and religious characteristics. *Journal of Research in Personality,* 20, 145-157.

Fernandez-Berrocal, P., Alcaide, R.; Extremera, N., & Pizarro, D. (2006). The Role of Emotional Intelligence in Anxiety and Depression among Adolescents. Retrieved from www.idr-journal.com 4(1)

Frankl,V. (1984). *Man's Search for Meaning,* New York: Simon & Schuster.

Gallagher E.N. & Vella-Brodrick, D.A. (2008). Social support and emotional intelligence as predictors of subjective well-being.*Personality and Individual Differences*. 44(7), 1551-1561.

Gartner, J. (1996). Religious commitment, mental health, and prosocial behavior: Are view of the empirical literature. In E. P. Shafranske (Ed.), *Religion and the Clinical Practice of Psychology,* 187-214. Washington, DC: American psychological association.

Gartner, J., D.B. Larson, & G.D. Allen. (1991). Religious Commitment and Mental Health: A Review of the Empirical Literature. *Journal of Psychology and Theology,* 2(11), 15-23.

Glenn, N. D., & Weaver, C. N., (1978). A multi-variate, multi-survey study of marital happiness. *Journal of Marriage and the Family,* 40, 269-282.

Goleman, D. (1996). *Emotional Intelligence,* London: Bloomsburry, Jens-Mular.

Gottleib, N. H., & Green, L. W. (1984).Life events, social network, life-style, and health: An analysis of the 1979 national survey of personal health practices and consequences. *Health Education Quarterly,* 11, 91-105.

Helliwell, T.(2001). Spiritual intelligence self test (International institute of transformation). Retrieved from http://www.iitransform.com/

Job, V., Langens, T. A. & Brandstätter, V. (2009). Personality and Social Psychology Bulletin, 35(8), 983-996.

Kaczorowski, J. M. (1989). Spiritual well-being and anxiety in adults diagnosed with cancer. *Hospice Journal*, 5(4), 105-116.

Kim, Y., & Seidlitz, L.(2002). Spirituality moderates the effect of stress. *Personality and Individual Differences*, 32, 1377-1390.

Kozma, A.(1996).Top down and bottom up approaches to an understanding of subjective well being.World conference on quality of life, university of northern British Columbia, Prince George, Canada.

Kulshreshtha, U.,& Sen, C. (2006).Subjective well being in relation to emotional intelligence and locus of control among executives. *Journal of the Indian Academy of Applied Psychology,* 32(2), 93-98.

Kumar, S., Rooprai, K. Y. (2009) Role of Emotional Intelligence in Managing Stress and Anxiety at workplace. Retrieved from http://asbbs.org/files/2009/PDF/R/Rooprai.pdf

Landa, J. M. A., Zafra, E. L., Antonano, R. M., Pulido, M. (2006) Percieved emotional Intelligence and life satisfaction among university teachers. Retrieved from http://redalyc.uaemex.mx/pdf/727/72709523.pdf

Llewellyn, D. J., Lang, I. A., Langa, K. M. & Huppert, F. A.(2008). Cognitive function and psychological well-being: findings from a population-based cohort. *Age and Ageing*, 37(6), 685-689.

Lucas, R. E., Diener, E., Grob, A., Suh, E. M. & Shao, I.(1998). Cross-cultural evidence for the fundamental features of extraversion: The case against sociability. Manuscript submitted for publication, University of Illinois at Urbana Champaign.

Maltby, J.; Lewis C.A., & Day L.(1999). Religious orientation and psychological well-being: The role of the frequency of personal prayer. British, 4 (4), 363-378

Martin, J. E., & Carlson, C. R.(1988).Spiritual dimensions of health psychology. In W. Miller & J. Martin (Eds.), *Behavior therapy and religion: Integrating spiritual and behavioral approaches to change*. 57-110. Newbury Park, CA: Sage.

Mathur, A. (2006). Hardiness and E.Q. as determinants of subjective well being in executive women. Paper presented in 32nd national annual conference of Indian association of clinical psychologist. Jaipur.

Maton, K. I. (1989). The stress buffering role of spiritual support: Cross sectional and prospective investigations. *Journal for the Scientific Study of Religion*, 28(3), 310-323.

Matthews, G., Emo, A.K., Funk, G., Robert, R.D., Costa, P.T. Jr. & Sxhulze, R.(2006). Emotional intelligence, personality, and task-induced stress. *Journal of Experimental Psychology Applied*, 12(2) 96-107

Matthews, D. A.; Larson, D. B., & Barry,C. P. (1994). The faith factor: an annotated bibliography of clinical research on spiritual subjects. National Institute for Health Care Research.1.Rockville, MD: John Templeton Foundation.

Mavroveli, A., Petrides, K.V., Rieffe, C. & Bakker, F. (2007). Trait emotional intelligence, psychological well-being and peer-rated social competence in adolescence. *British Journal of Developmental Psychology,* 25, 263-275.

Montes-Berges, B. & Augusto, J.M. (2007). Exploring the relationship between perceived emotional intelligence, coping, social support and mental health in nursing students. *Journal of Psychiatric Mental Health Nursing,* 14(2), 163-71.

Nilsson, K. W.; Leppert, J. Simonsson, B., & Starrin, B.(2009). A Reaserch report: Sense of coherence and psychological well-being: improvement with age. *J Epidemiol Community Health, 64* (4) *347-352.*

Ozer, D. J. & Benet-Martínez, V. (2006). Personality and the Prediction of Consequential Outcomes.*Annual Review of Psychology*, 57, 401-421.

Peterson, L.R., & Roy, R. (1985).Religiosity, anxiety and meaning and purpose: religion's consequences for psychological well-being. *Review of Religious Research*, 27(1), 49-61.

Rathi, N., & Rastogi, R. (2007). Meaning in Life and Psychological Well-Being in Pre-Adolescents and Adolescents. *Journal of the Indian Academy of Applied Psychology*, 33(1) 31-38.

Recker, G.; Peacock, E., & Wong, P.(1987). Meaning and purpose in life and well-being: A life-span perspective. *Journal of Gerontology,* 42, 44-49.

Ryff, C.D.(1995).Psychological well-being in adult life. *Current Directions in Psychological Science,* 4, 99-104.

Ryff, C., & Keyes, C.(1995). The structure of psychological well-being revisited. *Journal of Personality and Social Psychology,* 69, 719-727.

Scitovsky, T.(1976).*The Joyless Economy.* Oxford : Oxford University Press.

Seybold, K., & Hill, P.(2001).The role of religion and spirituality in mental and Physical health. *Current Directions in Psychological Science,* 10(1), 21-24.

Shek, D. (1992). Meaning in life and psychological well-being: an empirical study using the Chinese version of the purpose in life questionnaire. *Journal of Genetic Psychology,* 153, 185-190.

Slaski M., & Cartwright S. (2003). Emotional intelligence training and its implications for stress, health and performance. *Stress*, 19(4), 233-239(7).

Sreehari, R. (2006). Emotional intelligence and spirituality: A comparative study between coronary bye pass and non surgical cardiac surgery patients. Paper presented in 32 national annual conference of Indian association of clinical psychologist. Jaipur.

Sturgeon, R. S., & Hamley, R. W.(1979).Religiosity and anxiety. *Journal of Social Psychology,* 108, 137-138.

Summerfeldt, L.J.; Kloosterman, P. H.; Antony, M. M., & Parker, J. D. A. (2005).Social Anxiety, Emotional Intelligence, and Interpersonal Adjustment. *Journal of Psychopathology and Behavioral Assessment*, 28(1), 57-68.

Taylor, S. E., & Armor, D. A.(1996). Positive illusions and coping with adversity. *Journal of Personality,* 64, 873-898.

Unterrainer, K.H.; Ladenhauf, M.L.; Moazedie, S.J.; Wallner-Liebmannb, & A. Fink (2010).Dimensions of Religious/Spiritual Well-Being and their relation to Personality and Psychological Well-Being. *Personality and Individual Differences*, 49(3), 192-197.

Vaughan, F. (2002). What is Spiritual Intelligence? *Journal of Humanistic Psychology*, 42(2), 16-33.

Warr, P. B., & Wall, T. D.(1975).*Work and Well-being*. London: Penguin.

Wilson,W. R. (1960). An attempt to determine some correlates and dimensions of hedonic tone (Doctoral dissertation, Northwestern University, 1960). Dissertation Abstracts, 22, 2814. (University Microfilms No. 60-6588)

Winefield, A.H.,& Tiggemann, M. (1990). *Journal of Applied Psychology,* 75(4), 455-459.

Witter, R.A., Stock, W.A., Okun, M.A., & Haring, M.J.(1985). Religion and subjective well-being in adulthood: A quantitative synthesis. *Review of Religious Research, 26*, 332-342.

Wright, L. S., Frost, C.J. & Wisecarver, S.J (1993). Church attendance, meaningfulness of religion and depressive symptomatology among adolescents. Journal of Youth and Adolescence, 22(5), 559-568.

Zika, S. & Chamberlain, K.(1987). Relation of hassles and personality to subjective well-being *Journal of Personality and Social Psychology,* 53, 155-162.

Zimmerman, Marc A., & Maton, Kenneth I. (1992). Life-style and substance use among male African American urban adolescents: A cluster analytic approach. *American Journal of Community Psychology, 2,*(1).

Zohar & Marshall (2000).Spiritual intelligence: The ultimate intelligence, London: Bloomsburry.

●●●

6

Efficacy of Yoga Therapy for the Management of Anxiety, Stress, Negative Mood Regulation and Self-Esteem of Female Adolescents

Anup Sud, Rita Bhalla and Zinnia Sethi

Adolescence is a time of transition, which happens to place an individual on those transverse paths where adjustments and coping becomes difficult. Change by itself is stressful and when this change happens to be a part of a growing youth's physiological, psychological, social and environmental scenario, it is surely to increase the intensity of anxiety and stress. Anxiety, stress, negative mood and self-esteem are allied with all the age groups but these are higher in intensity in adolescence, primarily due to immense changes that are unfolded in their lives everyday.

Adolescence has been termed as the period of stress, storm and strain and has also been termed as the terrible teens (Mythili, Bharathi & Nagarathna, 2004). Though people's perceptions have changed, yet adolescent female students in India even today deal with higher authoritative practices and restrictions imposed on them by their parents and teachers. Making adjustments with one's own self, family, peers, teachers and society at large, imposed demands and their inability to stand up to all the expectations further results in anxiety, stress, negative mood, and low self-esteem.

Keith, Hodapp, Schermellch-Engle and Moosbrugger (2003) explain that according to Spielberger personality states are conceptualised to be mainly determine by situational characteristics and the personality traits are viewed as relatively enduring inter individual differences in tendencies to react and behave in a particular personality trait. The stronger a particular personality trait, higher is the probability that an individual will experience the emotional state corresponding to this trait. Test anxiety is a situation specific trait and is conceptualised to capture inter individual differences in the general tendency to react with anxiety in certain situations (Hodapp, Glanzmann & Laux, 1995). State, trait and test anxiety are inevitable regular components affecting their performance and relations too.

Stress is an unpleasant state of emotional and physiological arousal which individuals experience in situations that they perceive as threatening to their well being (Singh, Tomar & Khokhar, 2005). Stressors are apart of the daily lives of adolescents encompassing difficulties with their parent's expectations, teacher's authority, peer's rejection and arguments, failure in academic performance, dealing with opposite gender relations, personal inadequacies and illness. Negative affectivity is pervasive negative mood marked by anxiety, depression and hostility (Watson & Clark, 1984). Mood fluctuations and unexplainable behaviours too hinder the adolescents performance and life.

Self-esteem involves the values that an individual places in himself and is a judgement of whether his abilities and qualities accomplish or not, the standards on believes to be ideal (Pope, McHale & Carigheal, 1988). Adolescent's self esteem is easily susceptible to being thwarted due to their failures, rejection by peers, criticism faced from teachers and family, low achievement and felling of hopelessness.

State anxiety, trait anxiety, test anxiety, stress, negative mood and low self esteem do not exist as segregating components but are instead a multidimensional construct affecting each other and the adolescent personality and well being. Holistic approaches are thus needed to deal with adolescent's multi unified tribulations such that they develop into a healthy positive generation of tomorrow.

Yoga offers a way out of the whirlpool of stress and is a holistic solution to stress (Bhavanani, 2004). Yoga is an efficient holistic therapy taking into consideration the unity of the mind and body in dealing with an individual. Yoga includes rhythmic breathing, postures, conscious concentration, mediation, healthy habits and thought rectification. It also serves as a devise for an individual's well being, by serving as a preventive, curative and promotive therapy. Stress of the modern world is making adolescents its victim, who thus must learn to be more self controlled and calm to fight back all the hardships, for which yoga serves as their redeemer and serves as an indemnity for their future. The study aims to find out the influence of yoga therapy in curtailing state anxiety, trait anxiety, test anxiety and stress and in enhancing negative mood regulation and self esteem of Arts and Science female adolescent subjects.

METHODOLOGY

Quota sample of one hundred female adolescents (+1 and +2 students), within the age range of 16-19 was selected from Arts and Science subjects. 25 Arts and 25 Science subjects participated in yoga therapy treatment workshop. The rest 25 from each subject were taken as no treatment control groups. The sample was controlled in terms of educational qualification, gender, age and institute of study.

Experimental design: A (2x2x2) AXBXC analysis of variance design was used. 'A' here denotes two class of subjects (arts and science), 'B' denotes the two groups (yoga therapy treatment group and no treatment control group), and 'C' denotes the two trials (pre and post).

The *Inventories* for the assessment of relevant variables were as follows:

(1) ***(STAI-X1) State Trait Anxiety Inventory X-1 (Spielberger, Gorsuch & Lushene, 1970):*** The STAI-X1 form consists of twenty items. Each statement has four response options 'Not at all', 'Somewhat', 'Moderately so', and 'Very much so'. The highest score is 80 and the lowest is 20. Higher score on this scale shows higher anxiety, felt at a particular moment measuring the state anxiety. The Alpha coefficient of this scale, for high school female is .92. The concurrent validity of the scale is well established.

(2) ***(STAI-X2) State Trait Anxiety Inventory X-2 (Spielberger, Gorsuch, and Lushene, 1970):*** This inventory consists twenty items measuring trait anxiety. Each statement has four response options 'Not at all', 'Somewhat', 'Moderately so', and 'Very much so'. The highest one can score is 80 and the lowest is 20 revealing high and low levels of general anxiety. The test retest reliability of A-Trait scale for college under graduates ranged from .73to .86, and that for females is .76. The alpha reliability for high school female students is .92. The concurrent validity of this scale is well established.

(3) ***(TAI-H) Test Anxiety Inventory (Sud and Sud, 1997):*** This Hindi inventory comprises of twenty items, each consisting of four response options 'Almost never', 'Sometimes', 'Often', and 'Almost always'. The highest one can score is 80 and the lowest is 20. The inventory assesses individual differences in anxiety proneness in test or examination situations. Higher score on this scale shows higher test anxiety. The reliability of the Hindi TAI-H, in terms of a high alpha coefficient (.89 and .83) for high school boys and girls attested to the high degree of the internal consistency of the Hindi TAI. The concurrent validity (Sharma, Sud & Spielberger, 1983), construct validity of Hindi TAI (Rao, 1979; Sharma *et. al.*, 1983), and factorial validity of this test is well established. Worry and emotionality were the two factors that have been identified (Sud, Jutshi & Spielberger, 1987).

(4) ***(SI) Stress Inventory (Sethi, 2006):*** This English inventory comprises of thirty items, consisting of three response options 'Never Stressful', 'Sometimes Stressful', 'Always Stressful'. This inventory assesses the stress level of the adolescent female students only. The highest one can score is 60 and the lowest is 0. Higher score on this scale shows higher stress levels. The alpha internal consistency reliability for the whole Stress Inventory is.84 and that for its sub categories is family .72, education .69, friends .66, health .54, and behavioural and personal .74 all highly significant at $p<.001$ level. The test- retest reliability for this Stress Inventory is .69, $p< .001$. The construct validity of the Stress Inventory calculated shows that there is a high positive correlation between [SI -STAI-XI .54, SI - STAI-X2 .48 and SI -TAI-H .74 ($p<.001$)] and high negative correlation between [SI- NMRS -.34 and SI - SEI - .44 ($p<.001$)]. Thus, proving the Stress Inventory to be reliable and valid.

(5) ***(NMRS) Negative Mood Regulation Scale (Catenzaro and Mearns, 1990):*** This questionnaire comprises of thirty items, each consisting of five response options 'Strongly Disagree', 'Mildly disagree', 'Agree Disagree Equally', 'Mildly Agree', and 'Strongly Agree'. This questionnaire seeks to find out what people believe they can do about upsetting emotions. The highest one can score is 150 and the lowest is 30. A higher score indicates a high ability to regulate ones negative mood. The test-retest reliability obtained over an interval of three to four weeks and six to eight weeks for females was .74 and .78 respectively. The discriminant validity showed a high negative correlation between Negative Mood Regulation and Beck Depression Inventory (short form) ($r = -.39$, $p<.01$) for women. High correlation was found between Negative Mood Regulation Scale and Social Desirability Scale ($r = .23, p<.01$) in case of women.

(6) ***(SEI) Self - Esteem Inventory (Coopersmith, 1975):*** This inventory comprises of twenty- five items, consisting of two response options 'Like Me' and 'Unlike Me' . This is used to measure evaluative attitudes towards the self in social, academic, family and personal areas of experience. The highest one can score is 25 and the lowest is 0. A higher score is indicative of one's higher self-esteem. The Adult Form is used with persons aged sixteen and above. The Cronbach alpha reliability for the Adult Form of SEI for females is .83. The construct validity of the inventory along with concurrent and factorial validity has been well established (Kokenes, 1978; Cowan, Attmann & Pysh, 1978; Reasoner, 1982).

Yoga Therapy Programme

Everyday prior to the actual session 'Om Chanting' was carried out by the subjects in a relaxed posture. The workshop included pranayama, sukhsham vyam, mudars, asanas and meditation. The '*pranayamas*' taught to the subjects included suryabedi, sitali, sitkari, bhastrika, bhramri, ujjai and kapalbhati, each of them having their own special effects. The '*Mudras*' that were taught to the subjects were kaki, shambhavi, bhujangi, yoni and taragi. Further '*Sukhsham vyam*' was taught in order to provide flexibility to almost each and every part of the body, relaxing every muscle, tissue, bones and joints of the body. '*Asanas*' are postures that bring strength, equilibrium to the limbs of the body. The asanas that were included in this workshop were bhujang, nauka, aeri darshan, kon, trikon, pawanmukt, vriksh, ushtra, shalabh and shav asana/yoga nidra. The '*Meditation*' procedure involved the recitation of the mantra Om in a relaxed posture and then followed by sitting in complete silence and trying to achieve a no thought state. This is a tool for relaxing oneself and improving one's power of concentration thereby introspecting oneself. The workshop profile was scheduled for a period of four weeks each week comprising of six days and forty-five minutes of daily practice. That which was performed one day was rehearsed the next day, with new add-ons.

No Treatment Control Group: These groups of subjects were not given any intervention. However the gap between the pre and post assessment trials was same as that for the yoga therapy subjects.

Hypotheses

It was assumed that Yoga therapy will be effective in curtailing state anxiety, trait anxiety, test anxiety and stress and will enhance negative mood regulation and self esteem of the treatment group subjects of arts and science [TG1 (A) and TG2 (S)].

RESULTS

A one way analysis of variance has been performed on the pre trial scores of all the dependent variables, of arts (treatment and control group) and science (treatment and control group) subjects individually. The treatment and control groups of arts class did not differ significantly in terms of their pre trial scores of all the dependent variables. Whereas the treatment and control groups of Science class were significantly different from each other on the pre trial mean scores of (STAI-X1) *State Trait Anxiety Inventory (df1/48, F=8.69, p< .005)*, (STAI-X2) *State Trait Anxiety Inventory (df1/4, F= 9.07, p< .005, (NMRS) Negative Mood Regulation Scale (df1/ 48, F=7.72, p<.01) and (SEI) Self - Esteem Inventory (df1/48, F=5.24, p<.05)*. Thus revealing that the pre intervention mean score for STAI-X1 *(47.8, 41.6)*, STAI-X2 *(49.48, 42.44)*, NMRS *(101.84, 111.56)* and SEI *(12.84,15.76)* of Science treatment group differ significantly from their control group counterparts respectively.

Since treatment and control groups of science class differed significantly on the pre trial scores, the analysis of covariance has been used to analyse the effect of treatment on all the dependent variables, for both arts and science students.

The analysis of covariance of all the dependent variables, under treatment and control groups, for both Arts and Science subjects, is illustrated in Table-1.

TABLE 1

Pre, and Post adjusted Means, Analysis of Covariance and Analysis of Variance (pre-post trials) of STAI-X1, STAI-X2, TAI-H, SI, NMRS and SEI for the treatment and control groups of Arts and Science Subjects.

STAI-X1	*PRE MEAN*	*POST MEAN*	*POST ADJUSTED MEAN*	*ANCOVA*	*ANOVA (pre-post trials)*
TG1(A)	45.88	42.04	41.71	F=3.36 p<.025	F=6.06 p<.025
CG1(A)	45.28	46.32	46.02		F=0.58 NS
TG2(S)	47.8	41.68	40.47		F=6.87 p<.025
CG2(S)	41.6	42.4	44.01		F=0.42 NS
STAI-X2					
TG1(A)	44.52	41.2	41.70	F=7.49 p<.001	F=5.26 p<.05
CG1(A)	45.84	47.16	47.03		F=0.83 NS
TG2(S)	49.48	40.28	38.38		F=18.99 p<.001
CG2(S)	42.44	42.6	44.11		F=0.01 NS
TAI-H					
TG1(A)	43.28	39.8	40.02	F=2.85 p <.05	F=2.92 NS
CG1(A)	43.72	43.2	43.18		F=0.16 NS
TG2(S)	45.68	39.2	38.11		F=13.58 p<.005
CG2(S)	42.08	42.72	43.60		F=0.07 NS
SI					
TG1(A)	30.24	26.96	27.65	F=5.07 p<.005	F=5.53<.05
CG1(A)	29.88	29.64	30.55		F=0.13 NS
TG2(S)	32.72	25.96	22.06		F=14.70 p<.001
CG2(S)	27.64	29.44	31.73		F=1.04 NS
NMRS					
TG1(A)	104.92	107.28	107.48	F=6.13 p<.001	F=1.83 NS
CG1(A)	102.56	98.24	100.09		F=8.99 p<.01
TG2(S)	101.84	108.88	111.23		F=4.71 p<.05
CG2(S)	111.56	104.92	100.50		F=8.30 p<.01
SEI					
TG1(A)	15.88	16.56	15.98	F=3.51 p<.025	F=0.83 NS
CG1(A)	15.84	14.96	14.41		F=2.54 NS
TG2(S)	12.84	16	17.61		F=12.39 p<.005
CG2(S)	15.76	16.36	15.86		F=0.77 NS

In order to reveal if such a difference is also evident from pre to post trial score a separate single group analysis of variance was performed and is reported in the same table.

Notes: Arts treatment group one TGI(A), arts no treatment control group one CGI(A), science treatment group two TG2(S), science no treatment control group two CG2(S), (STAI-X1) State Trait Anxiety Inventory X-1, (STAI-X2) State Trait Anxiety Inventory X-2, (TAI-H) Test Anxiety Inventory, (SI) Stress Inventory, (NMRS) Negative Mood Regulation Scale and (SEI) Self - Esteem Inventory.

STAI-X1 (State Trait Anxiety Inventory X-1)

Table 1 reveals that for STAI-X1 the post (adjusted) mean score of arts yoga therapy treatment group (41.71) is significantly less than the mean score (46.02) of its no treatment control group counterpart ($p<.05$). The post (adjusted) mean score of Science yoga therapy treatment group (40.47) appear to be lower than its no treatment control group counterpart (44.01), but the difference is not significant according to the Duncan's Multiple - Range Test.

However, to show if such a difference is also evident from pre to post scores a separate single group analysis of variance was performed.

The post mean scores of Arts and Science treatment groups (42.04, 41.68) turned out to be significantly less than their pre mean scores of (45.88, 47.8) respectively. Further these changes were not significant for their respective control groups.

STAI-X2 (State Trait Anxiety Inventory X-2)

Table-1 shows that the post (adjusted) mean scores of arts (41.70, 47.03) and science (38.38, 44.11) yoga therapy treatment group are significantly less than the mean scores of their no treatment control group counterparts ($p<.01$), according to the Duncan's multiple - range test. Further, a significant difference is also evident from pre to post score on performing the single group analysis of variance. The post mean scores of arts and science treatment groups (41.2, 40.28) have turned out to be significantly less than their pre mean score (44.52, 49.48) respectively. These changes were not significant for the control groups of these respective classes.

TAI-H (Test Anxiety Inventory- Hindi)

Results reveals that the post (adjusted) mean scores of science yoga therapy treatment group *(38.11)* is significantly less than the mean score (43.60) of its no treatment control group counterpart (p<.05). The post (adjusted) mean score of arts yoga therapy treatment group (40.02) appears to be lower than the mean score of its no treatment control group counterpart (43.18), but this difference is not significant according to the Duncan's multiple - range test.

A significant difference however is evident from pre to post score for only the science treatment group on performing the single group analysis of variance. Where the post mean score of the science treatment group *(39.2)* is significantly less than its pre mean score *(45.68)*.

SI (Stress Inventory)

Results reveals that even though the post (adjusted) mean scores of Arts yoga therapy treatment group (27.65) appears to be lower than its no treatment control group (30.55), the difference is not significant according to Duncan's Multiple-Range Test. Whereas the post (adjusted) mean scores of Science yoga therapy treatment group (22.06) is significantly (p<.01) less than its no treatment control group (31.73) counterpart, according to the Duncan's multiple- range test.

However, the post mean scores of arts and science treatment groups (26.96,25.96) are significantly less than their pre mean scores (30.24,32.72) respectively. Further these changes were not significant for the control groups of these respective classes.

NMRS (Negative Mood Regulation Scale)

Results reveals, the post (adjusted) mean scores of arts (107.48,100.09) p<.05 and science yoga therapy treatment group (111.23,100.5,) p<.01 are significantly higher than the mean scores of their no treatment control group counterparts according to the Duncan's multiple - range test.

However the single group analysis of variance revealed that the post mean score of the science treatment group (108.88) to be significantly higher than its pre mean score (101.84). Whereas, no significant pre to post mean score difference has been seen for the arts treatment group subjects. Although, the control groups of both arts and science have shown significant differences in their post mean scores (98.24, 104.92) which are significantly lower as compared to their pre mean scores (102.56, 111.56) respectively. This decrease in their post trial scores as compared to their pre trial scores shows a decline in their ability to regulate their negative mood.

SEI(Self - Esteem Inventory)

Results reveals that even though the post (adjusted) mean scores of arts (15.98, 14.41) and science (17.61, 15.86) yoga therapy treatment group appear to be higher than their no treatment control group counterparts, the difference is not significant according to the Duncan's multiple- range test. A significant difference is evident from pre to post score for only the science treatment group on performing the single group analysis of variance. The post mean score of the science treatment group (16.00) is significantly higher than its pre mean score of (12.84). However, no significant pre to post mean score difference has been seen for the arts treatment group subjects.

DISCUSSION

Stress and strain in life extensively affects not only an individual's daily life activities, but also makes him prone to, or a victim of disease. Not being able to cope effectively with stress, anxiety and its other related components is a common problem of today's individual. Stress not only affects a person's mood, self-esteem, and academic performance but also leads to psychological, behavioural and cognitive inconsistencies, adversely affecting one's social life too. Stress and its related problems arise out of a person's complicated and undisciplined lifestyle.

Yoga has been defined as a methodised effort towards self perfection of one's latent potentialities (Aurobindo, 1955), as a science of mental control (Udupa, 2000) and also as a science of individual's well being harmonising the mind and the body (Sinha, 2002). Yoga is that multidimensional therapy which has made a mark for itself proving itself in the field of science and technology today. With the problems of adolescents being multiconceptual in nature, the therapy to resolve the issues also needs to be multifaceted.

The present study reveals a significant decrease in the post scores of both Arts and science treatment groups after receiving yoga therapy, on state anxiety, trait anxiety and stress inventories. However with regard to test anxiety, this decrease was evident only for the Science treatment group subjects.

Yoga therapy in the present study consisted of a multidimensional programme, included pranayamas, mudras, asanas and meditation. In a number of earlier studies, meditation has played a role in reducing stress (Goleman & Schwartz, 1976; Linden, 1973; Patel, 1993) and decreasing the levels of trait anxiety (Davison, Goleman & Schwartz, 1984). Yoga including asanas, pranayama and kriays has showed effective decrease in anxiety (Kocher, 1972). Yoga nidra has shown significant decrease in the stress levels and anxiety (Kamakhya, 2004) and has shown significant reduction in trait anxiety (Bhushan & Sinha, 2001). The short term Iyengar yoga course revealed significant decrease in self-reported symptoms of trait anxiety (Woolery, Myers, Sternlieb & Zeltzer, 2004).

Campbell and Kathleen (2004) revealed low average levels of symptoms of anxiety and stress after the yoga was performed. Jain & Sharma (2005) in their study have shown decrease in stress levels after performing yoga.

Relaxation is a prime aspect while performing yoga. In many studies, relaxation training has been found to be effective in alleviating general anxiety (McMilan & Lynn, 1986; Lindsay, Gamsu, McLaughlin, Hood & Espie, 1987; Somasundaram, 2002), study anxiety (Richardson & Suinn, 1973) and help students who find it difficult to catch up with stress of college life (McCreary, 1982; Whitehouse, Dinges, Orne, Keller, Bates, Baurer, Morahan, Haupt,

Carlin, Bloom, Zaugg & Orne, 1996). Relaxation training in general has been found to be significantly effective in reducing test anxiety in India and the West (Barbara & Steve, 1988; Broota & Sanghvi, 1994; Doan, Plante, Degregorio & Manuel, 1995; Prabha, 1990; Topp, 1989, Sud & Prabha, 1995).

In the present study yoga therapy has been found to be effective in enhancing the negative mood regulation and self esteem of only the Science treatment group subjects. This research stands on its own merit since very few studies have been carried out to know the effect of yoga therapy on the psychological variables such as negative mood regulation or self-esteem. Thus certain referred studies give an inferential view of the effect of yoga therapy on the aspects related to negative mood regulation and self-esteem. Thereby deriving assumed conclusions of the effect of yoga on factors associated to negative mood and self esteem. Few of such studies have been included to highlight the efficacy of yoga vis-à-vis negative mood regulation and self esteem.

It has been shown that yoga could be used for modifying affected behaviour, promoting mental health and achieving higher states of consciousness (Balodhi, 1986). Studies have shown that meditation and yogic exercise have had effective results on personality further showing decline in tension and emotional maturity (Kolswalla, 1978) producing significant improvement in the positive approach towards life, self concept, changing negative approach, ability to handle problem situations and in the development of perseverance and tenacity (Vinod, Vinod & Rajguru, 1998). Physical and mental activeness has also been maintained due to practice of asanas, yogic kriyas and meditation (Jain & Sharma, 2005). Yoga helps one to control emotions effectively (Sequeria, 1994), Pestonjee (1992) reported Sahasi, Mohan & Kacker (1989) study which showed increase in the locus of control showing increased self and inner control on using yoga techniques. Woolery, Myers, Sternlieb & Zeltzer (2004) observed changes in the acute mood, with subjects reporting decreased levels of negative mood and fatigue following yoga.

The present study has shown a significant decrease in the negative mood regulation scores for the arts and science control group subjects who were not given any intervention. This lowered efficiency of control groups in regulating their negative mood could have been a result of a lot of activities (regular tests, severe preparation for the twelfth board exams, annual day function rehearsals, project work etc.) being carried out in that particular month as revealed by subjects receiving yoga therapy. Since the control and treatment group subjects of the present study involved students of one institute, the schedule of work hours, tests, exams and curricular activities were somewhat similar for both group of subjects leading to personal pressures and hassles for all. This result also accounts for a common notion that during adolescence mood fluctuations are very frequent. The present study thus not only reveals heightened efficacy of Yoga therapy for the treatment group of the science subjects, showing an increase in their negative mood regulation, but deterioration of negative mood regulation for control group highlights the need for yoga therapy for all students.

Anxiety, stress, negative mood, low self-esteem are allied with all the age groups but these are higher in intensity in adolescence, primarily due to immense changes that are unfolded in their lives everyday. Anxiety, stress, negative mood and low self esteem among adolescents may be a result of their facing novel situations in all possible domains of development. Though people's perceptions have changed, yet adolescent female students in India even today deal with higher authoritative practices and restrictions imposed on them by their parents and teachers. Making adjustments with one's own self, family, peers, teachers and society at large, imposed demands and their inability to stand up to all the expectations further results in anxiety, negative mood and low self-esteem. Yoga therapy authenticates itself as an effective means of changing the diverse complications that an adolescent is confronted with. It helps an adolescent to be collected within himself / herself, deal with stress and anxiety, refuel lost energies, cope with negative mood and perceive the world and himself / herself positively.

REFERENCES

Aurobindo, S. (1955). *On Yoga*. Vol.1, 4. Pondicherry: Sri Aurobindo Ashram, International University Centre.

Balodhi, J.P. (1986). Perspective of raja yoga in its application to mental health. *NIMHANS Journal*, *4*(2), 133-138.

Barbara, S., & Steve, I. (1988). Effectiveness of progressive relaxation on test anxiety and visual perception. *Psychological Reports, 63*(2), 511-518.

Bhushan, S., & Sinha, P. (2001). Yoganidra and management of anxiety and hostility. *Journal of Indian Psychology*, *19* (1-2), 44-49.

Broota, A., & Sanghvi, C. (1994). Efficacy of two relaxation techniques in examination anxiety. *Journal of Personality and Clinical Studies,* 10(1-2, March-September) 29-35. (Special section: -Relaxation techniques and Psychological Management).

Campbell, D.E., & Kathleen, A.M. (2004). Yoga as a preventative and treatment for depression, anxiety, and stress. *International Journal of Yoga Therapy*, *14*, 53-58.

Catenzaro, S.J., & Mearns, J. (1990). Measuring Generalised Expectancies for Negative Mood Regulation: Initial Scale Development and Implications. *Journal of Personality Assessment*, *54*(3&4), 546-563.

Coopersmith, S. (1975). Building Self esteem in the classroom. *In Developing Motivation in young Children.* San Francisco: Albion Publishing Company.

Cowan, R., Attmann, H., & Pysh, F. (1978). A validity study of selected self-concept instruments. *Measurements and Evaluation in Guidance*, *10,* 211-221.

Davison, R.J., Goleman, D.J., & Schwartz, G.E. (1984). Attentional and affective concomitants of meditation: A cross sectional study. In D.H. Shapiro, & R.N.Walsh (Eds.), *Meditation: Classic and contemporary perspectives* (227-231). New York: Aldine.

Doan,Boa-TranT., Plante,Thomas G., Degregorio, Micheal P., & Manuel, Gerdenio M. (1995). Influence of aerobic exercise activity and relaxation training in coping with test anxiety. *Anxiety, stress & coping: an international journal, 8*(2) 101-111.

Goleman, D., & Schwartz, G. (1976). Meditation as an intervention in stress reactivity. *Journal of Consulting and Clinical Psychology, 44*, 456-466.

Hodapp, V., Glanzmann, P.G., & Laux, L. (1995). Theory and measurement of test anxiety as a situation specific trait. In Spielberger, C.D. & Vagg, P.R. (Eds.), *Test Anxiety. Theory, Assessment and Treatment*, 47-58. London: Taylor and Francis.

Jain, M., & Sharma, S. (2005). Art of Living: Its significance in Management of stress and general health. *Indian Journal of Applied Psychology, 42*, 13-18.

Keith, N., Hodapp, V., Schermellch-Engle, K., & Moosbrugger, H. (2003).Cross sectional and longitudinal confirmatory factor models for the German Test Anxiety Inventory: A construct validation. *Anxiety, Stress and Coping, 16*(3), 251-270.

Kocher, H.C. (1972). Yoga practices as a variable in neuroticism, anxiety and hostility. *Yoga Mimamsa, 15*(2), 37-46.

Kokenes, B.A. (1978). A factor analytic study of the Coopersmith Self Esteem Inventory. *Adolescence, 13,* 149-155.

Linden, W. (1973). The relationship between the practice of meditation by school children and their levels of field dependence and independence, test anxiety, and reading achievement. *Journal of Clinical Psychology, 41*, 139-143.

Lindsay, W.R., Gamsu, C.V., McLaughlin, E., Hood, E.N., & Espie, C.A. (1987). A controlled trial of treatments for generalised anxiety. *British Journal of Clinical Psychology, 26,* 3-15.

McCreary, M.H. (1982). Reduce stress by teaching relaxation techniques as coping skills for adolescents, *Dissertation Abstracts International, 42*(10).

McMillan, C.L., & Lynn, R. (1986). Differential assessment and the treatment of alcoholism. *British Journal of Clinical Psychology, 25,* 261-273.

Misra, O.P., & Srivastava, S.K. (1990). *Manual Costello Achievement motivation Scale*. Hardwar: Gurukul Kangri University.

Mythili, B., Bharthi,T., & Nagarthna, B. (2004). Adjustment Problems of Adolescent Students. *Journal of Community Guidance & Research, 21*(1), 54-61.

Patel, C. (1993). Yoga based therapy. In P.M. Lehrer & R.L.Woolfolk (Eds.), *Principles and practice of stress management* (89-138, 2nd edn.). New York: Guilford Press.

Pestonjee, D.M. (1992). *Stress and Coping: The Indian Experience.* New Delhi: Sage Publications.

Pope, A.W., McHale, S.M., & Carighead, E.W. (1988). *Self esteem enhancement with children and adolescents. New York*: Pergamon.

Prabha, I. (1990). A study of the effectiveness of cognitive / relaxation therapy in reducing the self reported anxiety and improving the performance of test anxious students. Unpublished Doctoral Thesis, Himachal Pradesh University, Shimla.

Rao, U. (1979). *Effect of self-acceptance. Test anxiety, and intelligence of achievement in different school courses.* Unpublished Master of Philosophy dissertation. Shimla: Department of Psychology, Himachal Pradesh University.

Reasoner, R. (1982). *Building Self Esteem: Teacher's guide and Classroom Materials.* Plato Alto, CA: Consulting Psychologists Press.

Richardson, F.C., & Suinn, R.M. (1973). A comparison of traditional systematic desensitisation, accelerated massed desensitisation and anxiety management training in the treatment of mathematics anxiety. *Behaviour Therapy*, *4*, 212-218.

Sequeria, H. (1994). Psychotherapy and Yoga- a clinical Psychologist speaks. *Yoga and Total Health*, 6-8.

Sethi, Z. (2006). *Efficacy of Yoga therapy for the management of anxiety and stress of adolescent female students.* Thesis for Doctor of Philosophy in Psychology. Shimla: Department of Psychology, Himachal Pradesh University.

Sharma, S., Sud, A., & Spielberger, C.D. (1983). Development of the Hindi form of the test anxiety inventory. In H.M. Van der Ploeg, R. Schwartzer, & C.D. Spielberger (Eds.), *Advances in Test Anxiety Research*, *2*, 183-190. Lisse: Swets and Zeitlinger Earlbaum.

Singh, V., Tomar, A.S., & Khokhar, C.P. (2005). Stress: Causative Factors and Remedies. In R. Singh, A. Yadava, & N.R. Sharma (Eds.), *Health Psychology*. New Delhi: Global Vision Publishing House.

Sinha. P. (2002). *Yoga: Meaning, Values and Practice.* Mumbai: Jaico Publishing House.

Somasundaram, D. (2002). Using traditional relaxation techniques in health care. *International Medical Journal, 9*(3), 191-198.

Spielberger, C.D., Gorsuch, R.L., & Lushene, R.E. (1970). *Manual for the State- Trait Anxiety Inventory.* Plato Alto, CA: Consulting Psychologists Press.

Sud, A., & Sud, P. (1997). *Manual of Test Anxiety inventory Hindi (TAI-H).* Varanasi: Rupa Psychological Centre.

Sud, A., Jutshi, C., & Spielberger, C.D. (1987). The factor structure of the Hindi version of the Test Anxiety Inventory. *Personality Study and Group Behaviour, 7,* 27-35.

Sud, A., & Prabha, I. (1995). Test anxiety and academic performance: Efficacy of cognitive / relaxation therapies. *Psychological Studies, 40*(3), 179-186.

Topp, R. (1989). Effect of relaxation or exercise on under graduates' test anxiety. *Perceptual & Motor Skills, 69,* 35-41.

Udupa, K.N. (2000). *Stress and its Management by Yoga.* Banglore: Motilal Banorsidas Publishers Private Limited.

Vinod, R.S., Vinod, S.D., & Rajguru, M. (1998). Effects of Yoga on Positive Approach Towards Life. *Yoga Mimamasa, XXXII* (4), 13-28.

Watson, D. & Clark, L.A. (1984). Negative Affectivity: The disposition to experience aversive emotional states. *Psychological Bulletin, 96,* 465-490.

Whitehouse, W.G., Dinges, D.F., Orne, E.C., Keller, S.E., Bates, B.L., Bauer, N.K., Morahan, P., Haupt, B.A., Carlin, M.M., Bloom, P.B., Zaugg, L., & Orne, M.T. (1996). Psychosocial and immune effects of self-hypnosis training for stress management through the first semester of medical school. *Psychosomatic Medicine, 58,* 249-263.

Woolery, A., Myers, H., Sternlieb, B., & Zeltzer, L. (2004). A yoga intervention for young adults with elevated symptoms of depression. *Alternative Therapies in health and Medicine, 10*(2), 60-63.

●●●

7

Impact of Yogasana on the Mentally Challenged

Sunita Malhotra, D.K. Diwan and Mukesh Kumar

Mental retardation is not something we have, like blue eyes or a bad heart, nor is it something you are - like short or thin. It is not a medical disorder nor a mental disorder. Mental retardation is seen more as a social problem than as an inadequacy in the individual. Mental retardation is a particular state of functioning that begins in childhood and is characterized by limitation in both intelligence and adaptive skills. It is a state of impairment or incomplete mental development. A mentally retarded person is considered to be an individual who has an undeveloped mind and thus has inadequate social adjustment, reduced learning and a slow rate of maturation. It is not a disease entity but just a symptom in response to various causes. Mental retardation may exist alone or in association with any other neuro-developmental disorder; mentally retarded individuals have similar feelings as others and are subject to the same emotional and behavioural problems as those of normal learning ability. They may have complex medical needs or be as healthy as the population at large. Because they may have limited common sense and problem solving capacity as well as communication difficulties, they may pose particular problems for the physician attempting to diagnose their mental state, and in this population both health promotion and health maintenance can be challenging.

The American Association on Mental Retardation (AAMR) arguably the leading professional organization in the field of mental retardation, offered the following definition of mental retardation that it is a disability characterized by significant limitations both in intellectual functioning and in adaptive behaviour as expressed in conceptual, social, and practical adaptive skills. It is a disability due to interplay of several genetic and ecological factors and no single factor can deal effectively with various facets of mental retardation. In the field of mental retardation the innovations have been taken up from three view points: (i) the mental retarded child - Yoga and its effects, (ii) the catalysts - augmentative intervention, (iii) the community - community participatory rehabilitation. This disability originates before age 18 years. (Luckasson, *et. al.*, 2002).

Western literature pays very little attention to yogic excercises in helping the mentally retarded. It is purely Indian in origin in temperament and in practice. Yoga means to bring two things together, to meet and to unit. Yoga is known for its time tested power of increasing concentration and imparting self-discipline for children and adults. It is a practice that enables one to achieve a higher level of performance previously impossible. It offers enormous scope to help overcome various human problems, both mental and physical. "Whatever place, whatever time, the ancestors have framed yoga practices to suit them all. Only the attitudes and circumstances of human beings change" (Desikachar and Jayachandran, 1983).

There are many branches of Yoga. The popularly used one is Hatha Yoga, which involves expression and conservation of energy. This type of yoga incorporates asanas along with pranayama. The word 'Asana' means posture. Posture simply refers to a particular position. The word asana originates from the Sanskrit word as means 'to be', 'to stay', or 'to remain' in a particular position. The two qualities of an asana are: i) The individual should maintain a certain amount of steadiness in the posture without much effort or tension ii) He should also experience comfort in that posture. To achieve both these qualities a long period of practice is needed. The comfort and steadiness in a posture is most often achieved through total concentration of the mind on the posture. The practice of an asana is always coordinated with breathing. According to Smith (1980) the asanas can be performed in various positions. They are as follows:

(a) Standing (*Tadasana*)

(b) Sitting, Kneeling (*Pascimatanasana*)

(c) Supine - Lying on back (*Apanasana*)

(d) Prone - Lying on stomach (*Bhujangasana*)

(f) Inverted (*Sarvangasana*)

The word 'Pranayama' means regulated breathing. While doing pranayama the person has to deliberately control and direct his breathing in a planned way. Pranayama is usually practised in a comfortable sitting position. The principle of pranayama are the posture must be comfortable, the body must be relaxed, the change from asanas to pranayama should be gradual, it should occur in a suitable sequence and the body must be rested before starting pranayama. When the mind is fully focused on the different parts of the breathing cycle it is known as pranayama. When we applied yoga on the individual it means, to avoid distraction and to help one focus all his attention, to arrive at a certain level where the activities of the mind and body work as one and to advance towards achieving higher levels of performance, that are presently existing only as capabilities within the individual which have not yet come out.

In relation to mental retardation, the common physical problems which occur along with the condition are paralysis, fits, defects in speech, sight and hearing and poor health. The mentally retarded people refers to a group of people with different level (mild, moderate, severe and profound retardation) and with different problems. However all of them have a common factor and that is low intelligence (below IQ 70). Many of the mentally challenged persons usually face a lot of difficulty in learning activities of daily living (ADL). They also have difficulty in co-ordination, concentration, to attend a particular task for the required amount of time and poor attention span. All these factors are responsible for the normal adjustment in the social life.

Some studies have been conducted among the mentally challenged to find out the effects of yogasanas. A significant improvement was reported in general health from yogasanas practices even in a short period of time. As a result of this gain, absenteeism had come down, thereby time available for learning has increased, and the improved general health facilitated the persons to learn more effectively without disruption and disturbance in their training schedule. Studies by Krishnamacharya Yoga Mandiram and Vijay Human Services among the mentally challenged have shown improvement in terms of reducing hyperactivity (Jeyachandran, 1981), appetite and in sleep motor skills and correcting posture (Pushpa, 1981), reduction of obesity and control of dribbling (Usha, 1982) and the disappearance of facilities (Annamma, cf. Vijay Human Service, 1988). Kasthuri. (1983) reported that the yoga practitioners - whoever they may be, special educators, psychologists, parents or other professionals - do realise that a systematic yoga practice will increase both the physical and mental well being of any individual. Desikachar and Jeyachandran (1983) hypothesized and proved that when yoga is applied for the mentally challenged person it helps the person to co-ordinate the activities of the mind and body and to improve his activities of daily living to a degree which could not be achieved before. It also tend to reduce the distracted state of mind and to concentrate on the present activity. Based on the above hypotheses the practice of yoga should be aimed at improving general health, concentration, social relationships and the self-reliance of the mentally retarded persons. As per Vijay Human Services, it was found that yoga has helped the mentally challenged persons in correcting postures, reducing obesity, controlling dribbling sleep, improving appetite, bringing down hyperactivity and general health. Uma, Nagendra, Nagarathna, Vaidehi and Seethala (1989) found yoga as an effective therapeutic tool in the management of mentally retarded children.

Yoga as a form of physical exercise is being used in special schools for the mentally retarded children/person to develop gross and fine motor skills and to improve general health. But there are differences between physical exercise and yoga.

(*i*) Yoga is exercise without visible movement, exercises emphasize movement,

(*ii*) Yoga induces relaxation, balance and self control, exercises develops strengths, flexibility and endurance.

(*iii*) The frequency of repetitions is not increased in yoga rather the duration of time in which each asana is being held, increases in accordance with ease of performance. The exercises usually entail some pain and discomfort.

(*iv*) Yoga stresses on a single slow contraction of certain muscles followed by relaxation, exercises usually involve a number of several bounces / stretches in a given time. Yoga is being practised with mental retardation to reduce hyperactivity, control seizures, increase attention span, improve social and communication skills and improve their general health.

An educator who works with the mentally challenged should have - the right understanding of asana and pranayama which is essential in teaching yoga to the mentally challenged; a desire to serve the mentally challenged; have knowledge of human development and limitations; to be responsible and to achieve the instructional goals; knowledge of nature, causes and management of mentally challenged persons; high tolerance and patience. He should be concerned, compassionate and able to communicate with mentally challenged at any level. With this empirical background regarding Yogasanas, in the specific context of mentally challenged, an observation was made to study the observable improvement on the status and behaviour of the mentally retarded children (of different level) with the intervention of Yoga by using the following methodology.

Method

Design: The pre-post observation was made for studying the impact of yogasana on the skills and problematic behaviour of three mentally retarded cases of 8, 12 and 14 years old (chronological age).

Sample: For present purpose group consisting of five mentally challenged was selected from the special school for mentally challenged children from Rohtak. After interacting with the group for 4 days, only three cases (two cases of moderate mentally retarded with Down's syndrome (IQ 45 to 49 and IQ 40 to 45 respectively) and one case of mild mentally retarded (IQ 50 to 55) who was highly motivated for practising yogasanas were selected for the study.

Procedure: Participative observational technique was used for studying the behavioural change in three cases of mentally retarded. The descriptive observations of three cases have been reported in the preceding section.

CASE I

Name	Radhika (not real name)
Father Name	Mr. Gopi Nath (not real name)
Age	14 years
Medical & Psychological	The medical and psychological diagnosis report reported her as being moderately mentally challenged with Down's syndrome, with an IQ 45 to 49.

Observation in Pre-intervention stage	Intervention (Yoga therapy)	Observation in post Intervention stage
- Considerable difficulty in expressing herself.	(*i*) A course of different yogasansa (from simple to complex) was being practised continuously for seven months on group basis. These yogasanas were:	Although not too confident but sufficiently well in expressing herself.
- Deficiency in fine motor skills	(a) Tadasana, (b) Uttanasana, (c) Parsva-Uttanasana	Improvement in the fine motor skills.

	(d) Vajrasana (e) Dvipadapitham,	
- Protruding tongue.	The practice of yogasana was minutes done twice a day for twenty closed in the institution. This practice was followed by a chain of warming up exercises (aerobics)	Most of the time mouth (no protruding).
- Over weight due to habit of over eating	(*ii*) Chanting of word 'OM' was also introduced after completion of five asanas twice a day for 2 minutes in a relaxing sitting position.	Weight dropped and look became healthy
- Lethargic		Active with less or no lethargic symptoms.
- Wide open mouth.		Mouth remained relatively closed
- Destructive behaviour (throwing objects).		Destructive behaviour reduced considerably.
- Difficulties in squatting.		Comfortable while squatting and doing different activities
-Low acceptance among the family members and siblings due to learning impairment and temper tantrum.		The acceptance and intimacy among the family members increased. The sibling realised that their sister had learnt the different skills which was not possible before. Temper tantrums considerably reduced.

Thus, there was an observable change in the physical appearance as well as in the behaviour of Radhika, she started her mouth close, lost her weights and looked healthy. Consequently she became active due to reduction in her weight and there were remarkable change in physical activities, and her interaction with the family members also increased.

CASE II

Name	Ashish (not real name)
Father Name	Mr. Suresh (not real name)
Age	12 years
Medical and Psychological	The medical and psychological diagnosis report reported him as being moderately mentally challenged with an IQ 40 to 45.

Observation during Pre-intervention stage	*Intervention by implementing of Yogasanas*	*Observation during post Intervention stage*
- Difficulty in self-expression	(*i*) A course of different yogasansa (from simple to complex) was being practised continuously for seven months on group basis. These yogasanas were:	Self-expression improved
- Deficiency in gross motor activities	(a) Tadasana, (b) Uttanasana, (c) Parsva-Uttanasana (d) Vajrasana (e) Dvipadapitham,	Improvement in the gross motor activities.
	The practice of yogasana was done twice a day for twenty minutes in the institution. This practice was followed by a chain of warming up exercises (aerobics)	
- Hyperactive and self hyperactivity and completion of five	(*ii*) Chanting of word 'OM' was also injurious behaviour self injurious behaviour asanas twice a day for 2 minutes in a relaxing sitting position.	Reduction in introduced after
- Lethargic		Became quite active
- Poor self help skills		Better self help skills

- Non intelligible speech - Protruding tongue and drooling behaviour reduction in drooling behaviour		Intelligible speech Most of the time keeping tongue in his mouth and

Thus, improvement was observed in the physical and observable difficulties of Ashish, as he was doing his work actively and could perform the activities of daily living adequately to some extent. Slowly his problematic behaviours were reduced and he started expressing himself verbally and non-verbally, as a result attitude of the family members was changed and he was accepted at the dinning table. On different occasion they took Ashish with them for family outing.

CASE III

Name	Surender (not real name)
Father Name	Mr. Rajender (not real name)
Age	12 years
Medical and Psychological	The medical and psychological diagnosis report revealed him as being mildly mentally challenged with an IQ 50 to 55.

Observation during Pre-intervention stage	**Intervention by implementing of Yogasanas**	**Observation during Intervention stage post**
- Poor span of attention	(*i*) A course of different yogasansa (from simple to complex) was beingpractised continuously for seven months on group basis. These yogasanas were:	Span of attention increased.
- Poor eye hand coordination,	(a) Tadasana,	Improvement in eye hand
concentration	(b) Uttanasana,	coordination and concentration
	(c) Parsva-Uttanasana	
	(d) Vajrasana	
	(e) Dvipadapitham,	

- Poor self help skills	The practice of yogasana was done twice a day for twenty minutes in the institution. This practice was followed by a chain of warming up exercises (aerobics)	Improvement in self help skills.
- Non- intelligible speech.	(ii) Chanting of word 'OM' was also introduced after completion of five asanas twice a day for 2 minutes in a relaxing sitting position.	Speech became intelligible to some extent
- Self injurious behaviour		Relative improvement in self-injurious behaviour.
- Not able to distinguish different sounds		Started distinguishing different sounds
- Non-cooperative in the group play activities		Active participation in group play activities by interacting with other children and cooperation is increased

Thus there was considerable improvement in the behaviour of Surender which perhaps led to increased acceptance by the family members.

In all the three cases of Radhika, Ashish and Surender, the medical practitioners, the parents, sibling and the special educators, opined that yoga therapy is positively effective. Yogasana helped in developing the skills, if it is performed in a proper way, in positive environment with dedication and discipline and with regular examination.

Thus in all the three above mentioned cases despite different levels their mental retardation improvement was observed in reducing self injurious behaviours, intelligible speech, self help skills, eye hand coordination, concentration, attention span, reducing hyperactivity, expressing himself, gross motor activities, and in squatting. These improvements in different patterns of behaviour may be attributed to the intervention of Yoga therapy, which was given continuously for seven months (twice a day). Along with

Yoga therapy children also learnt free hand exercises (warming up with music) and did meditation. This might have increased their performance in daily life activities. The reports from Minovikas Kendra Calcutta, who worked on nearly 300 mentally retarded children, also confirmed that this therapy has worked wonders in improving the co-ordination of mind and body subsequently increasing the level of concentration. The Yogic exercises may have brought some physiological changes like release of endorphins from the opiate sensitive cells (receptors) in the body that may have cause the reduction in self-destructive behaviour and hyper-activity. Breathing exercises while chanting OM have augmented speech therapy, reduction in weight, improving bilateral activities, relaxation and bending exercises, promoting attention and concentration span.

It can be concluded that Yoga is a significant tool to help in developing the capacities which are not visible on face and also assisting in variety of activities related to therapeutic aspect, self help skills, fine motor and gross motor skills and activities of daily living etc. Yoga can be employed as a means of improving the academic achievement, social adjustment, increase attention span, improved their general health and reducing the hyperactivity of mentally retarded children.

Hence, on the basis of the present observational study it can be recommended that yogic exercises should strictly be incorporated in manpower development and training curriculum dealing with mental retardation (although few centres have already in corporated). The rich heritage, viz. the system of yoga, has today been universalized and endowed to humanity for its prosperity and its effectiveness has also been proved for persons with mental retardation.

REFERENCES

Desikachar, T.K.V. (1982). *The Yoga of T. Krishna macharya* Madras; Krishna macharya Yoga Mandiram.

Desikachar, T.K.V. and Jeyachandran, P. (1983). Yoga for the mentally retarded. In Vijay Human Service (1988) *Teaching Yogasana to Mentally Retarded Persons.* Madras.

Jayachandran, P. (1981). *The effectiveness of Yogasana on the Mentally Retarded.* Paper presented at the First National Conference of the Indian Academy of Yoga, Bangalore.

Kasthuri, D (1983). Teaching Yogasana to the mentally retarded. In Vijay Human Service (1988) *Teaching Yogasana to Mentally Retarded Persons.* Madras.

Luckasson, R., Borthwick, D., S., Buntinx, W.H.E., Coulter, D.L., Craig, E. M., Reeve, A. (2002). *Mental Retardation: Definition, Classification and System of supports* (10th ed.) Washington, DC: American Association on Mental Retardation.

Mervyn, F.A. (2003). *An Introduction to Neuro-Developmental Disorders of children.* New Delhi: The National Trust.

Pushpa (1982). Teaching Yogasana to the Mentally Retarded. In Vijay Human Service (1988) *Teaching Yogasana to Mentally Retarded Persons,* Madras.

Smith, M.J.N. (1980). *An illustrated guide to Asanas and Pranayama.* Madras: Krishna macharya Yoga Mandiram.

Uma, K., Nagendra, H.R., Nagarathna, R., Vaidehi, S., and Seethala, R., (1989). The integrated approach of Yoga: a therapeutic tool for mentally retarded children: A one-year controlled study. *Journal of Mental Deficiency Research* 33, 415-421.

Usha (1982). Teaching Yogasana to the Mentally Retarded. In Vijay Human Service (1988) *Teaching Yogasana to Mentally Retarded Persons.* Madras.

Vijay Human Services (1988). *Teaching Yogasana to the mentally retarded persons.* Madras: Vijay Human Services.

●●●

8

Psycho-physiological Responsiveness to Meditation in HIV Positive Patients

Sunita Gupta and Meenakshi Sharma

During the last two decades, HIV/AIDS (Human Immune Deficiency virus/Acquired Immuno Deficiency Syndrome) has become a pandemic around the globe. The increasing number of deaths occuring throughout the world due to HIV/AIDS has already reached an alarming state.

AIDS as the name holds means "Acquired Immune Deficiency Syndrome". The term acquired refers to what is caught as opposed to being inherited and Immune Deficiency describes the state in which the body's immune system is depleted, so that it is unable to defend itself against the development of certain conditions, particularly infections. Syndrome refers to group of sign and symptoms of illness, which result from the destruction of the body's defense by HIV.

The HIV is a unique virus which weakeans and ultimately destroys the immune system *i.e.*, defense system of the body. As a result, the effected individual becomes venerable to many life threatening infections. When we don't have a strong immune system to fight off the germs, our body becomes weaker and weaker gradually.

HIV infected person may continue to live a perfectly normal life without showing any physical symptoms, such a situation is called

"HIV Non-Symptomatic". Once the disease progresses, the person will begin to have different illnesses and will show certain physical symptoms. The situation is called "HIV symptomatic". The term 'AIDS' is used when disease has progressed and the person develops one or more serious infections or conditions.

HIV antibodies are detectable only three weeks to six months after the first infection. This invisible period is termed as the 'Window Period'. Any tests undertaken during this period may be negative even if the person is infected. But different types of tests are used to detect antibodies. Some of them may be (1) ELISA (Enzyme Linked Immuno Sorbent Assay). It is easy to perform, is reliable and sensitive. The basic principle of the test is to detect the antibodies against HIV virus that are present in the blood of an infected person. (2) Rapid test is a screening test for HIV, based on a single use qualitative immunoassay that can detect antibodies to HIV. Confirmatory tests are important to eliminate 'false positive' results (a positive HIV test result for a person who is actually HIV negative). The possible causes of Anxiety and depresion in HIV/AIDS patients could be because of an HIV test or a confirmatory test; the prospect of CD cell count or viral load test; a forth coming physical examination or some illness within the family.

HIV positive patients commonly experience Anxiety, the symptoms of which include trouble falling asleep, impaired concentration, fatigue, and psychomotor agitation. Discrete intense episodes of Anxiety that include a constellation of physical symptoms such as dizziness, chest pain, shortness of breath, paresthesias of the fingers, toes and lips and a sense of impending doom are panic attacks. Depression is a serious problem for HIV patients which may include feeling of sadness and hopelessness due to loss of ability in usual activities or loss of physical apperance due to weakness, poor concentration, isolating oneself and irritability which can further lead to suicidal feelings. Experts believe that lower household income, active drug use, sexual and physical abuse, relationship status and social support may lead to depression.

The neuropsychiatric manifestations of HIV infection is a progressive cognitive/motor impairment leading to AIDS Dementia

Complex (ADC). The patients with advanced ADC have Motor dysfunction such as no coordination, ataxia, and cognitive changes such as poor attention, slowed information processing speed and impaired memory (Tross et al., 1988). The cognitive abnormalities seen in HIV positive patients due to 'Pseudo dementia' *i.e.*, impaired neuropsychological performance is mainly attributed to depressive illness (Caine, 1986).

The onset of depression here in HIV positive patients is facilitated by many factors such as poor social support, poor social or health care, and problems involving poor accomodation, finances or employment, as well as personal or familial predisposition to effective illness. The risk of suicide in these individuals is there in relation to usual socio- demographic risk factor and the current mental status (Rundell *et al.*, 1988).

A large number of antiretroviral drugs are being used for the management of HIV cases. But these drugs donot cure the individual. At present there is no effective cure or vaccine available to combat this deadly disease. Since the role of medication is not very effective, Behavioural Medicine can play a very important role, which emphasizes the role of psychological factor in health. This include biofeedback, meditation and yoga and many other behavioural medicine techniques.

Meditation is thought to be the oldest form of relaxation. In simple terms, it is a mind cleansing or emptying process. At a deeper level, meditation is focused concentration and increased awareness of one's being when the mind has been emptied of conscious thoughts, unconscious thoughts can enter the conscious realm to bring enlignment to our lives. It is an increased concentration and awareness, a process of living in the present moment to produce and enjoy a tranquil state of mind.

The contextual approach to meditation proposed by Johnson (1982) believes that meditation is a skill which can be utilized to achieve any desired goal. The relaxing effect of yogic meditation has also been successfully reported in reducing post partum distress in mothers (Halonen and Passman, 1985); treatment of stuttering, migraine headache, asthma and even retarded ejaculation (Delmonte, 1986). Meditation can improve strength and flexibility, help in the management of physiological variables such as blood pressure, respiration, heart rate and metabolic rates and improve over all exercise capacity (Raub, 2002). Meditation has been found to be effective in the treatment of gastrointestinal disorders (Shannahoff, 2002); heart diseases (Schneider, Nidich & Salerno, 2001), and irritable bowel syndrome (Shannahoff, 2002). There is an utter dearth of studies regarding the effects of meditation in physical and mental health of HIV patients. Mayatech (1992) and Benner (2001) used herbal medicine and traditional medicine as an alternative approach in managing HIV disease which included relaxation, nutrition, herbs, ayurveda and massage. People with HIV/AIDS were found to manage their health to some extent with the help of these alternative therapies.

Dane (2000) conducted a study so as to explore the role of meditation on the immune functioning of Thai women infected with HIV/AIDS. The author found that the meditation provided great comfort to the persons living with HIV and influenced their immune functioning. Conradsen, Susan and Coll (2000) used mindfulness meditation to promote holistic health in individuals with HIV/AIDS and found that holistic approach to health promotion reduces stress along with reduction in negative effect and improvement in well-being. Bertucci and Marie (2000) used 'guided imagery body scan meditation' technique, three times per week for six weeks for responsiveness to relaxation of distress in HIV positive patients and found that guided imagery body scan meditation helped HIV positive patients to decrease their distress conditions. Gore - Felton *et al.* (2003) used alternative therapies of acupunture, massage among men and women living with HIV and found them to be effective in promoting the physical and mental health of the patients. Molassiotis and Maneesakorm (2004) used emotion focused coping method of meditation which improved the quality of life, and psychological status of Thai people living with AIDS.

Not even a single study has been conducted on HIV positive patients so far that has tried to investigate the effects of meditation on physiological Measures namely EEG frequency, Muscle action potential and blood pressure (Systolic and Diastolic) and psychological measures which assess Anxiety in terms of its four components namely cognitive, somatic, behavioural and feelings and depression. The present study is a step in this direction.

METHOD

Design

Pre-Post experimental design was used for the assessment of all the dependent variables.

Sample

Male indoor and outdoor patients in the age range of (21-40 years), diagnosed as HIV positive, on the basis of laboratory tests, served as the subjects who voluntarily attended the confidential and counselling centre, Microbiology Department, Government Medical College, Amritsar. Initially the study was started with the sample of 100 subjects (50 in control group and 50 in experimental group on the basis of random assignment). But out of 50 subjects in control group, 9 subjects dropped out in between testing and retesting sessions thereby leaving the sample of 41 subjects in this group. The number of patients who participated in the study was, therefore, 91. The subjects in both the groups used to visit the centre for counselling daily in addition to Medication prescribed by the physicians.

Tools

Physiological Measures

(1) The Alpha EEG Apparatus (Medicaid Systems, Chandigarh) was used for recording alpha EEG brain-wave pattern.

(2) The EMG Bio-trainer Apparatus (Medicaid Systems, Chandigarh) was used to measure the muscle action potential.

(3) Sphygmomanometer was used to measure both systolic and diastolic blood pressure.

Psychological Measures

(1) Four Systems Anxiety Questionnaire - FSAQ (Koksal and Power, 1990) was used to assess Anxiety on four components; somatic, cognitive, behavioural and feeling. The FSAQ consists of 60 items concerning difficulties that most people experience from time to time. Respondents were asked to indicate whether they have or have not experienced in accordance with the content of the item by ticking 'Yes' or 'No' option given against each item. The test provides measures for four 15- item subscales. Each item has been assigned a scale value and the patients scrores are calculated by adding the scale values of the items with which their agree. The means and standard deviations of the scale values as reported by the authors are: somatic ; M=5.49, SD= 2.73: Cognitive; M = 5.49, SD = 2.78: behavioural; M = 5.50, SD = 2.60: feelings; M = 5.49, SD = 2.51. The comparability and similarity in these values enables direct comparison of a person's scores across different components (Koksal and Power, 1990). This test has already been used in Indian setting (Gupta & Gupta, 1997).

(2) The IPAT Depression Inventory (Krug & Laughlin, 1976) was used to assess the depression level of the subjects. The tests consists of 40 statements about how people feel or think at one time or the other. There are no right or wrong answers. The subject has to pick the one that is really true for him or her and answers have to be marked in a, b, c order form. The split-half and test-retest reliabilities of the inventory as reported by authors are .95 and .93 respectively and the validity of the test, in terms of correlation with clinical Analysis Questionnaire,was .88.

Procedure

The blood pressure (systolic and diastolic) of each subject was noted down. The alpha EEG Measurements were taken using alpha EEG appratus. The electrodes were placed on the occipital, parietal and frontal regions of the head.

The muscle action potential was measured using the EMG apparatus. The electrodes were placed over the fore-finger. The measurements were automatically recorded in terms of Micro-volts per second. After the EEG, EMG, and Blood Pressure recordings, the FSAQ and Depression Inventory were administered on each subject. A gap of 5 minutes was given in between all the assessments whether physiological or psychological. For pre- and post-treatment assessments, each subjects was tested individually, asked to relax in the testing room for five minutes and then tested on the physiological and psychological parameters mentioned above.

The subjects in the meditation group were first kept on meditation practice for one week. The subjects were instructed to sit in the lotus position, close their eyes with their hands in 'Gyan Mudra'. The subjects were instructed to inhale deeply but slowly and then exhale slowly while chanting 'Om'. The subjects were instructed to focus on the movements of abdomen during the whole process. After one week's practice, the meditation procedure was continued for 20 minutes daily for 20 days before breakfast after emptying the bladder and bowel.

The pre-treatment testing was done a day before commencement of the meditation treatment, while the post-treatment testing was done a day after the meditation treatment was over.

The subjects in the control group were simply tested for physiological and psychological assessments and retesting was done after 20 days.

RESULTS AND DISCUSSION

The results of the present study are reported in Table I in which the means and standard deviations for scores on physiological and psychological measures under various groups and conditions are given.

The significance of differences between means was tested by t-test, two types of comparisons were made: intra group comparison, *i.e.*, pre- vs post-treatment comparison for the control as well as the experimental group, and inter-group comparison *i.e.* control vs experimental group comparison for the post-treatment condition.

For the control group, the pre- vs post-comparisons yielded significant results for the physiological measures of alpha EEG, EMG and psychological parameters of feelings, cognitive components of Anxiety and composite Anxiety. As the post treatment means of the psychophysiological parameters were found to be significantly higher then the pre-treatment means. It can be inferred, therefore, that the subjects in the control group were not responding to medication and counselling provided by the counsellors in between testing and retesting. The other pre-post comparisons in this group were found to be nonsignificant thereby again implying that mere medication and HIV counselling did not improve physical and mental health of HIV patients of this group.

The pre-post comparison for the experimental group provided statistically significant results for all the psychophysiological measures—a marked significant decrease in the post treatment means was reported except alpha EEG scores.

For the control vs. experimental group post treatment comparisons, the results were significant for all the psycho-physiological measures thereby revealing clear cut effects of meditation in the experimental group.

It can be inferred, therefore, that the meditation produced a highly beneficial effect on the physical and mental status of HIV positive patients. The results are therefore, consistent with the findings of Mayatech (1992), Dane (2000), Conradsen *et al* (2000), Gore - Felton *et al.* (2003) and Molassiotis and Maneesakorn (2004).

The results, therefore, clearly demonstrate that the practice of meditation for 20 minutes daily for 20 days leads to significant reduction in all components of Anxiety, depression, EMG and blood pressure (systolic and Diastolic) and increase in alpha EEG. The results, therefore, clearly demonstrate the relaxing and soothing effects of meditation on HIV positive patients.

The conceptualization of Anxiety in terms of its different components enables a researcher or therapist to assess a patient's Anxiety profile in a more detailed manner and this detailed information may be used by him to improve the treatment efficacy (Barlow, 1985; Koksal and Power, 1990; Ost, Jerramalm and Johansson,

1982). Koksal and Power (1990) suggest that "the primary treatment approach adopted for any Anxiety disorder may also be determined by the relative emphasis of the patient's Anxiety profile on cognitive, affective, behavioural and somatic components".

REFERENCES

Barlow, D.H. (1985). Dimensions of Anxiety disorders, In A.H. Tuma and J.D. Master (eds). *Anxiety and Anxiety Disorders*. Hillisdale, NJ: Lawrence Eribaum Associates, Inc.

Benner, H. (2001). Raising our voices: HIV Activism Breaking Down the Isolation of AIDS survivors. *AIDS Widows Group Project*—Roi—ET, Thailand, 2: 50-55.

Bertucci, N.M. (2000). Responsiveness to relaxation for distress in HIV positive patients. *Dissertation Abstracts*, 60, 4201.

Caine, E. (1986). The Neuropsychology of Depression: The Pseudomentia Syndrome. *The Neuropsychological Assessment of Neuropsychiatric Disorders.* In L. Grant and K.M. Adams (eds.), New York; Oxford University, Press.

Dane, B. (2000). Thai Woman: Meditation As a way to cope with AIDS. *Journal of Religion and Health*, Spring; 39, 5-21.

Delmonte, M.M. (1986). Meditation as a clinical Intervention strategy; A Brief Review. *International Journal of Psychosomatics*, 33: 9-12.

Gore, F., Vosvick, Power Koopman, Ashton; Bachmann, Israelsl and Spiegel (2003). A common Practice among Men and Women living with HIV. *Journal of the Associations of Nurses in AIDS care*, 14: 17-27.

Gupta, U. and Gupta, B.S. (1997). Indian Instrumental Music and Mental Relaxation. *Indian Journal of Clinical Psychology*, 24: 154-157.

Halonen, J.S. and Passman, R.H. (1985). Relaxation training and expectation in the treatment of Post Partum distress. *Journal of Consulting and Clinical Psychology*, 53: 839-845.

Johnson, W. (1982). *Riding the ox home; A history of meditation from Shamanism to silence.* Boston, M.A., Beacon Press.

Koskal, F and Power, K.G. (1990). Four System Anxiety Questionnaire (FSAQ): A self-Report Measure of Somatic, Cognitive, Behavioural,

Feeling Components. *Journal of Personality Assessment*, 54: 534-544.

Krug, S.E. and Lauglin, J.E. (1976). *Manual of Depression Inventory.* Institute for Personality and Ability Testing, American.

Logsdon - Conradsen, Berry, C. (2000). Using Mindfulness Meditation to promote holistic health in individuals with HIV/AIDS.

Mayatech, K. (1992). Traditional Medicine as a Alternative Approach to Managing HIV Disease. *Dissertation Abstracts*, 12: 3.

Molossiotis, A. and Maneesakorn, S. (2004). Quality of life, coping and Psychological status of Thai people living with AIDS. *Psychology, Health and Medicine*, 9: 350-361.

Ost, L.G.; Jerramalm; A.; and Johansson, J. (1982). Individual response patterns and the effects of different behavioural methods in the treatment of social phobia. *Behavious Research and Therapy*, 20: 445-460.

Raub, J.A. (2002). Psychophysiological Effects of Hatha Yoga on Musculoskeletal and Cardiopulmonary Function: A Literature Review. *Journal of Alternative Complementary Medicine*, 8: 797-812.

Rundell, J., Thompson, J., Zajac, R. and Beatty, R. (1988). *Psychiatric Diagnosis and Attempted Suicide in HIV infected USAF personnel.* Paper presented at Fourth International conference on AIDS at stockholm.

Schneider, R.H. and Nidich, S.I. and Salerno, J.W. (2001). The Transcendental Meditation Program: Reducing the Risk of Heart Disease and Mortality and Improving quality of life in African Americans. *Dissertation Abstracts*, 11: 159-60.

Shannahoff, K.D. (2002). Complementary Health Care Practices. Stress Management for Gastrointestinal Disorders, the use of Kundalini Yoga Meditation Techniques. *Gastroenterology Nursing*, 25: 126-9.

Tross, S., Price, R.W., Navia, B., Thaler, H.T., Gold, J., Hirsch, D.A. and Sidns, J.J. (1988). Neuropsychological characterization of AIDS Dementia complex; A Preliminary Report. *AIDS*, 2: 81-8.

●●●

9

Effect of Yogic Package on the Patients of Diabetes Mellitus

Charu Sharma

The present study examined the physiological effect of yogic package *(Dhanurasana, Gomukhasana, Kapalbhati, and Anulom-Viloma Pranayama)* in diabetes mellitus patients. The subjects were assigned by accidental sampling to two conditions namely, control (n=25) and experimental (n=25). The Subjects in experimental group were exposed to yogic package daily for half an hour for 40 days. Glucometer and Sinha's Anxiety Test were used as the measure and Data collection was done individually /in group and best attempts were made to avoid external distractions. The results of the study show that yogic package was found to reduce (positively lower towards normal) the fasting serum glucose level and post-prandial serum glucose level in patients of Diabetes Mellitus.

The World Health Organization has declared that the number of people with diabetes is rapidly increasing worldwide and has become of major public health concern (Alwan, & King, 1992; King, & Rewers 1991). Diabetes mellitus is currently a chronic disease, without cure, and medical emphasis must necessarily be on managing/avoiding possible short-term as well as long-term diabetes-related problems.

The discovery and ultimate wide spread production of insulin for use by diabetics, seemed to many patients and some physicians to be the first step in conquering a disease usually accompanied by a death sentence. According to Centre for Disease Control & Provention of Department of Health and Human Services (1997), however, after eight decades of research, there have been few steps as significant in the battle against this disorder. The prevalence of diabetes mellitus among the general population has increased year upon year without fail

Diabetes is a disease in which your blood glucose, or sugar, levels are too high. Glucose is a simple sugar found in food. It is an essential nutrient that provides energy for the proper functioning of the body cells. After meals, food is digested in the stomach and the intestines into glucose and other nutrients. The glucose in digested food is absorbed by the intestinal cells into the bloodstream, and is carried by blood to all the cells in the body. However, glucose cannot enter the cells alone. It needs assistance from insulin in order to penetrate the cell walls. Insulin therefore acts as a regulator of glucose metabolism in the body.

Insulin is known as the "hunger hormone". The corresponding insulin level rises with the eventual lowering of the blood sugar level and glucose is transported from the blood into the cell for energy. When the blood glucose levels are lowered, the insulin released from the pancreas is turned off.

When the blood sugar level drops below a certain level, hunger is felt. This often occurs a few hours after the meal. In normal individuals, such a regulatory system helps to keep blood glucose levels in a tightly controlled range. Cravings for sweets frequently form part of this cycle, which can lead to snacking, often for more carbohydrates. If the cravings are not fulfilled, sensations such as hunger, dizziness, moodiness, and a state of "collapse" can result.

This system of auto regulation and homeostasis is the function of the pancreas and it works around the clock. Dysfunction of this auto regulation system - either inability of the pancreas to secrete any or insufficient insulin, or pancreas overload from too much sugar ingested over a long period of time, or over compensatory mechanism, or a combination of these, results in the lack of insulin, and hence high blood sugar. This is the hallmark of diabetes mellitus (commonly called diabetes).

Insulin is a hormone that helps the glucose gets into your cells to give them energy. With Type 1 diabetes, your body does not make insulin. With Type 2 diabetes, the more common type, your body does not make or use insulin well. Without enough insulin, the glucose stays in your blood.

The early symptoms of untreated diabetes mellitus are related to elevated blood sugar levels, and excretion of it to the urine. High amounts of glucose in the urine can cause increased urine output and lead to dehydration. Dehydration causes increased thirst and water consumption. Some untreated diabetic patients also complain of fatigue, nausea, and vomiting. Patients with diabetes are prone to developing infections of the bladder, skin, and vaginal areas. Fluctuations in blood glucose levels can lead to blurred vision. Extremely elevated glucose levels can lead to lethargy and coma (diabetic coma).

The fasting plasma glucose test is the standard and preferred way to diagnose diabetes. Normal fasting plasma glucose levels are less than 110 milligrams per deciliter (mg/dl). If the overnight fasting blood glucose is greater than 126 mg/dl on two different tests on different days, the diagnosis of diabetes mellitus is made. Random blood glucose alone is seldom used because it is not reliable.

Over time, having too much glucose in your blood can cause serious problems. It can damage your eyes, kidneys, and nerves. Diabetes can also cause heart disease, stroke and even the need to remove a limb. Pregnant women can also get diabetes, called Gestational diabetes. Symptoms of Type 2 diabetes may include fatigue, thirst, and weight loss, blurred vision and frequent urination. Some people have no symptoms. A blood test can show if you have diabetes. Some of the most common treatment options are: oral medicines (Diabetes pills), dietary changes, exercise, insulin and islet cell transplantation. The oral medicines may have negative side effects. The side effects of the oral medicines include: nausea, diarrhea, metallic taste in mouth, low blood glucose, skin rash or itching, and weight gain.

In general, the rapid socioeconomic development which started in the 1970s has led to proliferation of educational establishments, health centres, hospitals and other medical facilities. These social advances have been accompanied by the characteristic cultural changes that are observed in rapidly developing societies Musaigar and Abdulaziz (1986). Alterations in lifestyle, unhealthy nutritional habits and a more sedentary life have led to an increase in obesity. A cure for Diabetes has not been found yet. However, it can be controlled. Ways to control diabetes are: maintaining blood glucose levels, blood fat levels and weight.

In order to get relief from their problems people go to the shelter of modern medicine. Modern science treats them by different medications such as Sulfonylurea drugs, Meglitinides etc. These medications stimulate your pancreas to produce and release more insulin. These medicines give temporarily relief but they also have some side effects. Such drugs include alcohol, MAO inhibitors like phenelzine (Nardil), beta-blockers like propranolol (Inderal), salicylates like aspirin (Bayer) or salsalate (Disalcid), and anabolic steroids like methyl testosterone (Android). Some techniques (Islet cell transplantation, Pancreas transplantation) are effective but they are time consuming and costly, every person cannot afford it. But this is a unique therapy package which is an integrated approach towards diabetes.

There is an exceptionally important role for patient education, dietetic support, sensible exercise, self glucose monitoring, with the goal of keeping both short-term blood glucose levels, and long term levels as well, within acceptable bounds. Careful control is needed to reduce the risk of long term complications. This can be achieved with combinations of diet, exercise and weight loss.

It is apparent that exercise used as prevention and therapy in the diabetic community is not a new concept. Prior to 1850, lifestyle modifications were primarily an adjustment of diet with exercise becoming a cornerstone of therapy by the early part of the 20th century. Currently, research concerning lifestyle modifications continues at various centres around the world. Diabetes Preventive

Program Research Group (2002) study focused on the prevention of diabetes mellitus using different methods. Subjects in this study were at risk of developing diabetes prior to their inclusion and these subjects varied widely in race, gender, economic and social standards. Three randomized were compared, a placebo group, a group who took daily doses of metformin an antihyperglycemic agent, and a group who underwent intensive lifestyle modifications consisting of diet and exercise intervention. By the end of this 24 week study, significant differences in the incidence of diabetes mellitus among the three groups were found. As expected, both the metformin and lifestyle groups showed much lower instances of diabetes mellitus. Yet even more striking was the significantly lower incidence of diabetes mellitus among those in the lifestyle group compared to the other group.

Exercise as a part of diabetes mellitus prevention and therapy has gained in popularity over the past two decades as more research has become available. However, its use is definitely not a novel approach in the management of this disease. According to the American College of Sports Medicine (ACSM) (2001), indications of the effectiveness of exercise in reducing glycosuria have been evident since 600 B.C. In Greece, another medical writer, Celsus (1812), had specifically prescribed exercise in the treatment of diabetes. Celsus advocated the use of exercise, massage and other treatments to improve the wellbeing of diabetics. Eventually, exercise became one of the three corners of diabetes therapy, which also include diet and medications.

In the ensuing decades opponents to exercise therapy would change their attitudes due to some of the first research in the area of exercise physiology. A group of French researchers led by Chaveau and Kaufman (1887) measured the uptake of glucose by working muscle and found it to be higher than resting muscle. In addition, a reduction in blood glucose levels with muscular exercise was apparent. With this new scientific evidence, the therapeutic benefits of exercise, so long held by Bouchardat, became common practice in other clinics for diabetics.

Therefore, yogic package is a unique package. It is an integrated approach towards Diabetes.

METHOD

Sample: The sample consisted of 50 subjects (25 in control group; 25 in experimental group) were selected from the Saharanpur district through the method of accidental sampling. The subjects of experimental group used to visit the centre for yogic therapy sessions for 40 days daily under the supervision of a yoga expert.

Tools

The GLUCOMETER to measure diabetes was used. A glucose meter (or glucometer) is a medical device for determining the approximate concentration of glucose in the blood. It is a key element of home blood glucose monitoring (HBGM) by people with diabetes mellitus or with proneness to hypoglycemia. A small drop of blood obtained by pricking the skin with a lancet is placed on a disposable test strip, which the meter reads and uses to calculate the blood glucose level. The meter then displays the level in mg/dl or mmol/l.

Design: Pre and post design was used in the present study. The pre-testing for diabetes test was one day before the commencement of yogic package sessions, while post treatment testing was done one day after sessions. (This lasted for forty days). The subjects in the control group were simply tested and retesting was done after forty days. No treatment was provided to these subjects. The subjects of both groups were regularly taking the medicines prescribed by the physician.

Procedure

Each subject was tested individually. The subjects in experimental group were given yogic package daily for half an hour for 40 days. Yogic package involves *Dhanurasana, Gomukhasana, Kapalbhati and Anulom-Viloma Pranayama.* It is advisable to take a light meal during this practice, plenty of clean, lukewarm water should be available and also extra hot water in case of temperature of the water falls below body temperature. No asana or physical work should be performed before commencing and no food or beverages should be taken. If the bowels are not evacuated prior to the practice it helps stimulate the peristaltic movement.

RESULT AND DISCUSSION

The results reported in Table 1 clearly reveal that the main effect of yogic package was statistically significant for fasting serum glucose level ($t=8.22$, $p<0.01$). So the hypothesis that yogic package significantly effect (positively lower towards normal) the fasting serum glucose level in patients of DM has been proved.

TABLE 1

For fasting serum glucose level.

	M	*S.D.*	*t-value*	*p<*
Experimental Group	114.84	16.16	8.22	0.01
Control Group	154.54	17.97		

TABLE 2

For post-prandial serum glucose level

	M	*S.D.*	*t-value*	*p<*
Experimental Group	155.18	18.25	11.79	0.01
Control Group	210.40	14.70		

The results reported in Table 2 clearly shows that the main effect of yogic package was statistically significant for post-prandial serum glucose level ($t=11.79$, $p<0.01$). So the hypothesis that yogic package significantly effect (positively lower towards normal) the post-prandial serum glucose level in patients of DM has been proved. The findings of Ramaiah (1986), Gore (1985), Dandona (1992), Notiya (2006), Souto (2006) support the research findings who also reported that there was a significant fall in plasma glucose, serum fractosamine, serum cholesterol values in NIDDM group, practicing yoga.

In the present study there were two groups one is experimental which practiced certain yogic practices like, and other group which did not practice any yogic practice. The result of study shows a significant change in fasting as well as post paradial serum glucose level of experimental group as compared with that of control group. Practice of asana increases blood flow to all the structure in the abdominal cavity including the pancreas. The practice of asana creates drop in the pressure, by 80 mmg of Hg in the intestine, this shows the negative intra abdominal pressure that is through the blood vessel that carry blood to abdominal organs. These arteries provide better oxygenation to intestinal wall liver spleen pancreas etc. (Srikant, et al., 2004). Abdominal squeeze is useful in controlling diabetes mellitus (Gore, 1985). The practice of yogic practice also involves abdominal squeeze and active manipulation of abdominal muscles, which is thought to be effective in controlling serum glucose level in the patients of diabetes mellitus. That is diabetes is best controlled and prevented by simple alterations of diet and physical activity.

REFERENCES

Alwan, A., & King, H. (1992). Diabetes in the Eastern Mediterranean Region. *World health statistics quarterly, 45*, 355-359.

American College of Sports Medicine. (2001). *ACSM's Resource Manual for Guild lines for Exercise Testing and Prescription* (4th Ed.) New York: Lippincott Williams & Wilkins.

Centres for Disease Control and Prevention. (1997). *National Diabetes Fact Sheet: National Estimates and General Information on Diabetes in the United* States. Atlanta, GA: U.S. Department of Health and Human Services, Centres for Disease Control and Prevention.

Celsus, (1812). Dictionnaire des Sciences Médicales : par une société de médicine et de chirurgiens. Panckoucke, Renauldin, 125-7 & 148-149.

Chaveau, M.A., & Kaufman, M. (1887). Expériences pour la determination du coefficient de l'activité nutritive et respiratoire des muscles en repos et en travail. *Comptes Rendus de l'Académie des Sciences, 104*, 1126-1132 .

Dandona. (1992). Integrated approaches of yoga therapy to Diabetes. *Journal of Complimentary Medicine Research*, 66-68

Diabetes Prevention Program Research Group, (2002). Reduction in the Incidence of diabetes mellitus with lifestyle intervention or Metformin. *The New England Journal of Medicine, 346*, 393-403.

Desai, B.P. (1985). Influence of yogic treatment on serum lipase activity in diabetics. *Yoga Mimamsa 23,* 1- 8,

Divekar, M.V. & Bhat (1981). Effect of yoga therapy in diabetes and obesity. *Clinical Diabetes Update.*

Gore, M.M. (1985). *Anatomy and physiology of yogic practices.* Kaivalyadham, Lonavala: Kanchan Prakashan,

King, H., & Rewers, M. (1991). Diabetes in adults is now a Third World problem. The WHO ad hoc diabetes reporting group, diabetes and other non-communicable diseases unit. *Bulletin of the World Health Organization*, *69*, 643-648.

Koshti (1972). Electrophoretic pattern of serum proteins in diabetes mellitus as influenced by physical exercises (Yogasanas). *Journal of the Mysore Medical Asso*ciation, *36*, 64-64

Musaiger, A.O. & Abdulaziz, S.A. (1986). Demographic characteristics of hospitalized patients with diabetes in Bahrain. *Bahrain medical bulletin, 8*, 73-6.

Notiya. (2006). *Role of Yoga-Nidra in controlling Diabetes Mellitus* paper presented in fifth international conference on Advances in Yoga Research and Therapy at Kaivalyadham Lonavala, Maharastra, India.

Patel, C.H., (1973). Yoga and Biofeedback in the Management of Hypertension. *The Lancet,* 1053-1055,

Ramaiah, S.A.A. (1986). *Yoga therapy for Diabetes*. Madras: Siddha Medical Board Govt. of Tamilnadu , India.

Rugmini, P.S. & Sinha, R.N. (1976). *Effect of yoga therapy in Diabetes mellitus*", Seminar on yoga, Science and man, Maharastra, 175-189.

Sahay, B.K. (1984). The effect of yoga in Diabetes. In J.S. Bajay (Ed.) *Diabetes Mellitus in Developing Countries* (pp379-381). New Delhi: Interprint

Souto, Alicia (2006). *Yoga practices in people with Diabetes.* Paper presented in fifth international conference on Advances in Yoga Research and Therapy at Kaivalyadham Lonavala, Maharastra, India.

Srikanta, S.S., Nagendra, H.R., & Nagendra, R. (2004). *Yoga for Diabetes*, Bangalore: Swami Vivekananda Prakashan,

Tulpule, T.H (1977). Yogic exercises and diabetes Mellitus (Madhumeh). *Journal of Diabetes Association, 17.*

World Health Organization, (1997). Ad hoc diabetes reporting group. Diabetes and impaired glucose tolerance in women aged 20-39 years. *World health statistics quarterly, 45*, 321-330.

●●●

10

Yoga and Psychophysiological Disorders

S.K. Srivastava and Sweta Maheshwari

Too much of stress and strain of life especially after the middle age, may lead to one of the stress diseases e.g. Hypertension, Asthma, Diabetes, Arthritis, Migraine, Headache etc. As the developing countries are also becoming more and more industrialised, the number of these diseases are increasing at a very fast rate. Hence, there is an urgent need for taking proper measures to prevent the development of such diseases and also to recognise and treat them in the early stages. Though recently innumerable tranquilizing agents have been discovered and marketed, all of them have certain toxic and habit forming properties. Hence, their use should be limited to the bare minimum followed by certain non-medical measures such as different type of yogic practice to control these diseases. So this paper attempts an evaluation of Yoga as a potent technique to manage stress which causes about 75 percent chronic bodily diseases.

Mankind has always tried to attain peace and happiness along with the ongoing process of development. The urgency of getting an ideal method of attaining mental peace has become great in view of the tremendous increase in the stress and strain of life especially in urban areas. Rapid industrialisation, competition, crowding, excessive hurry and worry are some of the major factors which lead to mental and physical changes. The person tries to adapt himself in these situations. However, if these situations are continued for a long time then the person fails to adapt himself and starts getting the manifestations of psychophysiological changes one by one. In the starting he gets psychic changes such as irritability, nervousness, sleeplessness etc. If these signs are not recognised and checked in time he gets some additional manifestations such as palpitation, increased pulse rate, rise of blood pressure etc. As these changes continue, the chain leading to higher order problem begins and the person becomes a victim of one of the psychophysiological disorders such as hypertension, peptic ulcer, diabetes mellitus, ulcerative colitis, bronchial asthma, migraine, rheumatoid arthritis, thyrotoxicosis, CHD etc.

Amongst all these disorders hypertension, diabetes and asthma seems to be most common. It is a worldwide phenomenon and the more advanced the country, the greater is the incidence of these diseases. What is most alarming is that the incidence is still increasing and is affecting more and more of younger generation.

As the number of stress related diseases are increasing day by day, there is an urgent need for taking proper measures to prevent the development of these diseases and also to treat them and recognize in the early stages. Though recently innumerable tranquilising agents have been discovered and marketed, all of them have certain toxic and habit forming properties. Hence, their use should be limited to the bare minimum followed by certain non-medical measures such as different types of yogic practices to control these diseases. For the treatment of stress related problems yoga has become a most common technique during the last three decades as it is economical, free from side effects (as in the case of drug therapy) and the cure is more or less radical. In fact, these seems to be on exposition of yogic practices all over the world, whether it is Patanjali's variety or some of its derivatives. All yoga therapy is psychotherapy as its aim is 'Chittavrittinirodha'. In fact, yoga is defined as science of mental control. It not only helps one to control one's mental state, but also to improve one's personality and behaviour, if it is practised regularly from childhood. One of the most distinguishing feature of ancient Indian thought including, of course, yoga with regard to human welfare in general and mental and physical health in particular is that it traces all man's sufferings essentially to the faulty perceptions of the individual.

In all the stress responses the impairment of cognitive functioning is very common which disturb the equanimity of the individual. Yoga aims at bringing back this equanimity by a change at the cognitive level. That is why harmony is called yoga samatyam yoga uchyate (Bhagvadgita, 2148).

Historical Background

The practice of yoga has come down from the pre-historical part. The references to yoga are available in Upanishads and Puranas composed by Indian Aryans in the later Vedic and post-Vedic period. The main credit of systematising yoga goes to Patanjali, who is the author of Yoga Sutra. He composed the treatise in brief code words known as "Sutras". Amongst the, who popularise the yoga system throughout the world, the name of Swami Vivekananda stands out most prominently. By giving a scientific interpretation of yogic methods and by supplementing them with the philosophical thoughts as described in Bhagved Gita, he made the greatest contribution to the physical and mental harmony throughout the world. In recent years Sri Aurobindo also made many original contributions in the field of mind and consciousness. While the practice of yoga started nearly 6000 years ago, yoga did not emerge as a fully developed practice until 500 B.C. In its traditional form, yoga is considered a compete life-style that provides a path to spiritual enlightment.

The practices of yoga came to the United States in the 1890s as a result of the teachings of Swami Vivekananda. It gained popularity in the 1960s because of a rising interest in and cultural acceptance of alternative modalities and mind-body therapies. Today, yoga is often practised as an exercise form separated from its traditional spiritual roots. In this form, yoga exercise is taught at health clubs, yoga centres and is often part of disease prevention and management programs in hospitals, such as stress reduction courses for people with high blood pressure and heart diseases.

Yoga, derived from the Sanskrit word meaning "union" is a spiritual practice that uses the body, breath, and mind to energize and balance the whole person. This mind-body therapy involves physical postures, breathing exercises, and meditation to improve overall well being. It has been stated that daily practice of yoga would help a person to maintain a perfect homeostasis of the mind and body throughout his life. According to Swami Chidanand (1985) our entire personality is nothing but a combination of body, prana and mind and all the troubles are due to disharmony among these three. Such disharmony can be removed and harmony can be achieved through yoga. Yoga helps in harmonious personality development. Practice of yoga helps not only in regaining and improving physical· and mental health but in the improvement of intellectual functioning and adjustment in all spheres. Gita has aptly said 'Yoga Karmushu Kaushalam'. That is, yoga brings efficiency in action. Practice of yoga helps in attaining concentration. Patanjali defines yoga as a control of the fluctuations of mind stuff (Chitta).

Different Types of Yoga

As the different connections between the mind and body were explored, various branches of yoga developed. These include:

Astanga or Power Yoga: Modern day variations of yoga developed for people who prefer a physically demanding workout.

Bhakti Yoga: The goal of this form of yoga is to take all of the love in one's heart and direct it to God. By worshipping God, the person who practises regularly becomes filled with respect for all life and is encouraged to be sacrificial and to treat others generously.

Bikram Yoga: a series of 26 asanas (postures) practised in a room that is 105 degrees in order to warm and stretch the muscles, ligaments and tendons and to detoxify the body through sweating.

Hatha Yoga: Emphasis is placed on the physical postures or exercise known as asanas, with the goal of balancing the opposites in one's life.

Jnana Yoga: Emphasises deep contemplation. Practitioner seek Jnana or 'wisdom' through meditation. The goal of this form of yoga is to be one with God.

Karma Yoga: Based on the philosophy that "yesterday's actions determine today's circumstances". Practitioner of Karma Yoga believe that by making today's action positive, they hope they can improve tomorrow's circumstances for both themselves as well as for others.

Raja Yoga: Known in India as 'the royal (raj) road to reintegration'. The goal of this type of yoga is to blend the four layers of self: the body, the individual consciousness, the individual sub-consciousness, and the universal and infinite consciousness, Raja Yoga, being most concerned with the mind and spirit, places its emphasis on meditation.

Working of Yoga

Scientists don't know exactly how yoga produces its healthful effects. Some say it works like other mind-body therapies to reduce stress, and others believe that yoga promotes the release of endorphins (natural pain killers and mood elevators) from the brain.

All of the branches of yoga previously mentioned incorporate three major techniques: breathing, exercise (asana or postures), and mediation. These three techniques have been shown to improve health in many ways. Patanjali has recommended eight stages of yoga discipline. They are Yama (restrains), (1) Niyama (observances), (3) Asana (Physical postures), (4) Pranayama (Breathing control), (5) Pratyahara (withdrawl of sense organs) (6) Dharana (contemplation), (7) Dhyana (Meditation) and (8) Samadhi (Attainment of superconsciousness). Though Patanjali has described all these stages in great detail, some modification is necessary to suit them to the modern society. The results of these practices can be enhanced much more if one follows all the recommended restraints and observances in everyday life. It may not always be possible to follow them very strictly in everyday life, but one should try one's best to get better results.

Psychic Disciplinary Exercises:

1. **Yamas**: These are five in number

(i) **Ahimsa** or non-violence including avoiding bodily or mental injury.

(2) **Satya** or truthfulness in all the dealings of life.

(3) **Asteya** or non-stealing of anything in life such as money, material, ideas, speeches or writings.

(4) **Brahamcharya** or celibacy, which means refraining from all the activities related to sexual enjoyment directly or indirectly.

(5) **Aparigraha** or non-possession *i.e.* keeping one's requirement to the bare minimum.

2. **Niyamas**: Patanjali has prescribed five Niyamas.

(1) **Shaucha** or cleanliness of body and mind.

(2) **Santosha** or contentment one should always develop a habit of contentment even under adverse circumstances.

(3) **Tapas** or austerity with regard to food, exercise, rest and recreation which will ultimately lead to the development of integrity in one's characters.

(4) **Svadhyaya** or intensive study in order to make life healthy, happy and peaceful. It is essential that we make an extensive study of the subjects.

(5) **Ishvara Pranidhana** In order to attain peace it is always better to dedicate the fruits of our actions to God Almighty.

Psychosomatic Energising Exercies:

3. **Asana** refers to stable and easy posture. According to patanjali asana is one that brings steadiness and pleasentness to the individual. He accepted to select only those postures that are comfortable. However, it is an established fact that there are some asanas, which provide relaxation and help in the regularisation of glandular secretions. Amongst various yogic measures, the practice of Shavasana, a yogic relaxation posture, was found to be of much use not only as a curative measure but also as a measure for preventing the development of hypertension. Datey of Bombay (Datey *et al.,* 1969) and Chandra Patel of London (Patel, 1973a) used this method quite extensively with improvement in a significant number of hypertensive patients. They postulated

that the relaxation postures possibly produce their beneficial results by reducing the adrenergic and noradrenergic activity in the brain stem and the peripheral organs and the tissues.

4. **Pranayam** or **Breathing**: Prana is that vital, which pervades the whole cosmos. It is in all things and it is the bioenergy that activates the human organism. It is closely related to the air we breathe, which is our main source of prana. However, air is only the vehicle, it is not Prana itself. Prana is the medium that links body and soul. It is the connecting force between consciousness and matter and can be regarded as a very subtle aspect of both matter and physical energy.

   Yama means control. Thus, pranayama is a series of techniques that aim at stimulating and increasing the vital energy in the body by directing it to particular areas for special purposes, including healing. Pranayama ensures that the flow of vital energy in the body is free and unimpeded, helping to maintain good health. Pranayam has three parts.

1) Purak or drawing in of breath.
2) Kumbhak or retaining the breath.
3) Rechak or expelling the breath.

   The time proportion is suggested as 1:4:2 for example if purak takes 10 sec, Kumbhak should take 40 sec and Rechak should take 20 second.

5. **Pratyahar** (Psychic sublimating exercise): Pratayahar is the withdrawl of mind from all the senses and practically it is the complete mastery over the senses. It is done by two ways, *i.e.* neither the sense should be affected by the stimulus nor the sense should disturb the mind by their sensation. It is not the incapacity of senses. They are healthy as usually. It is the complete mastery over the psyche of individual. Such process is really very difficult. It requires daily long practice, free association and analysis of learning.

Psychic Supernormal Attainment (Siddhi) Exercises:

6. **Dharana:** Steadiness of mind and concentration are the two main features of Dharana. One has to bind his mind to a restricted contour or frame within which the object of attention is confined called steadiness and squeezing mind. Dharna can best be understood as allowing the attending process to flow only within a limited circle that is immediately related to the objects of attention.
7. **Dhayan (Meditation):** It is the unity of mind with the idea of some object. The preliminary steps for Dhyan should be taken with care. Quite and calm environment is essential so that the session of meditation may be held without disruption. As a method of process towards psychic relief or growth, they can be looked upon as two systems of exercises in attention and concentration. In one, the focus is on the body, it begins and ends with attention to the functions of a body organs like heart, lungs, skin-temperature etc, which are not ordinarily amenable to conscious control. The other system operates by fixing the attention on some external stimuli like light or sound and/or some internal stimuli like following a thought process effortlessly or building it up to a crescendo. The immediate aim of Dhayan is to reach a state of deep relaxation by shutting most channels of sensory stimuli and keeping open one single channel on which attention is focused.
8. **Samadhi:** This is the final stage of Inner yoga. Patanjali defines samadhi as "the very same stage of Dhyan reflecting in consciousness, the object alone, emptied of its form."

Yoga and Psychophysiological Disorders

It has been stated that daily practice of yoga would help a person to maintain a perfect homeostasis of the body and mind throughout his life. In fact, the practices of Hatha Yoga and Meditation tends to bring about normalcy in our psychophysiological functions. It has been claimed that such persons would be less prone to psychosomatic imbalance resulting usually from stress and strain of life.

As we know that the main initiating factor in the development of psychophysiological disorders is the increased liberation of neurohumours like acetylcholine, catecholamines, and histamine by the excessively stimulated cerebral cortex. Therefore, it is understandable that if one can learn to restrain the cerebral cortex, especially its psychic centre, one can be free from the development of various psychosomatic disorders throughout one's life. It is here that yoga can be of immense help to all in preventing the development of stress diseases, and thereby living a long happy and healthy life. In fact, yoga is defined as science of mental control. It not only helps one to control one's mental state, but also improves one's personality and behaviour, if it is practised regularly from childhood.

Various studies lend support to the above discussion. Oken *et al.*, (2006) found improvements in physical and quality-of-life measures among healthy elderly people in the yoga or exercise group compared to the waiting list control group. Manjunath and Telles (2005) also found that the practice of yoga significantly improves the length and quality of sleep in the elderly. Galantino *et al.*, (2004) randomised 22 participants between the ages of 30 and 65 with chronic low back pain to either a yoga based intervention, or to waiting list. Potentially important trends showed improved balance and flexibility and decreased disability and depression for the yoga group awareness/learning. Woolery *et al.*, (2004) results also suggest that yoga asanas could potentially be useful in the management of depression. More studies with larger groups and more complex study designs are necessary

These yogic practices not only help in reversing the progress of these psychophysiological diseases but also improve the resistance of the body at the psychophysiological level. Such non-medical measures should be adopted to overcome the stressful situations and to maintain an alert mental state. This would largely avoid severe mental depression resulting from too much use of tranquilisers.

The famous sage Patanjali says that a few people in society are resistant by nature to every type of disorders of stress, a few others develop such resistance after birth by the prolonged use of some of the retroactive medicines, and most of the other people can develop such resistance only by the practice of various types of yoga. Postures (Asanas), breath holding exercise (pranayama) and meditation (dhyan) are the important ones for bringing the neurohumoral pattern to normalcy. Thus, if there is an excess of a neurohumour, it becomes less, and if these is less of other harmones they become increased, to come to the normal level. In addition, it also improves the functional efficiency of all the organs and tissues by improving their microcirculation. But the most important thing to remember in this context is that yogic practice can play a great role in the prevention of various diseases provided it is practised with all sincerity and in a regular manner.

As per survey and review of literature conducted by different investigators like Weiner (1977), Selye (1950), Udupa and Singh (1977), Patel (1973b), pointed out that yoga therapy is more effective in the present scenario. Most of the cases indicate that 60% of the cases are cured, 25% cases relieved from their psychosomatic diseases and about 15% cases showed no effective results due to yoga therapy.

REFERENCES

Burchfield, S. R. (1985). Ed. *Stress*. Washington: Hemisphere Publisher Crop.

Datey, K. K., Deshmukh, S. N., Dalvi, C. P. and Vinekar, S. L. (1969). Shavasan: A yogic exevices in the Management of Hypertension. *Angiology, 20*, 325.

Galantino, M.L., Bzdewka, T.M., Eissler-Russo, J.L., Holbrook, M.L., Mogck, E.P., Geigle, P. and Farrar, J.T. (2004). The impact of modified Hatha yoga on chronic low back pain: a pilot study. *Alternative Therapies in Health & Medicine, 10*, 56-59.

Manjunath, N.K. and Telles, S. (2005). Influence of Yoga and Ayurveda on self-rated sleep in a geriatric population. *Indian Journal of Medical Research, 121*, 683-690.

Oken, B.S., Zajdel, D., Kishiyama, S., Flegal, K., Dehen, C., Haas, M., Kraemer, D.F., Lawrence, J. and Leyva, J. (2006). Randomized, controlled, six-month trial of yoga in healthy seniors: effects on cognition and quality of life. *Alternative Therapies in Health and Medicine, 12,* 40-47.

Patel. C. H. (1973a). Yoga and Biofeedback. Management of Hypertension, *Lancet, 2,* 1053.

Patel. C. H. (1973b). Twelve months follow up of Yoga and biofeedback: Management of Hypertension, *Lancet,* 1, 62.

Selye, H. (1950). *The stress of life.* New York: McGraw Hill Book Co.

Singh, R. H. and Udupa, K. N. (1977). Psychobiological studies on some hathyogic practices, *Quarterly Journal of Surgical Science, 13,* 290.

Udupa, K. N. (1985). *Stress and its Management by Yoga.* Delhi: Motilal Banarasidass.

Vivekananda, Swami. (1970). *Raja Yoga,* Calcutta: Advaita Ashram.

Weiner, H. (1977). *Psychobiology and Human Disease,* New York: Elsvier.

Woolery, A.; Myers, H.; Sternlieb, B. and Zeltzer, L. (2004). A yoga intervention for young adults with elevated symptoms of depression. *Alternative Therapies in Health & Medicine, 10,* 60-63.

●●●

11

Reducing Anxiety through Yogic Practices

Bishamber Singh and Surendra Kumar Sia

In the present study an attempt has been made to examine the impact of yogic practices upon trait anxiety of the respondents. The study was conducted upon 38 under graduate and post graduate students of Punjabi University, Patiala. Out of them 26 were boys and 12 were girls. The study adopted a pre-post design to compare the level of trait anxiety before and after the yogic interventions. The session continued for 3 months. At the beginning of this three month session it was started with 'suksham byayams' (warming up exercies) and gradually more advanced yogic practices were introduced. After three months, the trait anxiety scores were collected and compared with those of pre-intervention scores through't' ratio, which came out to be significant. The finding has been discussed in light of related literature.

Healthy life has become a matter of great importance for everybody including academicians, counselors, professionals, researchers etc. It includes physical, mental as well as social dimensions. Yoga has been suggested to be an effective and comprehensive way for remedy as well as maintenance of these dimensions. Taking an Indian perspective of health and well being, Kiran Kumar (2006) mentions that *'Tusti' (contentment)'* is more important than *'Tripti (pleasure)'* and *'Sukha (happiness)'*. The ultimate or ideal contentment comes from within through the realization of transcendent self. Hence, self-realization should be accorded greater prominence than self-actualization. Kumar also views that, the practices which incorporate strategies of realizing the transcendent self, are known as 'yoga'. There are different systems of yoga suited to persons at different levels of evolution.

Based upon the *'Yoga Sutras'* of Patanjali, Pandit (2008) mentions that true nature of reality, within and without, is *'satchitanand'*. 'Sat' is described as existence, essence and quality; 'Chit' is used as intelligence, intuition and cognition; and 'Anand' refers to experiential fullness of quality. But there are certain barriers which obstruct us from reaching that reality. Mind, which changes from time to time, filters and obscures this reality. If the mind is restless, that not only affects the social relationships and academic performance, but also distorts the quality of life (Pandit, 2008). Quality of mind is an integral component of health. In other words, we may mention that we should focus upon the methods that can influence both mind as well as body positively. Yoga is one of the best comprehensive procedures for this purpose.

Yoga is a path for self-liberation through expansion of consciousness. In this path an attempt is made to refine one's attention, increase one's bodily awareness and greater control over body. This is done through the practices of different procedures such as '*asanas* (physical postures)', '*pranayam* (breathing practices)', '*bandhas* (procedures for sealing energy)', '*mudras* (gestures and attitudes), and '*shatkriyas* (cleansing procedures). As a result of this process, defective functioning at the physical, psychological and emotional levels may be rectified in a natural and systematic manner (Rani & Rao, 2005).

Jensen and Kenny (2004) found that yoga is an effective intervention for a broad range of childhood difficulties. Children treated with yoga were found to carry out their duties being more attentive and remain relaxed. Manjunath and Telles (2003) observed that yoga training produced a significant increase in spatial test scores, which indicates that *'yoga'* improves performance in right hemisphere-specific memory test. A study by Abadi *et. al.* (2008)

indicates the positive effect of yoga programme on children with ADHD. A study by Rani and Rao (2005), through a two-week long yoga training programme, reveals a significant decrease in depression as a result of yoga practice.

The above mentioned theoretical expositions as well as empirical findings suggest that yogic practices can reduce in the negative aspects of an individual's personality. The present study has taken up such an aspect – anxiety. It can be defined as a response to an unidentifiable threat or an anticipated danger, while fear is a response to a clearly identifiable danger (Sharma, 2002). It is quite possible for anybody to experience anxiety at one time or other. In other words we may say that anxiety as a momentary emotional state is experienced by most of us at many points of our life. However, there are same individuals who are more prone to anxiety. This is in line with the distinction between 'state' and 'trait' anxiety. The concepts of state and trait anxiety were first introduced by Cattell (Cattell, 1966; Cattell & Scheier, 1963) and have been elaborated by Spielberger (1966, 1972, 1976, and 1979). State anxiety may be defined as an unpleasant emotional state or condition which is characterized by subjective feelings of tension, apprehension and worry, and by arousal of the autonomic nervous system, whereas, trait anxiety refers to a relatively stable personality disposition. However, trait anxiety does not imply chronic anxiety rather a higher tendency to experience anxiety (Spilberger, 1972). In the present study, an attempt has been made to examine the impact of 'yogic practices' upon the level of trait anxiety of the participants.

Sample

The present study was conducted on 38 undergraduate and post-graduate students of Punjabi University, Patiala. Out of them, 26 were boys and 12 were girls. A Pre-Post design was followed for the present study to compare the level of their trait anxiety before and after the yogic practices (*yoga bhyas*).

Tool Used

Spielberger's State-Trait Anxiety Inventory (STAI) was used to gather responses from the participants. It consists of two self-report scales- one for measuring 'state' anxiety and the other for 'trait' anxiety. But both the scales are printed on the opposite sides of a single page test form. The item numbers 1 to 20 which constitute form Y-1, representing state anxiety, evaluate how respondents feel "right now" at this moment. Item numbers 21 to 40, on the opposite page constitute form Y-2 representing trait anxiety. It assesses how people generally feel. Form Y-2 has been used in the present study. Participants' scores on items 21, 23, 26, 27, 30, 33, 34, 36 and 39 were reversed. Test retest reliability of form Y-2 with an interval of 30 days was 0.71 for males and 0.75 for females. The concurrent validity of STAI with IPAT Anxiety scale is .75, with Taylor Manifest Anxiety Scale is 0.80 and Zuckerman Affect Adjective Checklist is 0.52.

Procedure

The participants performed the yogic practices (yoga bhyas) under the guidance of the first author, who himself is the yoga instructor in the Physical Education department of Punjabi University, Patiala. The session continued for three months except Saturday and Sundays from 6 am to 8 am in the morning. For the first 15 days, the participants practiced *'suksham byayam'* (warming –up exercises) for effective movement of different joints. After 15 days they performed easy *Asanas, Pranayamas* and *Shatkarmas* along with the warming-up exercises. The asanas included *Uttan Padasana, Pawan Muktasan, Shalav Asana, Bhujangasana, Surya Namaskar, Vajrasana, Makarasana* and *Sabasana*. Under the supervision of the instructor, the participants practiced pranayamas, which at this stage included *Anulom-Bilom* and *Nadi Sodhan*. Three bandhas, namely *jalandhar, Mool* and *Uiddiyan* were introduced as corollaries of pranayams. Two Shatkarmas, *Neti* and *Kunjan* were also performed by them. This continued for 15 days *i.e.* till the first month.

After the first month, advanced asanas and pranayams were introduced along with those already being practiced by the participants. The advanced asanas were – *Dhanurasan, Ardha-matsyendrasan, Gomukhasan, Paschimttasan, Sarvangasan* and

Matsyasan; the advanced pranayamas were – *Syrya Bhedan, Vijjayi Shitkari, Bhastrika* and *Bhramri.* All these continued till the end of the session *i.e.* third month. During this programme, *Mudra* and *Dhyana* (meditation) were introduced after the second month. *Dhyana*, which basically consisted of '*Om*' recitation and '*Gayatri Mantra*' were done for 30 minutes each day. The participants had progressive improvement upon the asanas as well as pranayams due to which they were gradually taking lesser and lesser time for the previously practiced asanas. The whole activities were performed in a sequential manner as below:

Asanas ⟶ *Pranayam* + *Bandha* ⟶ *Mudra* ⟶ *Dhyan*

The instructor was present with the participants through out the whole session and monitored their practice diligently by providing feedback as and when required.

RESULT AND DISCUSSION

The result of the study indicates that there is a significant reduction in the trait-anxiety score after the session of the yogic practices. The't' ratio for mean differences between pre and post yogic session came out to be 2.634, which was significant at $p < 0.01$. The mean trait anxiety score at the pre-Yogic session was 44.5, which was reduced to 38.65 at the post-Yogic session. Inputs from interactions with the participants also substantiate this result. Some participants reported that, after this regular yogic practice, they felt less nervous, calm and cool; experience fewer disturbing thoughts; improvement in their self-confidence.

The finding of this study validate the objective of Yoga. According to Yoga-Sutra, the practice of Yoga has a purpose of controlling *citta vrittis*. *Citta* refers to the functional mind. The conscious mind is a stage of perpetually changing and shifting scenes of awareness called *Vrittis.* The vrittis are fluctuating states of mind that are cognitively loaded and affectively coloured. They are considered to be inimical for attaining the goal of *kaivalya*, which is the state of self-realization. The *citta-vrittis* are many and varied. Yoga classifies those under five heads. The first category is true cognitins based on pramanas (valid sources of knowledge); the second category is *viparyaya i.e.* false cognitions which includes doubts and uncertain cognitions; the third is *vikalpa,* which refers to an idea which has no corresponding material object; *nidra* (sleep) and *smriti* (memory) are other two categories (Rao & Paranjape, 2008). According to them, if the mind is a sea, the vrittis are its waves. The disturbed minds are like turbulent seas and the goal of human endeavour for self-realization is one of stilling the mind by controlling its fluctuations *(vrittis)*. We may opine that anxiety *(Duschinta),* being a manifestation of disturbed mind can be controlled by yogic practices like that of other disturbances. A physiological explanation may also be put forth for this finding. The emotional or autonomic reactions which take place owing to the evaluations of the unforeseen situation can be controlled optimally through yogic practices. Some recent studies upon test-anxiety also hint at this physiological base (Sud, 2001; Sud & Sud, 2002; Sud & Prabha, 2004). The findings of the study corroborates with the view by Dalal and Misra (2006) about Yoga as a traditional healing system in India. They opine that Yoga as a therapeutic intervention involves physical practice as well as a way of cultivation of consciousness. It treats liberation as healing. Researches also indicate that meditation has been effective in reducing the physiological and psychological stress and related illness (Chopra, 1991; Easwaran, 1991; Yogi, 1995).

Inputs from Interaction

The participants came for the yogic practices regularly. During this three month long session the participants had very good rapport among themselves, with the instructor (first author) and also the second author. Many a days, the second author took part in yogic exercises along with other participants. In the course of interaction with them some interesting facts came-up.

Most of them echoed the fact that practicing along-with other participants was very conducive for them in comparison to their practice at home on holidays. Saints and sages, particularly of ancient times, are said to practice '*asanas*', '*pranayams*' and '*dhyan*' alone at secluded places, but here the participants had a contradictory view. It may be due to their nascent stage at yogic practice. We cannot say that they have been engrossed in yogic way of life. They are just at a learning stage, in which participants corrected their postures through instructor's guidance as well as by seeing postures of other participants. They suggested that, beginners like them should practice in the presence of the 'yoga instructor', because they themselves could not identify their faults properly at the time of practice. It was the instructor who could observe and find out the mistakes in their postures at a glance and provided feedback accordingly.

At the beginning, the participants had difficulty in following accurately the 'asanas' and 'pranayams', but as time passed, they were at ease with them. The university being closed on Saturday and Sunday, the participants did not come on those days. During the initial phase, they could not perform on holidays. This implies that the 'yoga centre' itself worked as an activating stimulus for the participants. Many of them also reported that, initially they were not serious about their practice, but gradually this routine like activity was so much ingrained in their mind that, they felt as if it was a food for their life. Here, we may equate this with the concept of 'functional autonomy' advocated by Allport (1965).

Some practitioners mentioned that, even till the end of the session, they could not concentrate properly during '*pranayam*'. Their mind fluctuated from one situation to another, though its intensity reduced at the ending phase from that of the initial phase. Perhaps, they needed some more practice and/or some further assessments may be made about their personality make-up, way of living, family-environment etc. because these can provide certain input for necessary changes in their practice.

However, most of the participants reiterated the view that, after completing the session, they felt mentally stable, concentrated better, improved eye-contact and enhanced their self-confidence. In comparison to the previous days they remained calm and composed even in disturbing situations.

Limitations and Implications

In the present study only one variable has been taken, *i.e.* trait anxiety. Some additional relevant variables could have been included. Secondly, the sample size was 38, which was not too large. But this study was an initial attempt. The authors are in the process of conducting a further study with more variables and participants at different places.

Yogic science, being an indigenous area of India, needs to be explored more and more. Empirical as well as qualitative studies may be conducted to delineate specific behavioural impact of specific yogic posture and *pranayam*. Yogic interventions may be conducted at different times of the day, like morning, evening, day-time etc to examine the timing impact. Likewise, those may be practiced at different locations to see the effects of settings. Yogic activity may be combined with music like *Nada* (Flute) and *Tal* (Tabla) etc. to investigate their interactive effect, if any. And more, Yoga is not only the 'asanas' and 'pranayams', but is a way of life covering various concepts. That is why Pattanjali describes it as *'Ashtanga Yoga Sutra'* covering eight stages. There are individual differences upon their extent of adherence to the different stages. Different people might have reached at different stages; many people might not have practiced even the elementary stage. So, studies may be conducted to scientifically establish the differential behavioural outcomes of the people reaching/practicing at different stages. These are some, but not the exhaustive list of avenues to explore the psychological correlates of *'Yoga'*.

REFERENCES

Abadi, M.S., Madgaonkar, J. and Venkatesan, S. (2008). Effect of Yoga on children with attention deficit/hyperactive disorder. *Psychological Studies, 53*(2), 154–159.

Allport, G.W. (1965). *Letters from Jenny.* New York: Harcourt, Brace & World.

Cattell, R.B. (1966). Patterns of change: Measurement in relation to state dimension, trait change, ability and process concepts. *Handbook of multivarious experimental psychology*. Chicago: Rand McNally & Co.

Cattell, R.B. and Scheier, I.H. (1963). *Handbook for the IPAT anxiety scale (2nd Edition)*. Champign, IL: Institute for Personality and Ability Testing.

Chopra, D. (1991). *Creating health: How to wake up the body's intelligence.* New York: Houghton – Miffin.

Dalal, A.K. and Misra, G. (2006). Psychology of health and well being: Some emerging perspectives. *Psychological Studies, 51* (2-3), 91-104.

Easwaran, E. (1991). *Meditation: A simple eight point programme for translating spiritual ideas into daily life.* Tomales, CA: Nilgiri.

Jensen, P.S. and Kenny, W. (2004). The effects of Yoga on the attention and behaviour of boys with attention deficit/hyperactivity disorders (ADHD). *Journal of Attention Disorders, 7*(4), 205–216.

Kiran Kumar, S.K. (2006). Happiness and well being in Indian tradition. *Psychololological Stuides, 53*(2), 154–159.

Manjunath, N.K. and Telles, S. (2004). Spatial and verbal memory test scores following Yoga and fine art camps for school children. *Indian Journal of Physiol and Pharmacol, 48*(3), 353-356.

Pandit, S.A. (2008). Assessing quality of life from Yogic perspective: A preliminary investigation. *Psychological Studies, 53*(2), 150 – 153.

Rani, N.J. and Rao, P.V.K. (2005). Impact of Yoga training on body image and depression. *Psychological Studies, 50 (1),* 98–100.

Rao, K.R. and Paranjape, A.C. (2008). Yoga psychology: Theory and application. In K.R. Rao., A.C. Paranjape. and A.K. Dalal (Eds.), *Handbook of Indian psychology.* New Delhi: Foundation Books, Cambridge University Press.

Sharma, S. (2002). Anxiety in students. *Psychological Studies, 47*(1-3), 49-53.

Spielberger, C.D. (1966). Theory and research on anxiety. In C.D. Spielberger (Ed.), *Anxiety and behaviour*. New York: Academic Press.

Spielberger, C.D. (1972). Anxiety as an emotional state. In C.D. Spielberger (Ed.), *Anxiety: Current trends in theory and research (Vol 1.).* New York: Academic Press.

Spielberger, C.D. (1976). The nature and measurement of anxiety. In C.D. Spielberger and R. Diaz-Guerrero (Eds.), *Cross-cultural anxiety.* Washington, D.C. : Hamisphere/Wiley.

Spielberger, C.D. (1979). *Preliminary manual for the state-trait personality inventory (STPI).* University of South Florida.

Spielberger, C.D. (1983). *State-trait inventory for adults.* Palo Alto, California: Mind Garden.

Sud, A. (2001). Test anxiety research in India: 20th century in retrospect. *Psychology and Developing Societies, 13*(1), 51-69.

Sud, A. and Sud, A. (2002). *Test anxiety: A brief overview of research in the 20th century.* Unpublished manuscript.

Sud, A. and Prabha, C. (2004). Perfectionism, procrastination and test anxiety. *Journal of Commuity Guidance and Research, 26*(3), 330-337.

Yogi, M.M. (1995). *Maharishi's vedic approach to health.* Viodrop Holland: Maharishi Vedic University Press.

●●●

12

The Samkhya, Yogic and Gita Models of Stress and Coping

C.B. Dwivedi

Man has been distressed by a number of stressors right from his existence and there have been efforts to understand and alleviate them by employing suitable measures. Although the usage of the term stress has changed in the Western literature, we come across its first usage there in the 14th century in the sense of hardship and adversity. However, there appears to be uniformity in its meaning since the 17th century in the work of prominent physicist/biologist Robert Hooke (see Lazarus, 1993). In contrast to this scenario, the Indian systems of thought present an uninterrupted position regarding the nature, intensity and methods for overcoming stress. It is pertinent to mention here that the Indian concept of stress is not synonymous with that of the West where we find several models to explain the stress in the post World-War-II era.

An overview of the dominant trends of usage of the term stress reveals that there have been three different approaches to the study of stress, namely, the stimulus-oriented approach, the response-oriented approach and the organism-oriented or interactional approach (see Cox, 1990; Derogatis, 1982). Stimulus-oriented approach uses stress as a potential residing within the stimulus properties of an organism's environment and accordingly those aspects of the environment that are demanding or disorganizing to the individual impose stress upon him. This approach essentially states that each individual has an innate capacity to withstand environmental stressors such as time demands, internal and external noxious conditions, *etc.* Response-oriented approach defines stress in terms of the response of an individual (strain) to the events of the environment. Cognitive aberrations, altered affect states, and disorganized interpersonal and social relationships reflect the presence of stress in an organism. The interactive point of view emphasizes the characteristics of an organism as major mediating mechanisms between stimulus characteristics of the environment and the responses they invoke (see for a review Cox, 1990; Lazarus, 1993). More recently, Matthews, (1995) and Matthwes and Deary, (1998) have suggested that a person's reactions to a stressful event should be studied across three distinct domains of subjective experience namely, emotional (such as mood states), motivational (such as task effort), and cognitive components (such as worry, Anxiety, *etc.*).

This brief description of the models of stress and stress state brings out that contemporary psychology regards stress as an analytical concept with varied emphases on stimulus, environment, or the organism. As against this analytical perspective, the Indian approach is a holistic one (see Falk, 1943) in which the root cause of stress has been elucidated with prescriptions for getting rid of it. In the present article an attempt has been made to highlight the Samkhya, the Yogic, and the Bhagavadgita's perspectives of stress and stress states along with techniques for their management.

The term stress has not found any expression in Indian sources and the concepts which appear to be very closely related to the discussion of stress and stress states are *duhkha* (suffering), *avidya* (nescience or wrong cognition), *klesa* (afflictions), *vasana/trsna* (unending desires), and the tapatraya (three varieties of human misery).

The Samkhya Framework of Stress and Coping

The samkhya system of thought offers a metaphysical description of the root cause of stress which is wrong cognition (*viparyaya*).

Five forms of wrong cognition have been discussed which denote its graded intensity. These are obscurity (*tamas*), perplexity (moha), extreme perplexity (mahamoha), gloom (tamisra), and blind gloom (andhatamisra). Each of them has been further classified. Eight types of each of tamas and moha, 10 types of mahamoha, and 18 types of each of tamisra and andhatamisra have been elaborated in the 48th aphorism of the Samkhya-Karika. Emancipation from wrong cognition has been suggested by the acquisition of true cognition (*vidya*) qua discriminative knowledge (*viveka*). It requires a continuous effort and liberation from tridimensional prakrti (the *sattva*, *rajas*, and *tamas*) which is made possible by an arduous effort. This process has been referred to as pratisancara (successive cessation). In this process the 16 vikrtis which comprise 11 modes of cognition and action (mind, 5 senses, and 5 motor organs), and 5 gross somatic components (*panca sthulabhuta*) are gradually attenuated. This is followed by the merger of *sapta-prakrtis* (seven premordia) which are namely the mahattattva (*citta*), the ahamkara (self-consciousness), and *panca-tanmatras* (five abstract forms of matter) in the moola *prakriti* (the premordial nature) to achieve a complete harmony.

These epistemological descriptions, however, remain only at a conceptual level if effort under proper guidance of a Guru is not invested in it. A resemblance of stress and its resolution can be seen in this model in which manifestation of one into many ramifies the stressful perception and reverting back to the origin resolves the stressors as well as their manifestations.

Yogadarsana's Framework of Stress and Coping

The Yogadarsana takes the samkhya framework as its theoretical base and offers a well-developed practical procedure for attaining self-realization (stress free state). Elsewhere it has been shown (Dwivedi, 1968) that the yogadarsana can become a nucleus for synthesis of entire Indian psychology. Recently Rao (1983a, 1983b) and Palsane, Bhavsar, Goswami, and Evans (1986) have attempted a description of the concept of stress in the Indian tradition. An exposition of the model of stress according to yogadarsana can not be conceived without discussing the *vrttis* (modes) and *klesas* (afflictions) followed by their resolution mechanisms. A brief description of these is attempted below.

Patanjali has described five types of *vrttis* (modes) which have been further divided into two types: *klista* (afflicted) and *aklista* (non-afflicted). The five modes are pramana (knowledge acquisition), *viparayaya* (wrong cognition), *vikalpa* (objectless imagery), *nidra* (sleep), and *smrti* (memory). During the course of severe affliction these vrttis generate excessive stress which has been termed as *klista*. On the other hand, there is a lessening of affliction in the *aklista* where a gradual dissipation of stress occurs. Three types of pramana have been described which are *pratyaksa* (perceptual), *anumana* (inferential), and agama (scriptural). These can become sources of stress when we turn outward in which case they are called afflicted (*klista*) whereas when subjective experiences work as an agent to resolve stress they are called unafflicted (*aklista*). Similar mechanisms of stress resolution have been hinted for other modes also.

Apart from these in aphorisms 30* and 31* of *yogasutra*, *Petanjali* has described somatic, affective, and cognitive components of stress. The somatic components are vyadhi (somatic diseases), angamejayatva (somatic tremors), and svasaprasvasaviksepa (respiratory disturbances and dyspnoea). The affective components are styan (mental inactivity), pramada (evasion) alasya (laziness), avirati (incesant desire), duhkha (grief), and daurmansya (uncomfort). The cognitive components are samsaya (doubt and indescisiveness), bhrantidarsana (wrong perception), alabdhabhumikatva (non-attainment of goal), and anavasthitattva (instability). After enumerating and expounding them, Patanjali has prescribed measures for their redressal which are given in aphorisms 33 (behavioural approach) and 34 to 38 (cognitive approach).

Vyadhistyansamsayapramadalasyavirtibhrantidarsanalabdhabhu mikatvanavasthitatvani chittaviksepasteantarayah (Yoga sutra I: 30).

Dukhdaurmansayangmejyatva svasprasvasviksepasahabhuvah (Yoga sutra I: 31)

Maitrikarunamuditopeksanasukhduhkhpunyapunyapunyavis-hyanam bhavanataschittaprasadanam (Yoga sutra I: 33).

Prachhardanavidharanabhyam va pransya (Yoga sutra I: 34)

Visayavati va Pravrttirutpanna mansah sthitinibandhini (yoga sutra I: 35).

Visoka va jyotismati (Yoga sutra 1: 36).

Vitaragavisaym va chittam (Yoga sutra I:37)

Swapnanidra jnanalambanam va (Yoga sutra I: 38).

Avidyaksetramuttresham prasuptatanuvichhinnodaranam (Yoga sutra II:4)

Tadbhavatsamyogabhavo hanam taddriseh kaivalayam (Yog sutra II: 25).

To bring home this point further, Patanjali has described at length the five types of affliction namely avidya (nescience), asmita (egoism), raga (attachment), dvesa (hatred), and abhinivesa (fear of death). Four intensities of these afflictions have been elucidated (Yoga sutra: 2:4). The root of all these klesas according to Patanjali is wrong cognition (avidya) and in aphorisms 25 & 26 the methods of overcoming them have been proposed. Space does not permit us to elaborate cognitive model of overcoming stress as proposed by Patanjali. However, it offers a model of continual appraisal and modification at behavioural, affective, and cognitive levels which alone can provide real knowledge or self-realization.

The Bhagavadgita's Model of Stress State and Cognitive Appraisal

Arjuna's *visadayoga* described at length in the first chapter of Bhagavadgita presents a vivid picture of stress state. A brief description of stress state as presented there will enable us to adequately understand the Gita's model of stress as well as its management. Stress researchers have usually employed situational stress conditions as the antecedent or independent variables and studied their effects on several consequent or dependent variable measures. Most of these studies have focussed on the effects of various stimuli on an individual's response patterns which have been labelled as behaviour under stress, somatic effects of stress, or performance under stress. However, very little effort has been devoted to study the influence of individual's behaviour itself, such as the effect of his activity, task effort or task-performance on the stress reactions *per se*. It is now increasingly realized that behaviour under stress is not just a one-step, unidirectional process. There is a continual self- regulation on the part of the individual and a proper assessment of this self-regulation needs to be done for a comprehensive analysis of stress.

There is, however, little information available about the temporary state of stress which is presumed to comprise a variety of distinct dimensions of subjective experiences (Dwivedi & Singh, 1996). Matthews (1995) and Matthews and Deary (1998) have suggested that at least three distinct domains of subjective experience are visible to have been influenced by stressful environment. These are the domains of emotional component such as mood states, motivational component such as task-effort and task-performance, and the domain of cognitive component such as worry, Anxiety, task-irrelevant thoughts, and self-focus of attention. These are temporary states and suitable measures are required to assess stress states instead of using more stable personality trait qualities.

In view of the brief description of stress state presented above, an analysis of Arjuna's *visadayoga* presents a true picture of the presence of distressed mood states, disoreintation, lack of concentration, depleted thoughts, lack of motivation and task effort in him. A warrior of the status of Arjuna who had fought many fierce battles single handedly finds himself in a state of utter stress. He shrinks with remorse and dismay as his cognitive-affective framework receives a jolt on perceiving his own kith and kin in the opposite camp. Compassion for his kinsmen and sudden arousal of self-abnegating love of humanity unhinged Arjuna's courage and presence of mind... He is confronted with a critical situation which clouds his thoughts and blocks his cognitive orientation. It renders him anxious and makes him flee from reality. Arjuna states in real anguish - "Seeing these kinsmen, O Krishna!, who have assembled here battle-bent, my limbs wither and my mouth becomes parched. My whole body trembles and sweats and my skin hair stands on end, my bow Gandiva slips from my hand and my skin fiercely burns. I am not able to remain firm seated, my mind wanders and I see omens of evil" (Dristvemam svajanam Krisna yuyutsu samupasthitam, sidanti roam gatrani mukham ca parisusyati, vepathus'ca sarire me roma harsasca jayate gandivam sransate hastat tvakcaiva paridahyate, na ca saknomyavasthatum bhramativa ca me manah. Nimmittani ca pasyami viparitani kesava" Bhagavadgita, chapter 1. 28-31).

Arjuna exhibits symptoms of Anxiety, confusion, phantasy, sweating, weakness, tremulousness, and palpitation. He is in depressed mood (visidantah) and excited (samvigumanah). However, his cognitive faculty is intact and he rationalizes that "by this war - the family tree will be torn" and - "injury will be inflicted on the friends". Realizing that Arjuna was in a state of stress Lord Krisna very patiently heard him first. He realized that once Arjuna ventilates the reasons for his anguish, depression, cognitive disorientation and ego defences, it would be easy to counsel him. Lord Krisna begins by dubbing Arjuna's state as cowardice (klaivyatvam), weakness of heart (hrdayadaurbalya), dirt (kasmala), unbecoming of a man (anarya) which is without any glory (akirtikara). The first task that Lord did was to induce an insight into Arjuna which he did by analyzing the problem from diverse angles. He first counselled for Arjuna's concern for his kinsmen, which in a sense was Arjuna's concern for his own self. Krisna began with an exposition of true nature of the self which is unborn, immortal, immutable, intangible and immeasurable. He distinguishes between ephemeral body and eternal self. This was meant to wipe out the somatic concerns of Arjuna. At length Lord Krisna counselled Arjuna and preached him of svadharma. To maintain an equipoise Lord described the sthitaprajna who is devoid of pain and pleasure, free from longing and dread. To bring a real feel Lord showed his cosmic vision (visvarupa) wherein Arjuna could see all his kinsmen entering the mouth of the Lord. He further tells arjuna "all these men are already destined to die by me and you act as an instrument only" (Maya eva ete nihitah purvameva, nimitta matram bhava savyasacin, 11.33).

In Chapter 18 Arjuna gains his normal self when he says "my infatuation has ceased, I have gained back my mind and cognition, I am now firm, free from doubt by your grace and shall indeed do as you guide" (*Nasto mohah smrtir labddhva tvat prasadanmayacyuta sthitosmi gata sandehah karisye vacanam tava*, 18.73). Arjuna gets orientation, becomes well-motivated and adjusted, ready to perform the task at hand.

The Samkhya, the Yoga, and the Bhagvadgita offer indigenous models of stress and stress state. We suggest that research efforts aimed at validating these procedures are undertaken to generate rigorous experimental and clinical tests so that current models may get a fillip based on ancient Indian tradition.

REFERENCES

Cox, T. (1990). Adaption to stress. In M.W. Eysenck (ed.), *The Blackwell Dictionary of Cognitive Psychology* Oxford: Blackwell Reference.

Derogatis, R. (1982). Self-report measures of stress. In L. Goldberger, & S. Breznitz (eds.), *Handbook of Stress: Theoretical and Clinical Aspects.* London: The Free Press.

Dwivedi, C.B. (1968) Yoga darsana: A nucleus toward the synthesis of Indian psychology *Prabuddha Bharata.,72*, 69-73.

Dwivedi, C.B. & Singh, I.L. (1996). Validation of a multi-component questionnaire of stress state across the measures of task performance and well-being. Unpublished research project.

Falk, M. (1943). The oldest psychology: Terminus a quo and aspects. *Indian Journal of Psychology, 18*, 106-116.

Lazarus, R.S. (1993). From psychological stress to the emotion: A history of changing outlooks. *Annual Review of Psychology, 44*, 1-21.

Matthews, G. (1995). Validation of a questionnaire, Measure of multiple dimension of stress state. London: *MRC Research Project.*

Matthews, G., & Deary, I.J. (1998). *Personality Traits.* Cambridge: University Press.

Palsane, M.N., Bhavsar, S.N., Goswami, R.P., & Evans, G.W. (1986). The concept of stress in the Indian tradition. *Journal of Indian Psychology*, 5, 1-12.

Rao, S.K.R. (1983 a). The conception of stress in Indian thought I: The theoretical aspects of stress in Samkhya and Yoga systems, *NIMHANS Journal*, 1, 115-21.

Rao, S.K.R. (1983 b). The conception of stress in Indian thought II. The practical involvement in Gita and Ayurveda. *NIMHANS Journal*, 1, 123-131.

●●●

Part—II
Yoga and Health: Promotion, Practice and Research

- Yoga and Health
- Yoga and Health Promotion
- Mental Health Management in Yoga-Sutra
- Yogic Practice as a Moderator of Mental Health
- Research in Yoga as a Holistic Model of Health

13

Yoga and Health

Prem Verma

There is a Roman saying, "Mens sana in corpore sana, *i.e.*, A sound mind in a sound body. Physical fitness or health and yoga are very much interrelated. Unless one has good health, one cannot aspire to attain self realization. Yoga occupies an important place in the scheme of spiritual practices. The conclusions about yoga are based not on mere theory or speculation, but on facts that have been tested time and again through practice. Its approach to life's problems is objective and analysis of the problems is scientific. Patanjali defined yoga as "subjugation of the thought waves of the mind". (Patanjali, yoga aphorisms 1.2). The mind is like a lake that remains constantly agitated by distracting thought waves (Vritti). Hence one does not see the self that is the bottom of the lake. The aim of yoga is to control the outgoing tendencies of the mind, the senses, and the body. The methodology of yoga is to control the subconscious with the help of conscious efforts. Restlessness of the body is to be overcome by the practice of postures (Asanas) conducive to tranquillity. Irregular breath, an indicator of restlessness is to be made regular by breathing exercises. Impure thoughts and the tendencies of the mind must be countered by the cultivation of moral and ethical virtues. The Raja Yoga system employs an eightfold system of practice (ashtang yoga) consisting of the following steps or "limbs":

1. *Yama* (Restraint) calls for the cultivation of five virtues :

(a) Non violence (*ahimsa*) - it does not mean merely abstinence from killing, but also refraining from injuring others either by word, thought or deed.

(b) Truthfulness (*Satya*) - This also means to be true in one's thoughts, words, and deeds under all circumstances.

(c) Non-stealing (*Asteya*) - Not claiming anything that does not belong to us. This means to control the propensity of the mind for greed.

(d) Continence (*Brahamacharya*) - It is observance of chastity in thought, word, and deed continence re-creates the body, mind, and nerves, infusing them with new vigor.

(e) Non-receiving of gifts (*Aprigraha*) - remaining free and independent from the influence of others.

2. *Niyam* (Discipline) - constitutes five observances :

(a) Cleanliness (*Shaucha*) - not only external but also internal.

(b) Contentment (*Santosh*) - remaining satisfied with a few material necessities procured without great effort.

(c) Austerity (*Tapah*) - practicing control of body, speech, and mind. It increases will power.

(d) Study of sacred books (*Suadhyay*) - study those books which help you to understand the reality of the absolute.

(e) Self surrender to God (*Eshvarpranidhanani*) - by surrendering the fruits of action to the Divine, one grows in devotion, which culminates in concentration on the chosen ideal.

3. *Asana* (Posture) - Raja yoga stresses on a steady and pleasant posture with the limbs of the body remaining restful, and conducive to concentration and meditation. In Hatha yoga, however. there are 84 postures of sitting as means to the practice of yoga. Some of them are beneficial for the physical body. The idea is to gain control over the body.

4. *Pranayama* (Control of breath) - The derivative form of pranayama is prana and ayama. Prana signifies the life force and ayama means to control. The breath supplies power to all parts of the body. When the breath is regulated, the mind becomes calm. Pranayama consists of breathing in (Puraka), restraining the breath (Kumbhaka), and breathing out (Rechaka) in proper proportion.
5. *Pratyahara* (Withdrawl of mind) - It consists of training the mind to detach itself at will from each sense organ. When we are in a perfectly concentrated state of mind, we would not hear any external noise.
6. *Dharna* (Concentration) - It means the gathering of mental energies that are scattered in all directions, and focusing them on an object for a certain length of time without interruption.
7. *Dhyana* (Meditation) - When concentration becomes effortless and continuous, there begins meditation. Patanjli says, "Meditation is the uninterrupted concentration of thought on its object. This itself turns into *Samadhi* when the object itself shines and the thought of meditation (and of the meditator) is lost, as it were".
8. *Samadhi* (Absorption) - Is attained when meditation becomes constant and continuous, and the mind merges in the object of meditation.

It is common to refer to the first four steps inclusively as Hatha yoga and the last four which focus more directly on mental realm as 'Raja Yoga' (Rama, Bellentina and Ajaya, 1993). Hatha yoga is inseparable from Raja yoga. Raja yoga begins when Hatha yoga ends. Hatha yoga prepares a person to take up Raja yoga. Hatha yoga relates to the restraint of breath, asanas, bandhas, and mudras. It aims at psycho physiological balance while Raja yoga brings predominantly, the yogic thought system, *i.e.* attaining objective perception of reality or liberation from false hood or 'avidya'.

Prana is described in the scared texts of yoga and Vedanta as having five modifications, according to its five different functions. These are prana, apana, samana, udana and vyana. The function of prana is respiration; of apana,. excretion; of samana, digestion; of udana, swallowing of food, helping in sleep; and of vyana, circulation of blood. The seat of prana is the heart; of apana, the organs of evacuation; of samana, the area of naval; of udana, the throat; while vyana is all - pervading and moves throughout the body, guarding it against disease and maintaining equilibrium.

Yoga helps to reduce stress through various techniques. With a better control over mind one feels that the world is, after all, not that uncongenial a place to live in. Relaxation through meditation, asanas, and pranayama is very effective in reducing stress that reduces the defence mechanism of the body. The regular practice of asanas and pranayama strengthens the nervous system and helps people deal with stress more effectively by reducing the steroid hormones, uric acid, free fatty acids and cholesterol, etc.

Goleman (1973) compared 30 meditators and 30 non meditators in an anxiety arousing situation and found that those who were experienced meditators, responded to threat with less subjective anxiety. Schwartz (1973) on the basis of a comparison between 38 meditators, 50 about to begin meditation and 39 non meditators, found that the meditators reported a general increase in positive mood states, being less stressed and leading a more regular life style that the typical American. Kocher (1972) reported a significant reduction in anxiety level and general hostility An group of forty yoga performers. Udupa (1985) reported to have treated 1007 cases of various stress disorders with a combination of the practice of asana, pranayama, and meditation. Granath, *et.al.* (2006) concluded on the basis of a 4 months systematic cognitive behaviour therapy on one group and the Kundalini yoga programme on the other group that both cognitive behaviour therapy and yoga are promising stress management techniques. The findings of Michalsen, *et.al.* (2005) showed that compared with the control group, yoga group showed significant reduction in stress, anxiety, fatigue, depression, headaches, and back pain. The yoga group also showed significant increase in well being. Kirkwood, *et al.* (2005) reviewed a number of studies on yoga. It was reported that in several studies, which compared yoga with anti-anxiety medication, greater improvements were found from yoga than medication.

Researchers have also reported positive results of yoga on cardiovascular endurance (Bera and Rajapurkar, 1993; Ganguli, 1981; Gharote, 1973, 1976). Lolage and Bera (2002) too found that Pranayamas were useful in improving cardiovascular endurance of Kho Kho players as measured by 8 minutes run test and 1600 M run test.

Prasad, *et al.* (2005) found that men (N=41) showed reduced levels of serum triglycerides and VLDL cholesterol at the end of 30 days practice of pranayama, and increased levels of HDL cholesterol and reduced levels of free fatty acids at the end of both 30 days of pranayama practice and 3 months session of pranayama and asanas together. Women (N=23) showed reduced levels of free fatty acids at the end of both 30 days as well as 3 months sessions, and also showed reduced levels of total cholesterol, triglycerides, LDL and VLDL cholesterol by the end of 3 months session.

Mamtani and Mamtani (2005) on the basis of a review of research on the use of ayurvedic treatments (including yoga practice) concluded that there is sufficient evidence to support the use of yoga in treating heart disease and hypertension. Patel (1973, 1975) too reported that biofeedback training when combined with yogic relaxation had lasting effects in lowering blood pressure. Improvement was sustained twelve months after training had been complete. The asana practices (Surya namaskar, trikon asana, tadasna, pawanmukta asana etc.) and bhastrika pranayam have been reported to be effective in lowering the blood glucose levels of insulin dependent diabetics (fasting as well as post prandial) (Malhotra, *et al.*, 2005)

Yoga stresses on adopting a life style based on proper behaviours including yama (restraints) and niyama (discipline). This would make the person more self efficacious to follow the desired routine.

The practice of yoga as documented above, keeps us away from many ailments. It enhances ,esistance, tolerance and will power. Yoga acts as an antioxidant counteracting many ill effects of various environmental hazards like bacterial infections. It keeps a balance between vat (wind) pitt (bile) and kaf (phlegm) in our body. Regular practice of surya namaskar, having twelve postures activates the seven charkas (muladhar, swadhisthan, Manipur, anhat, vishudhi, jnan, and shasrar), the energy centres, which when activated, maintain the tone of the nervous system. Other asanas like bhujang, shalabh, makar, matsya, shav, etc. are as effective. Pranayama (comprising poorak, kumbhak, and recheck) results in inhaling more oxygen and consuming less energy. It has been found to have beneficial effects on heart and lungs and an increase in longevity. A glance on the following table would reveal the relationship of breath with life span.

TABLE 1

Relationship of breath with life span

Living being	Breaths per minute	Life span
Tortoise	4-5	200 yrs.
Snake	7-8	150 yrs.
Humans	15-16	100 yrs
Horse	20-22	40 yrs.
Dog	28-30	14 yrs.

Considering the different aspects of yoga, one can conclude after Patanjali that yoga is a live art that promotes a long healthy life. However, the ultimate goal of yoga is not just to achieve and maintain good health only. Health / well being should be considered as only supportive of the internal practices of yoga *viz.*, concentration, meditation, and *samadhi*. Meditation endows a person with increased capacity of the mind by releasing its dormant power. By participating in the peace and serenity of the soul, the mind becomes rejuvenated and strengthened and regains its lost vigor, resulting in increased capacity for tolerating the frustrations of life. The ultimate goal of yoga is self realization. By realizing the true self (dredging through the five sheaths, *i.e.*, Koshaas), an embodiment of bliss free from the taint of sin and fear of death, a mortal individual attains the highest fulfillment (Adiswarananda, 2004).

REFERENCES

Adiswarananda, S. (2004). *Meditation and its practices*. Kolkata: Advaita Ashrama.

Bera, T.K., and Rajapurkar, M.V. (1993). Body composition, cardiovascular endurance and anaerobic power of yogic practitioners. *Indian Journal of Physiology and Pharmacology*, 37, 225-228.

Ganguly, S.K. (1981). Effect of short term yoga training programme on cardiovascular endurance. *SNIPES Journal*, 4, 45-50.

Gharote, M.L. (1973). Effect of yogic training on physical fitness. *Yoga Mimamsa*, 15, 31-35.

— (1976). Physical fitness in relation to the practice of selected yogic exercises. *Yoga Mimamsa*, 18, M-23.

Goleman, D., (1973). *Medidation and Stress Reactivity* Dcotoral dissertation, Harvard University.

Granath, J., Ingvarsson, S., Von thiele, U., and Lundberg, U. (2006). Stress management; a randomized study of cognitive behavioural therapy and yoga. *Cognitive Behaviour Therapy*, 35, 3-10.

Kirkwood, G., Rampes, H., Tuffrey, V., Richardson, J., Pkilkington, K., and Ramaratnam, S. (2005). Yoga for anxiety a systematic review of the research evidence. *British Journal of Sports Medicine*, 39, 884-891.

Kocher, H.C. (1972). Anxiety, general hostility and its direction as a result of yogic practices. *Yog Mimamsa*, 17, 73-82.

Kristal A.R. Littman, A.J., Benitez, D. White, E. (2005). Yoga practice is associated with attenuated weight gain in healthy middle - aged men and women. *Alternative Therapies in Health and Medicine*, 11, 28-33.

Lalage, R.S., and Bera, T.K. (2002). Effect of Pranayama on cardiovascular endurance in Kho Kho players. *Yoga Mimamsa*, 34, 13-26.

Malhotra V., Singh, S., Tandon, O.P., and Sharma, S.B. (2005). The beneficial effect of yoga in diabetes. *Nepal Medical College Journal*, 7, 145-147.

Mamtani, R., and Mamtani, R. (2005). Ayurveda, yoga and cardiovascular disease. *Cardiology in Review*, 13, 155-162.

Michalsen, A., Grossman, P., Acil, A., Langhorst, J., Ludtke, R., Esch, T., Stefano, G.B., and Dobos, G.J. (2005). Yoga reduces stress and anxiety among distressed women. *Medical Science Monitor*, 11, 555-561.

Patel, C.H. (1973). Yoga and Biofeedback in the Management of hypertension. *The Lancet*, Nov., 1053-1055.

— (1975). Twelve months follow up of yoga and biofeedback in the management of hypertension. *The Lancet January*, 62-67.

Prasad, K.V.V., Sunita, M., Raju, P.S., Reddy, M.V., Sahay, B.K., and Murthy, K.J.Y. (2005). Impact of Pranayama and yoga on lipid profile in normal healthy volunteers. *Journal of exercise physiology*, 9, 1-6.

Proskauer, M. (1969). Breathing Therapy, In J. Mann, and H. Otto (Ed.) *Ways of growth*. New York: Viking Press.

Rama, S. Bellentina, R., and Ajaya, S. (1993). *Yoga and Psychotherapy : The evolution of consciousness*. The Himalayan Institute Honesdale, PA.

Schwartz, G.E. (1973). *Pros and cons of meditation; current findings on Physiology and Anxiety, Self Control, Drug Abuse and Creativity* (Paper presented at the APA convention, Montreal.

Udupa, K.N. (1985). *Stress and its management by yoga*. Delhi: Motilal Banarsidass.

●●●

14

Yoga and Health Promotion

Chandra Shekhar and Sunil Sharma

Modern medicine and yoga are rational, scientific and universal in outlook and hence are natural allies which bound to come together. Their combination has the potential to provide us with a holistic health science that will be a boon for the psychosomatic health of our masses. Improved health of the general population will result in reduction of pressure on our hospitals, which are under-staffed, over-crowded and fund-starved. Yoga and modern medicine are not exclusive, but complementary systems. Their enlightened collaboration will have a significant impact on our health care system. Yoga involves a holistic approach to healing and well being and integrates healing with the culture, diet, environment, and tradition. Modern allopathic medicine that originated from Greco-Roman medicine and Northern European traditions is built on the science of anatomy, physiology, and biochemistry and the structure-function relationship between cells, tissues, and organs. Allopathic medicine focuses on diagnosis, treatment, and cure for acute illnesses via potent pharmaceutical drugs, surgery, radiation, and other treatment modalities.

We are today faced with numerous debilitating chronic illnesses related to aging, environment, and hedonistic lifestyle, such as cancer, diabetes, osteoporosis, and cardiovascular diseases as well as many incurable diseases such as AIDS. Modern medical advancements provide the rationale for the integration of various traditional healing techniques including yoga to promote healing, health, and longevity. It is imperative that advances in medicine include the holistic approach of yoga to face the current challenges in health care. The antiquity of yoga must be united with the innovations of modern medicine to improve quality of life throughout the world.

At first glance, allopathic medicine and yoga may seem to be totally incompatible and in some ways even antagonistic to each other. Practitioners of either system are often found at loggerheads with one another in typical modern one-upmanship. It would of course be much easier to build a bridge between yoga and ayurveda as both share many similarities of concepts such as the Trigunas, Tridoshas, Chakras and Nadis. They also understand that a healthy balance between body, mind and soul leads to total health. Diet and behaviour are given importance in both systems and the ultimate goal of both is the attainment of *Moksha.*

Though allopathy may not share all of these concepts with yoga, it is to be seen that there are a great many 'meeting points' for the construction of a healthy bridge between them. Both allopathy and yoga understand the need for total health and even the Word Health Organization has recently added a new dimension to the modern understanding of health by including spiritual health in its definition of the "state of health'. Spiritual health is an important element of yoga and now that even the WHO has come around to understanding this point of view, there is hope for a true unification of these two systems. Modern medicine has the ultimate aim and goal of producing a state of optimum physical and mental health thus ultimately leadings to the optimum well being of the individual. Yoga also aims at the attainment of mental and physical well being though the methodology does differ. While modern medicine has a lot to offer humankind in its treatment and management of acute illness, accidents and communicable diseases, yoga has a lot to offer in terms of preventive, promotive and rehabilitative methods in addition to many management methods to tackle modern illnesses.

While modern science looks outward for the cause of all ills, the yogi searches the depth of his own self. This two way search can lead us to many answers for the troubles that plague modern man. The *Shiva-Samhita* lists the characters of a fully qualified disciple (*Shishya*) as follows. "Endowed with great energy and enthusiasm, intelligent, heroic, learned in the scriptures, free from delusion..." Doesn't a true modern medical scientist require these very same qualities?

Anatomy and Physiology

The study of anatomy and physiology is a great meeting point for modern medicine and yoga. Yoga therapists and practitioners can benefit from the intricate and detailed 'break-down study' of modern medicine where the body is broken down into many systems, then into many organs, many tissues and finally into billions of cells. On the other hand the yogic " holistic" view of the *Pancha Kosha* (the five sheathed existence) can help modern doctors realise that we are not just, 'one-body' organisms but have four more bodies that are equally if not more important. We are a manifestation of the Divine and have, not only the physical body but also an energy body, a mental body, a body of wisdom and a body of eternal bliss. An understanding of the psychic anatomy and physiology of Nadis, Chakras and Bindus when coupled with the practical understanding of the details of the physical body can inspire real knowledge of the self in all health care personnel. Maharishi Mahesh Yogi has tried to correlate 37 areas of human physiology with 37 areas of intelligence or consciousness as available in Vedic literature. Some of the examples are the correlation between *Nyaya* and the thalamus as well as *Samkya* and the types of neuronal activity (Feuerstein, 1996).

In his excellent book, *The Shambala Guide to Yoga*, Dr. Georg Feuerstein (1996) says, "Long before physicists discovered that matter is energy vibrating at a certain rate, the Yogis of India had treated this body-mind as a playful manifestation of the ultimate power (*Shakti*), the dynamic aspect of reality. They realized that to discover the true self, one has to harness attention because the energy of the body-mind follows attention. A crude example of this process is the measurable increase of blood flow to our fingers and toes that occurs when we concentrate on them. Yogis are very careful about where they place their attention, for the mind creates patterns of energy, causing habits of thought and behaviour that can be detrimental to the pursuit of genuine happiness".

Prevention of Disease

Modern medicine has come to realise the importance of prevention only in recent times but the role of preventive medicine is still very limited. The Yogic lifestyle that includes the *Yama* and *Niyama* can help prevent a great many of the modern diseases like Hepatitis B and AIDS. Cleanliness that is taught through *Soucha* can help prevent and limit the spread of contagious and infectious diseases. Mental peace and right attitudes of Yoga such as *Pratipaksha Bhavanam* (taking the opposite view), *Samatvam* (equanimity of mind) and *Vairagya* (dispassionate detachment) can help prevent many of the psychosomatic ailments running wild in the modern world. If these yogic values as well as practices such as Asanas, Pranayamas, Kriyas and Dhyana are inculcated in the modern human race, we can prevent virtually all diseases that abound today. Communicable diseases as well as degenerative disorders of the body can be well prevented in true manifestations of the adage, "A stitch in time saves nine". However the 'will' to do so is also of paramount importance as there is no money or fame in prevention and we don't know what we have prevented because we have prevented it from happening (Champaneria, 2002).

To quote the eminent neurosurgeon Padma Bhushan Dr. B. Ramamurthi, (2000) "The revival of the science of yoga bades good for mankind. All the technological advances in the third millennium will not lead to the happiness of mankind as man has a severe aggressive tendency and is likely to destroy himself because of this aggression. The only way out of this mess is through the science of yoga, which transcends all religions and cults. It is a science of the mind and the body and needs to be practiced by all human beings to ensure their own future".

Health Promotion

Yoga is an excellent tool of promoting health that can enrich modern medicine. The practice of Yoga leads to the efficient functioning of the body with homeostasis through improved functioning of the psycho-neuro-endocrine and immuno system. A balanced equilibrium between the sympathetic and parasympathetic wings of the autonomic nervous system leads to a dynamic state of health. According to Ramamurthy, (2000) yoga re-orients the functional hierarchy of the entire nervous system. He has noted that yoga not only benefits the nervous system but also the cardiovascular, respiratory, digestive, endocrine and immune systems in addition to bringing about general biochemistry changes in the yoga practitioners. He has also said that the science of yoga has been India's greatest contribution to mankind.

Management of Diseases and Disorders

Yoga doesn't negate the use of drugs and other methods of modern medicine. Patanjali in his *Avatar* as *Charaka* didn't shy away from the need to use medicinal herbs as well as surgical methods when necessary for the benefit of the patient. The system of Ayurveda is more in tune with the yogic views of healing in this regard but definitely the modern antibiotic treatment of infectious diseases as well as the emergency medical and trauma-management techniques of modern medicine must be understood to be life-savers in times of need. No yoga therapist in his or her right mind should try to treat an acute myocardial infarction or an unconscious accident victim by yoga alone. A symbiotic relationship between the techniques of modern medicine and yoga can help the patient more than a dogmatic refusal to see the 'other side'. Yoga has a lot to offer in terms of psychosomatic disorders and in stress related disorders such as diabetes, asthma, irritable bowel syndrome, epilepsy, hypertension, back pain and other functional disorders. Yoga can help reduce and in some cases eliminate drug dosage and dependence in patients suffering from diabetes mellitus, hypertension, epilepsy, anxiety, bronchial asthma, constipation, dyspepsia, insomnia, arthritis, sinusitis and dermatological disorders.

Brena, (1972) has said that yoga is probably the most effective way to deal with various psychosomatic disabilities along the same, time-honored, lines of treatment that contemporary medicine has just rediscovered and tested. Asanas are probably the best tool to disrupt any learned patterns of wrong muscular efforts. *Pranayama* and *Pratyahara* are extremely efficient techniques to divert the individual's attention from the objects of the outer environment, to increase energy potentials and 'interiorize' them, to achieve control of one's inner functioning. Moreover, in restoring human unity, the yoga discipline is always increasing awareness and understanding of ourselves, adjusting our emotions, expanding our intellect, and enabling us not only to function better in any given situation, but to perform as spiritual beings with universal values.

Yoga therapists must work in tandem with medical doctors when they are treating patients who have been on allopathic treatment. There are many instances where the patient stops medical treatment thinking that it no more necessary as they have started yoga. This leads to many catastrophes that could be easily avoided by tandem consultations with a medical specialist. Similarly, many allopaths tend to tell the patient to take up yoga or relaxation and forget to mention to the therapist what they actually want the patients to do. Most allopathic medications need to be tapered off in a progressive manner rather than being stopped suddenly. We often find this mistake in regard to corticosteroids as well as cardiac medications where sudden stoppage can be harmful. We must remember Plato's words when he said, that the treatment of the part shouldn't be attempted without a treatment of the entirety, meaning that the treatment of the body without treating the mind and soul would be a useless waste of time.

Rehabilitation

Yoga as a physical therapy has a lot to offer patients of physical and mental handicaps. Many of the practices of physiotherapy and other physical therapies have a lot in common with yoga practices. Mentally challenged individuals can benefit by an improvement in their IQ as well as in learning to relate to themselves and others better. As their physiological functions improve with yoga, the combination of yoga and physical therapies can benefit such patients as well as those with learning disabilities. Musculoskeletal problems can be treated by the combination to improve function as well as range of movement, strength and endurance abilities. Balance and dexterity can also be improved by the combination therapy. The use of yoga can help those recovering from accidents and physical traumas to get back on their feet faster and with better functional ability. An example of this was Swami Gitananda Giri (1996), who managed to get back on his feet and function normally after a debilitating stay in a full body cast for more than six months. Swamiji used to say, "Modern medicine kept me alive, but yoga gave me back my life as otherwise I may have been a cripple for life". Yoga also has a lot to offer those suffering from drug and substance abuse in assisting them to get back to a normal life. Yoga helps develop their self-control and will power and also gives them a new philosophy of living. This is vital as otherwise they will lapse into their old negative habits.

Healthy Diet

This is a place that modern medicine and yoga can help give a patient as well as normal person the proper holistic values of a proper diet. This is important for the person to know how much of each constituent of food is to be taken in the proper quantity. Yoga can help a person to learn the right attitude towards food as well as understand concepts based on the Trigunas and Tridoshas for better health. Yoga teaches us that the cause of most disease is through under (*Ajjeranatvam*), over (*Atijeeranatvam*) or wrong (*Kujeeranatvam*) digestion. Yoga also teaches us about the approach to food, the types of food as well as the importance of timings and moderation in diet. A combination of the modern aspects of diet with a dose of yogic thought can help us eat not only the right things but also in the right way and at the right time thus ensuing our good health and longevity.

Relaxation

Most medical doctors understand that it is important to relax in order to get better. The problem is that, though the doctor tells the patient to relax, they don't tell them how to do so and maybe in fact they don't know the answer themselves in the first place. Hatha Yoga and Jnana Yoga relaxation practices help relax the body, emotions and mind. Relaxation is a key element of any yoga therapy regimen and must not be forgotten at any cost. Shavasana has been reported to help a lot in hypertensive patients and practices such as Savitri Pranayama, Chandra Pranayama, Kaya Kriya, Yoga Nidra, Anuloma Viloma Prakriyas and Marmanasthanam Kriya are also available to the person requiring this state of complete relaxation. It is important to remember that relaxation on its own is less effective than relaxation following activity.

Coping Skills

Yoga has a lot to offer those who unable to cope with death and dying as well as those suffering from incurable diseases. The yoga philosophy of living sees death as an inevitable aspect of life that cannot be wished away. Swami Gitananda Giri (1976), used to tell that the whole of life is, but a preparation for the moment of death, so that we can leave the body in the right way. Those who are taking care of the dying as well as those taking care of patients of incurable diseases and major disabilities are under an extreme amount of stress and yoga practice as well as its philosophy helps them gain the inner strength necessary to do their duty. Yoga can help break the vicious spiral of pain-drug dosage-pain and by doing so help reduce the drug dosage in patients suffering chronic pain. It has been reported that yoga helps improve the quality of life in patients suffering from cancer and also helps them cope better with the effects of treatment. It relaxes them and helps them sleep better. Yoga may not be able to always cure but it can surely help us to endure (Carlson, 2003).

Expenditure

Modern medicine is often criticized for the cost involved in its methods of treatment. Yoga offers an inexpensive method of health that can be added to the medical armory when required. Yoga only requires the patient's own effort and really doesn't need any paraphernalia. Of course the modern yoga industry would rather have us believe that we need tons of yoga equipment to start yoga, but they are awfully of the mark in this case. Reduction in drug dosage and avoidance of unnecessary surgeries in many cases can also help reduce the spiraling cost of medicare (Sri, 1997).

Aging

Aging is inevitable and yoga can help us to age gracefully. Modern medicine tries to help retard aging and help people look better by costly surgical methods that are only an external covering over the underlying aging process. Healthy diet, regular exercise, avoidance of negative habits and cultivation of the positive habits and a healthy lifestyle can help us to age with dignity. Yoga can also help our 'silver citizens' retain their mental ability and prevent degenerative disorders such as Parkinson's disease, Alzheimer's and various other dementias. Physical accidents such as falls can be minimised and many an artificial hip, knee or shoulder replacement surgery can be avoided. Swami Gitananda Giri, Yogashri Krishnamacharya, Kannaiah Yogi, Swami Suddananda Bharathi, Yogeshwarji, Yogendraji and Padma Bhushan BKS Iyengar are but a few of the Yogis who have shown us that it is possible to grow old without losing any of the physical or mental faculties of youth (Gitanada and Meenakshi, 1991).

Psychotherapy

In the field of psychotherapy and psychoanalysis we can find a lot of ancient yogic concepts being reiterated time and again. Many modern psychotherapeutic concepts such as identification, projection, and transference are similar to concepts in yoga psychology. Yoga psychology integrates diverse principles within a single body. Jung had a great interest in yoga and the eastern thought and said, "Chakras represent a real effort to give a symbolic theory of the psyche". His 'Centre of Personality' concept based on dream analysis is very similar to the yogic concept of a central psychic or spiritual personality. He also correlated Chakras to the archetypes that abound in the collective unconscious. Yoga helps the psychotherapist in training self awareness, and in the self regulation of body, diet, breath, emotions, habit patterns, values, will, unconscious pressures and drives. It also helps in relating to the archetypal processes and to a transient being. It offers an integrated method rather than one that is found in isolation in many different therapies. The theory of Kleshas is an excellent model for psychotherapy while emotional therapies of yoga include Swadyaya, Pranayama, Pratyahara, Dharana, Dhyana and Bhajans. Development of proper psychological attitudes is inculcated *via* the concepts of *Vairagya*, *Chitta Prasadanam* as well as Patanjali's advise on adopting the attitudes of *Maitri, Karuna, Mudita* and *Upekshanam* towards the happy, the suffering, the good and the evil minded persons. Yoga also has a lot to offer in terms of spiritual therapies such as *Swadyaya, Satsangha, Bhajan* and Yogic counseling. It is also interesting to note that both yoga and psychoanalysis share common ground in understanding that symptoms of the disease are often willed by the patients. While all psycho analysists must undergo psychoanalysis themselves, it is taught in yoga that one must first undergo a deep *sadhana,* before attempting to guide others on the path. However, while psychoanalysis searches the unconscious, Yoga attempts to understand and explore the super conscious (Nagarathna & Nagendra 2001).

Life Style Changes

Yoga helps patients take their health in their own hands. They learn to make an effort and change their life style for the better so that their health can improve. Life style modification is the buzzword in modern medical circles and Yoga can play a vital role in this regard. Yogic diet, Asanas, Pranayamas, Mudras, Kriyas and relaxation are an important aspect of lifestyle modification. Dr. Dean Ornish, an eminent American medical doctor who has shown that Yogic lifestyle can reverse heart disease says, "Yoga is a system of perfect tools for achieving union as well as healing.

Women's Health

Women are the chosen ones blessed with the responsibility of the future of our human race. Healthy mothers give birth to healthy babies and a healthy start has a great future ahead. Yoga has a lot to contribute in combination with modern medicine to the health status of woman kind. Puberty and menopause become easier transitions with the help of yoga and many eminent yoginis have said that they were not even aware of a single menopausal symptom as they went through this difficult period in a woman's life. Similarly, our young girls can vouch for the fact that their pubertal changes and menarche has been relatively smoother than their counterparts who don't practice yoga. The benefits of yoga in terms of family planning are also an important aspect that needs further study, as they can be an effective part of the contraceptive armory. The risk of side effects is negated and the entire control restored to the individuals themselves. The Oli Mudras as practiced in the Gitananda Yoga tradition have great potential in this regard and also the Swara Yoga theories of conception have a lot of exciting possibilities. Once conception occurs, yoga helps the young mother to be, to prepare herself physically and mentally for the upcoming childbirth. Yoga helps open the joints of the pelvis and hip as well as strengthen the abdominal muscles for childbirth. Later, simple Pranayamas and relaxation techniques help the new mother relax and enjoy the new experience of her life. Post- partum introduction of simple practices along with breathing, relaxation and a lot of crawling helps her come back to normal earlier and this can be used in all maternity hospitals along with allopathic management. Yoga practices can also help reduce the drug dosage in medical problems that often complicate a normal pregnancy such as diabetes, asthma and hypertension (Anantharaman, 1976, 1983).

REFERENCES

Ajay, S. (1983). *Psychotherapy east and west.* Pennsylvania: Himalayan Institute.

Anantharaman, T. R. (1976). *Yoga as a science.* Souvenir: Seminar on Yoga, Science and Man. Central Council for Research in India, New Delhi.

Anantharaman, T. R. (1983). Yoga Vidya and Yoga Vidhi: *The Yoga Review*, *3*, 119-137.

Brena, S. F. (1972). *Yoga and Medicine*. New York: Penguin Books.

Carlson, L. E. (2003). Mindfulness based stress reduction in relation to quality of life, mood, symptoms of stress, and immune parameters in breast and prostate cancer outpatients. *Psychosomatics Medicine*, *65*, 571-581.

Champaneria, M. (2002). The new world of medicine: prospecting for health. *Nippon Naika Gakkai Zasshi*, *20*, 159-163.

Feuerstein, G. (1996). *The Shambala Guide to Yoga*. Boston: Shambala Publicaton.

Gitananda, G. S. (1997). *Frankly Speaking*. Pondicherry: Satya Press.

Gitananda, G. S. (1996). *Yoga the art and science of awareness*. Pondicherry: International Yoga Festival.

Gitananda, G. S. (1976). *Yoga: Step-by -step*. Pondicherry: Satya Press.

Gitananda, G. S and Meenakshi, D.B. (1991). *Bridging the gap between yoga and science*. Souvenir of the International Conference on Biomedical, Literary and Practical Research in Yoga, Pondicherry, India.

Nagarathna, R and Nagendra, H. R. (2001). *Integrated approach of yoga therapy for positive health*. Bangalore: Swami Vivekananda Yoga Prakashana.

Ramamurthi, B. (2000). *Uphill all the way*. Pondicherry: Guardian Press.

Sri, R.M. (1997). *Healthy mind and healthy body*. Pondicherry: Satya Press.

●●●

15

Mental Health Management in Yoga-Sutra

K.M. Tripathi

Yoga has been traditionally recognised as a metaphysical and spiritual science leading to the union of individual consciousness and cosmic being with integration of body, mind and spirit. The ancient form of Yoga has not been aimed at management of disorders, nevertheless certain aspects of health were covered in the foundation texts of Yoga (Svetasvataropanisad/2/12; Bhagavad-Gita/6/17, 23; Yoga Sutra/ 1/31-32 and 2/2). Later on during the, period of later Upanishads and Yoga- Samhitas, it was duly emphasised, that the practice of yogic postures and Yogic breathing are able to alleviate physical, mental and ethical disorders (Yoga Chudamani Upn./109; Hatha Pr./ 1/19 and 2/16-18; Yoga-Vashistha/6/1/ 81/ 12-42). In modem time, through the consistent medical researches, it has been properly established that Yogic practices maintains good positive health at the level of body and mind as well. Selected regimen of yogic practices in routine life can certainly lead to a happy and healthy life.

Because of being psychosomatic in nature, Yoga practices bring about a balance in the functioning of vital system, endocrine secretions and the activities of central as well as peripheral sympathetic nervous system. Since emotional excitations increase the sympathetic activity leading to the hyper metabolic state and it escorts somewhat disturbance in the orderliness of thought process by the way of modifying the thinking process negatively. Whereas the main purpose of Yoga practices is to lower down the possibilities of emotional excitations by the successful regulation of the hypothalamo-pituitary-aderno-cortico-neuro-axis and *vis. a vis.* instigating a hypo-metabolic state in human system. Emotionality and Yoga are the two ends at the continuum of affectivity. Calming down process of emotional excitation through Yoga practices not only checks these negative modifications in ones thinking process but also promotes conservation of psychic energy for the creative purposes and further psychic upliftment. Consequently, the practitioner gets energy and insight for attaining the solutions of his/her problems that further escorts placidity of mind (*Bhagavad-Gita*/2/64-65).

Since basic nature of all the Yogic practices is psycho-physiological, Yoga-practices have possibility of being helpful in the treatment' of neurotic illness. Thus Yoga more closely resembles with psychotherapy than a religion or a philosophy (Fritjof C., 1981). Many psychologists, neurophysiologists and psychiatrists are being inspired by the earlier published research reports and the own clinical experience with Yogic practices. Yoga practices were also found to be effective in the management of personality disorders (Singh 1986) mental retardation (Nagendra & Nagarathna, 1984 & Maria ullard 1985), hyperkinetic behviour (Subramanyama & Porkodi, 1981); and neurotic reactions (Meares, 1976; Puryear, 1976; Nagarathna, Horia & Nagendra 1984). Meti (1997) reported electrical activity in brain similar to the mild electroconvulsive seizure effect as a result of practices of Pranayama irrespective of their types. Orem-Johnson (1973) found an increased ability to resolve conflicts and higher score of self-esteem caused by Yoga-practices. Doubtlessly it may be observed that Yoga practices mayably cause relaxogenic effect, marked improvement in mental faculties, positively increased electrical activity in the brain (Meti, 1997) and integration among personality variables (Tripathi & Singh 2003).

Mental Health Management Devices in Yoga-Sutra

Certainly the Yoga-sutra of Patanjali visible does not aim at discussing the processes or techniques of mental health management nevertheless contingently the components of psychotherapeutic process were either directly or in indirect way but quite significantly covered in the Yoga-sutra. The neurotic, psychosomatic and physio-psychic disorder processing along with the symptoms and syndrome, are concisely discussed as Chitta Vikshepa and Antaraya in the very first chapter of Yoga-sutra (I/30-31) and the fundamental causes of mental problems are duly described as the Panch-Kleshas in the very beginning of second chapter (Yoga-Sutra/II/3).

In course of Yoga Sadhana (progressive higher Yoga practice), seekers of Yoga found that after a certain stage the course of Yoga practices are supposed to be a stressful and strenuous process. The stress and strain of higher Yoga practice depends upon the grade or intensity of the observance of ascetic regimen (Brahmacharya & Samyama) during the preceding life-time of the practitioner. The intensity and/or grading of regulated life and ascetic regimentation in the preceding life of the practitioner, used to be the deciding factor for the quality of initial success in the advance yoga practice. In otherwise conditions, it may usually cause certain mental and physical problem for the beginner for a while. In Yoga-sutra Patanjali has described these mental and physical problems and suggested effective measures for the management of these noticeable psycho-physical and mental disorders. These disorders should be treated as transient virtual problems and as a part of the essential purging out process of human psycho-physical system in order to be fit for coping up with the subsequent advance Yogic stages.

In the lack of essential intensity of morale (Achara) or psychic strength (Veerya), one is initially very much supposed to be psychically affected by languor or mental laziness that may further leads to the loss of trust for substantiality of advanced Yoga practices. Due to this reason the practitioner/beginner starts deviating from his/her regular regimen and observances and gradually become careless. All this brings about the tendencies of indolence and clinging to the sensual comforts or short-cuts. Slowly one successively goes in grip of paradoxical vision which finally leads to the strayed life style.

Actually the above mentioned symptoms, *i.e.,* physical problems, languor or mental laziness, carelessness, indolence, clinging to the sensual comforts, paradoxical vision and the strayed life style, taking place during the course of Yoga Sadhana, are also the manifested symptoms during the neurotic reactions as well. The Paradoxical vision and strayed life style later on escort the symptoms of unusual aggression and syndromes of depression (as also is commonly being observed in the present western materialistic world). Due to the depression some persons develop the symptom of tremor of limbs and/or errant kind of inhalation and exhalation which is the indication of the dysfunctioning of internal organs. This evinces the starting of psychosomatic vicious chain of reactions that lastly may end in the organic structural change or chronicity of a particular physical problem.

Pancha Kleshas (The Factors Afflicting the Human Psyche)

Yoga-sutra lists five etiological factors as *Pancha Kleshas,* five afflictions or the factors causing deviation or disorder into the human psyche. These *Pancha Kleshas* are *Avidya* (fundamental nescience or ignorance), *Asmita* (egoism or I-ness), *Raga* (affection or love), *Dwesha* (Aversion or hate) and *Abhinivesha* (will to live leading to the fear of death). Due to these *Pancha Kleshas,* the human psyche forms positive and negative kinds of impressions which are strongly sticked to the human psyche. The first and foremost primal affliction of human psyche is *Avidya* or ignorance. Because of certain functional limitations of human sensory system (Dey, 1981), the Avidya or ignorance is the usual destiny of human life. Thus until and unless we are living with the sensory system inherited by us, we are bound to be affected by the ignorance. Despite all efforts and measures, adopted to get rid of ignorance caused by the sensory system, particularly in case of the other category of ignorance, concerned with the lack of knowledge, there may be further possibility of ignorance about the intensity and amount of the ignorance related with the knowledge, still remains as uncovered. All this ignorance happens to cause a psychic blasphemy that further leads to the physical and mental ailments (Ch. Sam./Shareer/1/101-102). That's why the Indian traditional studies, in comparison to the other parts and cultures of world has been found to be sensitive and serious regarding all kinds of ignorance.

Asmita or I-ness is the product of *Avidya.* Due to the *Avidya* one feels himself as an individual entity somewhat apart from the whole world. All the psychological complexities of human life are the product of the *Asmita or* egoism. I-ness or egoism has been found to be main hindrance in the pursuit of spiritual height and emerges as the root cause of many psychosocial and psychological problems. In the area of psychology especially the school of psychoanalysis and among its forerunners particularly Alfred Adler, Carl Rogers and Eric Brown have stressed on the significance of ego or I-ness in the formation of individual personality, though Adler has emphasised on the creative role of psychological self or I-ness.

In the classical Indian psychology *Raga* and *Dwesha* are assumed as the ingredients of *'Kama'* that is sensual desires, lust or sexuality. Freud has given too much emphasis on the role of sexuality in the formation of human personality. So far as the *Raga* (affection or love), *Dwesha* (aversion or hate) are concerned, they are the foundation of almost whole western psychoanalytical thinking. Even in the Indian psychology, especially in Bhagavad-Gita, though in somewhat different terms, a great stress has been given on the role of *Raga* and *Dwesha* in camsing the negative modifications or complexities in the human psyche (*Bhag. Gita* /2/62-53; 3/37-40). The *'Abhinivesh'* has been signified as 'will to live or survive' as the basic instinct of human life, has got due recognition by the Karl-Jung, one of the great exponents of the school of psychoanalysis.

Thus the etiological factors and disorder processing at the psychic, psychosomatic and physio-psychic level, has been obliquely but concisely discussed by Patanjali as *Chitta Vikshepa* and *Antaraya* in the Yoga-sutra. Patanjali suggested effective techniques for the management of above said psychosomatic and physio-psychic problems in terms of *Chitta-Parikarma* and *Chitta-Prasadana (Yoga-sutra/I/32-39).*

The Role of Chitta-Parikarma and Chitta-Prasadana in the Psychic Management

There is a difference between the classical Indian approach and western approach of medicine. The western approach of medicine has been analytical and directly focuses on finding out and management of the instant cause of the disease whereas the classical Indian approach of medicine has been comprehensive and considerate in finding out the route cause of the disease and strengthening of the respective tissue systems. The concept and techniques of *Chitta-Parikarma* (Yoga-Sutra/I/33-39) nicely gives the clues of psychotherapeutic process and devices of psychic management, adopted classically in India where the main emphasis has been on the strengthening of morale and mental stuff. The techniques adopted for the psychic management, described as *Chitta-Parikarma* are as follows:

(i) One-pointed concentration: The first device described as *Chitta-Parikarma* is the practice of one-pointed concentration through which the mental functions or elements are brought under effective control. Though it appears to be very much resembling with the techniques of hypnotism, classically are being used for the psychic management, in reality it is the practice of determination. However among the psychologists it has been treated as a very primary gross device of psychic management—*Tatpratisedhrtham Ekatattvabhyasah* (Yoga Sutra/I/32).

(ii) Chitta Prasadana Methods: For the psychic management, further Patanjali described four gears of *Chitta Prasadana* (Yoga Sutra/I/33). They are *Maitri* (amicability or friendliness), *Karuna* (compassion or sympathy), *Mudita* and *Upeksha.* The concept of Chitta-Prasadana, as narrated by Patanjali in Yoga-sutra, is a sensitive device which is appears as a common element of approximately all the psychotherapeutic approaches nevertheless it very much resembles with the approach of the earlier psychoanalytical psychotherapy, propounded by the Freud and his successors— *Maitrikarunamuditopekshanam Sukhduhkhpunyapunyavisayanam Bhavanataschit-taprasadanam* (*Yoga Sutra*/I/32) .

Maitri or friendliness is not only the foundation of interpersonal relations but also an important component of personality integration. From psychotherapeutic point of view the *Maitri* may be taken as the initial rapport establishment process takes place during the initial sessions. The *Maitri* is the base of all psychotherapeutic processes which also includes gaining of trust, confidence and intimacy of the affected person. *Maitri,* in psychotherapeutic process is followed by the *Karuna.*

Karuna is the feeling of compassion; it is a wider feeling and takes in the feelings of empathy, sympathy, kindness, understanding, benevolence and so on. Initially after establishing a rapport or amicability with the client or disturbed person; when the process of interaction is on its due line, the succeeding sessions of psychotherapy should be full of *Karuna.* In the process of psychotherapy the *Karuna* or Sympathy plays significant role in the maintenance of mental health. A prolong absence of sympathy may bring about abnormal psychic tendencies even in a normal person whereas under the influence of proper sympathetic behaviour towards one's unusual laughing, crying, prancing, gabbling, and babbiing, by showing a sympathetic overlooking attitude, even a psychotic may gradually attains normalcy in a course of time. Attempts should be made to comprehend the problems of the suffering person by placing himself on the situation of the sufferer. At least there is a need of listening to the verbatim of the person and feelings with adequate involvement.

Mudita means expression of gladness or cheerfulness at the time of meeting with the client. *Mudita* conveys the sense of psychosocial acceptability of the client. During the psychotherapeutic sessions the client should always be welcomed gladly, especially when the psychotherapeutic process is on proper line. The intensity of the *Mudita* should be maintained to such an extent that it also ought to be transmitted up to the client to keep him relaxed and well during the psychotherapeutic sessions.

Upeksha actually connotes to the feeling of indifference, apathy or unconcern, however it usually takes in the reactions of aversion, overlooking and avoidance. Thus *Upeksha* may be categorised-into two general categories, *i.e.*, positive *Upeksha* and negative *Upeksha.* Positive *Upeksha* may be further classified into two major subcategories: (1) Renunciation, which is a higher verity of *Upeksha* or indifference, and (2) Sympathy that has application value while treating the mental disorders. The approach of sympathetic *Upeksha* towards the unorganised verbatim and neurotic reactions of the patient should be adopted during the psychotherapeutic process. Moreover, during the psychotherapeutic sessions, gradually an intimacy and affectionate relationship is established between the client and the psychotherapist, so lastly in order to terminate the psychotherapeutic process successfully, *Upeksha* in the sense of attitude of unconcern is also needed. Thus the psychotherapeutic process beginning with the *Maitri* in the initial sessions is followed by *Karuna,* and *Mudita* all through the succeeding psychotherapeutic sessions and finally ends with the *Upeksha* to terminate the psychotherapeutic process successfully.

(iii) Yogic Inhalation and Retention: Western approaches of psychotherapy may be effectively supplemented by the Yogic breathing techniques. By the deep or forceful exhalation and retaining the breath with an attentive and regulated way, followed by a number of deep and calm breaths, the fluctuations of mind can be successfully controlled in a easy manner for a considerable time — *Prachchhardana Vidharanabhyam va Pranasya* (Yoga Sutra/I/34).

A very notable relationship has been observed between respiration and emotional state. It is usually observed that when the breathing pattern is agitated ones psyche is also in the restless condition and vice versa. Due to this very relationship, the hyperventilation caused by the anxiety states, enhances metabolic changes and somewhat faster decay of the tender cells and tissues, which may be harmful to organismic system in the long run. On the other hand slow breathing causes mental relaxation by bringing about the alpha brain waves. But we have no hold on the controlling of the switch-on and switch-off process of said the relationship between respiration and emotion. So the practice of voluntary control on breathing or Pranayama can cause the ability of changing the state of mind through the variation in respiration as showed in the presentation as following:

Psychological Factors *Vs Respiration*

Fast/irregular respiration	anxious mental state
Moderate and consistent respiration	Normal mental state

Management of Psychological Factors through Pranayama

Slow and rhythmic deep abdominal respiration/Yogic breathing Composure of mind

The repetitions of deep or forceful exhalation and retention of breath, is positively bound to be followed by certain deep and calm breaths and gradually it brings about the capacity of voluntary control over the switch-on and switch-off process of bond between respiration and emotion and may cause the ability of changing the state of mind.

(iv) **Object Centred Activity:** Object centred activity associated with any sanctified or magnificent entity has also been prescribed for the effective control over the mental functions. It may also lead to the placidity of mind. It represents the higher kind of suggestive devices. The technique of Yoga-Nidra or Preksha Dhyana and different other popular methods of meditation may be took in this category of *Chitta Parikarma.* Virtually it might be compared with the technique of hypnotism— *Vishyavati Cha Pravittirutpanna manasah sthiiti nibandhini* (*Yoga Sutra*/I/35).

(v) Company of Sanctified Persons or Contemplation on Sanctified Objects: Moreover through the contemplation on a luminous state within which is free from sorrow and emotionality or company of the one, who is free from worldly attachments and/or by the supernormal realization, mind can be stabilised or calmed down —*Vishoka Va Jyotismati; VeetaragavisayamVa Chittam* (*Yoga Sutra*/ I/36- 37).

(vi) Analysis or the awareness of Sleep and Dream State: Through the analysis or attaining the awareness or insight associated with one's dream state and dreamless sleep situation, the mental problems may be managed down. It is also adopted as one of the important device in the psycho-analytical approach of psychotherapy as well. The dreamless sleep state may be compared with the states of transcendence in certain respect that many a time it used to be the source of insight for solution of certain crucial problems. The dream state is psychologically supposed to be a cathartic measure and a safer way of coming out of the unconscious mind. Normally we are devoid of having any linkage and effective control over the dream and dreamless sleep states. Once by efforts or practice if some linkage lines are developed with these states, we get some control over the psychic and neurotic processes— *Swapna-Nidra- Jnanavalambanam Va* (*Yoga Sutra*/I/38).

(vii)Meditation as per Personal Likings: Desired In addition, the meditation on the subject or the object as the liking of the person has also been prescribed as technique of psychic management— *Yathabhimat Dhyanat Va* (*Yoga Sutra*/I/39).

Out of the above described devices of *Chitta-Parikarma,* the IInd, Vth, VIIth are already adopted in the psycho-analytical approach of psychotherapy and also by the other schools of psychological management whereas the 1st, IIIrd, IVth and VIth are supposed to be the Yogic devices, which have a great potential of effectively complementing the classically established techniques of psychotherapy.

Despite the fact that it seems that the Yoga system of Patanjali does not aims at treatment of mental disorders, however, by incorporating or combining all the above said techniques, prescribed as *Chitta- Parikarma* devices an efficient methodology of psychic management can be structured for the welfare of humanity.

The Role of Astánga Yoga in the Management of Psychological Problems

The second chapter of Yoga Sutra comprehensively covered the methodology of psychic management *(Ashuddhikshaye/Yoga-Sutra/II28).* The *Astanga Yoga* (Eight-limbic approach of Yoga) system of *Patanjali* divides its eight limbs of Yoga into two categories or steps of Yoga, *i.e., Bahiranga Yoga* (exterior Yoga) and *Antaranga Yoga* (interior Yoga). *Bahiranga Yoga* (exterior Yoga) takes in the substantial techniques of psychic control.

Psychological Problems and Bahiranga Yoga

The psychological attitude or observance part of Astanga Yoga, *i.e.,* Yama and Niyama can help in resolving the conscious emotional conflicts. Through *Yama* and *Niyama* the interaction between individual and environment as well as the components of self (Yogic approach) may be modified. The observance of Yama and Niyama are also recommended as the prerequisites for Asana and Pranayama by the Patanjali. The practice of Asana and Pranayama may be utilised for the management of subconscious emotional conflicts, by the regular and sincere practice of *Asana* and *Pranayama,* the physiological and psychosomatic components are profoundly managed; it has been proved by a number of empirical researches. Asana and Pranayama produce harmonious effect in the state of emotional agitation. However to deal with the unconscious complexes and conflicts the regular, consistent and sincere practice of the practices of Antaranga Yoga or Samyama may play effective role. It is clear in the presentation as below:

Management of Emotional Conflicts through the Astanga Yoga:

Conscious conflicts by Varna and Niyarna

Subconscious conflicts by Asana and Pranayarna

Unconscious Conflicts by Pratyahara, Dharana and Dhyana

(1) **Psycho-spiritual Analysis of Yama and Niyama:** In modem psychology the behaviour of an individual is the psychical manifestation of the individual's personality towards physical and social conditions of his environment. In classical Indian psychology too, individual behaviour has been characterised as the interaction between one's 'self' and 'non-self' in terms of *'Atma-Anatma Antahkriya'*. Therefore, in order to ordain a harmonization between the 'self' and the 'nonself', the first and foremost preference should be given to the aspects of interaction. The physical, mental and spiritual aspects of the personality, including one's body, mind, intellect, ego and soul, are assumed as the component of one's 'self' (Katha Upan/1/3/3-4) whereas the different aspects of environment are treated as one's 'non-self'. The interaction between the environment and the individual personality is dependent on as well as influenced by the environment and personality of the individual simultaneously. Both the factors are also influenced by the 'interaction' as well. Thus, the regulation of 'interaction' and the refinement of the 'self' may be accomplished as a bipolar process. The 'self or the personality of an individual, because of being an internal unmenifest element, cannot be influenced directly, whereas

the extension and sovereignty of 'non-self in itself, is beyond the limits of control. Notwithstanding that the regulation process of the individual 'Self may be prolonged and complex, however, in comparison to 'non-self, it would be relatively easier and within the bounds of possibility. Individual behaviour or 'interaction' is a noticeable phenomenon and can be regulated by certain direct or indirect means and in the long run it may verily influence the 'self' and the 'non-self' both. That's why the *Astanga Yoga* system of Patanjali and the modem psychology as well has focused their attention on the modification of individual behaviour further followed by the refinement techniques of personality, in their respective systems.

Maharishi Patanjali, quite long back, had proposed *Yama* and *Niyama* for the modification of the Interaction aspects and the components of self by positioning them at the first place in his Astanga Yoga system. In order to establish a harmony with the environment or the non-self, the thoughts, speech and action of the aspirant are modulated through the *'Yama'* (self restraints) and various components of personality are amended through the observances of *'Niyama'* (self modification). This ultimately results into the all-round effectiveness of personality to establish a sublime adjustment with one's environment and to be fit for attaining the paramount states of Yoga (Tripathi & Singh, 1984).

(2) **Psychosomatic Effect of Asana and Pranayama:** Yogasana influences sympathetic and parasympathetic tone of the autonomic nervous system. It also brings about positive effect on higher nervous system by the voluntary control over somatic and psychic areas of the brain. Stability of the body achieved by the practice of Asana may lead to emotional stability and psychological well-being. Asana release tension which are subconscious in nature. It makes the body function harmonious and restores the natural

reciprocity function. Practice of Asana contributes the alignment of body by the changing postural reflex that naturally produces psychological changes. This psycho-physiological modeling is helpful to human life.

The ultimate object of Pranayama is to regulate the movement of bio-energy through the breathing process. In the *Kumbhaka* (retention of breath) component of Pranayama, breathing process is suspended temporarily. *Anuloma-Viloma* (alternate breathing) pattern in Pranayama keep balance between cooled and hot-mindedness. These practices control the autonomic nervous system and establish balance in the bio-energy system. It is discussed in the earlier paragraphs that there is a relation between respiration and emotion.

(3) **The Role of Antaranga—Yoga for Management of Psychological Problems:** Pratyahara helps to control the senses and manage the stresses of personal life. Patanjali in Yoga-sutra established that regular practice of Pratyahara helps in attaining a great control over the senses (Yoga-Sutra/II/54-55). Control over the senses not only incorporates the control over the external senses but also the mastery over the internal senses including proprioceptive, introspective and kinesthetic senses, moreover the sensory areas of ones brain as well. All this may finally result into the better control over the functioning of organismic system, at last leading to the control over the self. One can attain a complete isolation from interior and exterior stimuli through the practice of *Pratyahara* by controlling and marshaling the activities of senses at both internal and external levels which manages the stresses of personal life and brings composure. When one finds time to isolate himself for a constant and deep reflection, he finds that he has an exaggerated idea of his problems.

Here yoga provide a humane, individualised therapy to overcome the fears, anxieties and tension of day today living'. During the practice of Pratyahara when one sits calmly and tries to dissociate his senses from their respective external objects, it starts curbing the psychic energy, which was going to be waste through the sensory interactions with the material world as well as through the reactive attitudes. During Pratyahara initially as well as essentially one should adopt a secluded state to isolate him to conserve and/or to revive the psychic energy. As the external sensory involvement and the reactive tendencies, the by-product there of, calm down, it gradually promotes the realization of the actual locus of control, lying inside the brain, which further may cause the relaxation of autonomic sympathetic activities. Gradually by consistent practice, one is able to set up a better communication with the regulatory centres of autonomic sympathetic activities in the Brain. Consequently through a de-feedback process ones affective states may settle down. For the practice of Pratyahara in order to de-condition the mind out of its usual sensory affaires, closing the eyes, when one either tries to change the track of thinking and feeling or categorise the mental reflections and regulate the mental activity goes ahead step by step in a properly distinct direction, this effort, by and large also causes the calming down of mind. Thus a proper composed state and favourable environment for resolving the conflicts and complexes is created and the ways of the management of problem are being find out.

The psychotherapeutic efficacy of meditation has also been reported (Shafii, 1973; Kartikeya, 1973; Daniel, 1975; Ross, 1976; Miskiman, 1976). Transcendental meditation has been found to bring about reduction in muscle tone, blood lactate level caused by stress, slow down respiration, decrease in metabolism, and changes on electroencephalogram (Wallace 1970). Meditation stabilises the autonomic nervous system and reduces anxiety and hypertension. Meditation is being recommended by the medical doctors for the management of anxiety, insomnia and drug addiction. Shafii (1973) believes that clam introspection during meditation can be used as a technique of dynamic psychotherapy. Meditation has been found to plays promotive role in emotional stability and it increases ability to resolve conflicts.

REFERENCES

Bullard, M. (1985). Yoga with mentally handicapped and other disabled people. *The Yoga Review*, 1 and 2.

Daniels, L.K (1975). The treatment of Psychiatric disorders and T.M. *America. J. of Cl. Hypn.*, *17*, 267-270.

Dey, P.K. (1981). Human Brain and Consciousness. *The Yoga Review*, *1*(4), 153-164.

Fritjof Capra, (1981). *The Turning Point' Flamingo*, An Imprint of Harper Collins Publisher, London.

Kartikerya, K. (1973). A comparative study of the efficiency of T.M. relaxation techniques and Diazepam in patients with anxiety neurosis (Thesis submitted, NIMHANS, Bangalore, India).

Meares, A. (1976). The relief of anxiety through relaxing meditation. *Aust. Fam. Physician*, 5 (7), 906-910.

Miskiman, D.E. (1976). Long-term effect of the T.M. programmes in the treatment of insomnia. *Sc. Res. T.M. coll.* Papers, VoU, 229.

Meti, B.L. (1997). *A Glimpse on the Neurophysiological Aspects of Pranayama and Meditation.* Conference Handbook of *N.* International Conference on Frontier in Yoga Research and Applications, Bangalore, 22.

Nagarathna, R., Horia, C. and Nagendra, H.R. (1984). *Preliminary Investigation of Yoga Therapy for Anxiety Neurosis.* Vivekananda Kendra YOCTAS (1984) Report no. VK YOCTAS/ BNG/011/84.

Nagendra, H.R. and Nagarathna, R. (1984). *Initial Studies for Yoga Therapy for the Mentally Retarded.* Vivekananda Kendra YOCTAS (1984) Report no. VK YOCTAS/BNG/014/84.

Nespor, K. (1984). The combination of psychiatric treatment and yoga. Paper presented in a conference "Yoga and Rehabilitation" Bardejovke, Kupele (CSSR) Oct. AA-II, 1984.

Orme-Johnson, D.E. (1973). Autonomic stability and transcendental mediation. *Psychomomatic Medicine*, *35*, 347-349.

Puryear, H.B. (1976). Anxiety reduction association with mediation. *Home Study perc. Mot. Skills, 43*, 527-31.

Ross, J. (1976). The effect of the T.M. programme on anxiety, Neuroticism and Psychotism. *Sc. Res. T.M. Coli. Pap,* (1976) J. P. 594-96.

Shaffi, M. (1975). Adaptive and therapeutic aspects of meditation. *International Journal of Psychoanalytic Psychotherapy*, 2, 364-382.

Subramanyam, S. and Pokodi, K. (1981). Yoga-Its probable role in maintaining and restraining normal health. *The Yoga Review*, I(3).

Singh, R.H. (1986). Trends of Medical Research on Yoga. *Annals. of NAIM*, I, 1 59-77.

Tripathi, KM. and Singh, R.H. (1984). Astangic Yoga-Its Symmetrical Wholeness and Mutual Interrelations with Special Reference to Yama, Niyama and Samadhi. *The Yoga Review*, l and 2, Spring and Summer, 27-40.

Tripathi, K.M. and Singh, R.H. (2003). Role of Yoga in the Management of Anxiety and Depression. *The Yoga Review*, IX. 1 and 2, 23-38.

Tripathi, K.M. (1987). *A study of personality and behaviour pattern profile in psychosomatic disorders and the role of certain therapeutic interventions*, Unpublished Ph.D. dissertation, Banaras Hindu University, 1987.

Vallace, R.R. (1970). *Physiological Effects of Transcendental Meditation-A Proposed Fourth Major State of Consciousness*' Ph.D. Thesis, Deptt. of Physiology, University of California, USA, Published in Vol. I, Scientific Research on T.M. Programme, collected papers.

References from classical Indian Texts:

Bhagavadgeeta 2/62-53; 2/64-65; 3/37-40; 6/17 and 23.; Charaka Sarnhital Shareer Sthana /1/101-102).

Hatha-Pradipikal1/19 and 2/16-18; Katha-Upanisad/1/3/3-4; Shvetashvataropanisad/2/12;

Yoga- Chudamani Upnisad/l09; Yoga- Sutra/I /30-31; 32-39; II /2-3; 28-55 and III! 1-4;

Yoga- Vasisthal 6/1/81/12-42.

●●●

16

Yogic Practice as a Moderator of Mental Health

R.K. Mishra, O.P. Sharma and P. Sharma

The word Yoga has many connotations, etymologically it means integration of the various systems of body. The term integration and samatva of the Bhagawat Gita conveys the same meaning. Other terms like homeostasis, systemic integration or a balance, harmony, etc. more or less suggest the same connotation. The aim of yoga itself is integration of personality in all aspects.

Modern techniques generally lay stress on muscles and body development but neglect concentration and confidence part of the individual. By combining yoga these faults could be corrected. Even sports people who require heavy muscular activities do not know the techniques of relaxation which are described in yoga. Yoga stretching is relaxation that have additional advantage for significant gain in sports performance. Contribution of yoga to sports has been depicted with a view to emphasise the importance of Asanas for better promotion of different aspects of sports. Yoga, therefore, not only contributes to other sports but also is a sport by itself and help in harmonious development of physical and psychological aspect of personality.

The pressing problems facing human society today are over population and malnutrition and also violence amounting to organized terrorism when yoga sculpture is the dire-necessity for bringing psychological equilibriums among to achieve harmony in human behaviour and positive health a state of complete physical, mental and social well-being of the community. Physiology, which is natural science has highlighted its relevance to the modern era of stress and strain giving rise to several disorders. Thus, totally of man being increasingly recognized as yoga has always believed in the integrated body mind. The Natural laws in respect of diet-physical activity, meditation, and yogic postures in daily life are more relevant today then ever before for development of mental health. With the advent in medical science most of the people carry a wrong notion that for every disease in the human body there is a fixed and forgetting that nature has given enough defence mechanisms to overcome the physical disorders. Yoga in its totality is natural science as well as philosophy and way of living and not a religious dogma as envisaged by laymen.

The physical culture in yogic practice is neither traditional exercises and nor does it require the use of extra calories for maintaining body. Moreover, it does not put any stress on muscle development Asanas, Pranayams which are key practices in yogis. Emphasize relaxation of body and mind and bring the physiological balance by involving emotions and autonomic nervous system and endocrine glands. Thus, this system of the body is different in bringing out homedtedid so essential for proper function of the body. Asanas work on tone and equilibrium at physical and emotional level and one experience stably, comfort ease and promotion of health and fitness.

The physiological basis in yoga philosophy gives more emphasis on sensory tonic activities as different from motor cortex activities applied in conventional exercise for promoting health. Relaxative asanas are claimed to give rise to chittavishranti, tranquility and peace apart from developing stability, steadiness and lightness of body. This can be experienced in Shavasana by performing breathing activities. Paranayams through physiological activities have demonstrated beneficiary effect on cardio pulmonary efficiency because oxygen consumption and carbon and dioxide output increases. Along with kapalbharti these practices increase breath holding time. The cardiac output increases without increasing in heart beat which is attributed to the efficiency of cardiovascular system. Along with hematological picture gets improved and blood sugar levels decreases. Meditation is used for ordering the mental disorder. The techniques are used to remove the emotional disturbances like anger, frustration, Anxiety, tension which are the root cause of the present day ailments *i.e.,* insomnia, headaches, asthma, hyperacidity, colitis, hypertension, cardiac disorders and even drug abuse. It is worthwhile to maintain that yoga is scientifically employed as a medicine for preventive and recuperative and curative aspects of diseases.

Yogic practice by affecting and integrating somatic and autonomous nervous system proved a shift in parasympathetic activity and as a result of regular training fitness of individual with improvement in the function of body and mind is affected. A significant reduction in psycho-physiological disequilibria has been noticed and overall improved performance of the mental work and programmed memory has been observed. It has resulted in cardio-pulmonary improvement, renal efficiency and endocrine co-ordination. In blood fibrin lyric activity, lowering of blood cholesterol has been reported. Yogic therapy has also tremendous scope in the present day technological advanced society. It is also helpful to resolve socio-economic, socio-psychological and even socio-political tensions and conflicts for bringing out tranquility in human mankind. Yogic exercises are already showing results in psycho-somatic chronic disorders like bronchial asthema, diabetic hypertension and other disorders. Yoga has already emerged as important and vital discipline of modern community medicine to find a pride place for serving the future mankind.

Higher performance in any sport's activity is governed by several factors of physical fitness. The important ones may be mentioned: speed, strength, stamina, suppleness, stability and neuromuscular co-ordination of body. Although not many scientific researches have been done, the work of Devries (1962), Dhanraj (1974), Giri (1966), Gharote and Ganguly (1979) have shown enough evidence about how yoga could gainfully employed in the promotion of basic fitness factors. Using elaborate Fleischmann battery of basic fitness test, Ganguly and Gharote (1974) have shown how even a short-term yogic training could improve different basic fitness factors.

But basic levels of physical fitness must be maintained even during off-season. This can be attained excellently by indulging in yogic routine. Yogic exercise deals with the vital organs of the body on which health depends. The precursor of physical fitness has in the efficient working of the mental *viz.*, the brain and behaviour is primary aim of the yoga. The various selected asana give different movements to the spine under controlled respiration. Relaxation technique and concentration practice as a whole form an excellent technique to take care of the health of vital organs of the body (Singh and Sinha, *et al.*, 2007).

REFERENCES

Devries, Herbert, A. (1962). Evaluation of static stretching procedures for improvement of flexibility. *Research quarterly*. 33, 222-229.

Dhanraj, V.H. (1974). *The Effect of yoga and 5 Bx fitness plan on selected,* (physiological parameters). Ph.D. Thesis, The University of Alberta, Edmonton.

Ganguly, S.K. and Gharote, M.L. (1974). Cardiovascular efficiency before and after yogic training. *Yoga Mimansa*, 17/1, 89-97

Gharote, M.L. and Ganguly, S.K. (1979). Effect of a nine week yogic training programme on some aspects of physical fitness of physically conditioned young males. *Ind. Tour. Med. Res.*, 33/10, 258-263.

Giri, C. (1966). Yoga and physical fitness with special reference to athletics. *IATHPER Quarterly Journal*, Patiala, 2-6.

Singh, A. (2007): Effect of yoga on positive mental health. In *Health Psychology*. New Delhi: Commonwealth Publishers. 11-14,

Sinha, S.N. *et al.* (2007). Integral Yoga - Its Contribution to positive Health: Wellness. In *Health Psychology*, Commonwealth Publishers. 61-63

●●●

17

Research in Yoga as a Holistic Model of Health

Latha

The view presented here is in the capacity of a yoga practitioner and researcher with more than a decade of experience in the area of yoga therapy on one-to-one basis, which is the unique strength of the *Krishnamacharya* tradition of yoga, the sheet anchor of *Krishnamacharya Yoga Mandiram Chennai* a place where I teach yoga.

Today, a lot of research studies focus on mind-body medicine. Science acknowledges the interactive inter-relationship between mind and body. Though modern research in yoga has accepted the power of yoga as influencing both the body as well as the mind, very minimal studies have focused on evaluating the psychological parameters while physiological parameters are evaluated much in detail (Arpita, 1990; Berger, 1992; Miller1995; DeBerry, 1992). Psychological impact on physiological changes is concomitant and inter-related, but a thorough evaluation is yet to be demonstrated. The physiologists have overlooked the psychological components and psychologists or others studying psychological effects have disregarded the physical impact. Research in yoga has thus become piece meal with some groups focusing on body, some others emphasizing on specific personality factors and very few trying to see the impact of yoga on social factors. This specialization has become so reductionistic that people have started believing *asana* is for body, *pranayama* is for prana and *meditation* is for mind, etc. This compartmentalization in research activity has also compartmentalized yoga. The variety of yoga schools and styles that are mushrooming in different parts of the world stand proof to this myopic approach in yoga.

According to *Patanjali*, the focus of yoga is the "Mind". In fact, yoga is defined as a state of mind: "*Yogah citta vrtti nirodhah*" *(YS 1.2)*. Mind and its activities and the enormous possibilities of the mind, which is functioning at different levels is the subject matter of Patanjali's Yoga Sutra. Asana, pranayama and meditation are offered as some of the tools, which in fact, form only a small part of the whole spectrum of yoga tools to reach a state of mind.

The "*Pancha Maya*" model presented in our *Upanishads* by ancient Indian scientists beautifully demonstrates the inter-relationship between different levels of existence. The *Annamaya* (physical body), *Pranamaya* (energy body), *Manomaya* (Mental processes), *Vignanamaya* (special intellect, what we call discriminative power) and *Anandamaya* (emotional level) are closely interconnected and influence each other in such a way that a perfect harmony between these levels reflects good health and well being of an individual.

This means, no tool in yoga can be understood in isolation, as affecting one particular level or the other. If yoga is understood or evaluated that way, it would tantamount to undermining the holistic and comprehensive nature of this ancient system.

Current Research Methods in Yoga

Control *vs.* Experimental group designs or Randomized Control trials or Double blind studies ignore the core aspects of the process of an intervention but emphasizes on outcomes only. With more and more emphasis on quantification of effect or outcome, which are statistically significant, the researchers are at loss to understand the processes, which really influence the outcomes. The mechanism-oriented studies also emphasis on single outcome and refuse to acknowledge individual uniqueness. Yoga being a process-oriented training, outcomes may vary. Thus, the methodology that suits clinical or other psychological investigations are not appropriate for yoga (Latha, 2003). To emphasise this point further, I would like to present some of the empirical evidences obtained through Qualitative methodology.

The focus of scientific research in yoga should ideally incorporate study of psychological influences of practices without which it would remain skewed and superficial. Drawing empirical evidences from the studies conducted, it is evident that the emotional states are more amenable to yoga training and we see quicker responses in terms of reduced Anxiety, anger and enhanced sense of well-being (Shrimaty, 2002; Priyadharshini, 2001; Malathi, Shah & Patil 2000; Wood, 1993), but the deeper changes at cognitive levels, (thinking processes) is not uniform in all those receiving yoga training. In my studies I have observed those who responded better at the physical level, they were not able to show any change at the deeper level of experiences like optimism or sense of purpose and satisfaction with life (Latha, 2003). These psychological attitudes refer to spiritual orientation and almost border on to the core spiritual dimension of a person (Empirical evidence), which takes much deeper analysis scientifically. Individual difference in response to treatment is another gray area that is hardly being addressed. The qualitative analysis of the interviews conducted on practitioners of yoga revealed the health enhancing effects of daily practice on alertness, stamina, energy, freedom from cough, cold, enthusiasm *etc.*

An evaluation of experience of a sample of 22 yoga practitioners who underwent one-month intensive meditative practices reported various experiences during the practice. Interviews analyzed, using CDC TEXT software, themes such as relaxation, calmness, discomfort and distractions during the processes of meditation. Almost all the participants expressed their belief that a stepwise progression into meditation by preparing the body and mind was most effective. Their experience also indicated that one cannot enter into meditation straight away. It takes time to reduce the internal noise and distractions. In these meditative practices many strategies were applied to enhance the focus, sustain the focus and also stay with it. These sessions were held daily for 20 days. The participants were all from outside India and had an exposure to other techniques of yoga but not meditation. This study conducted in 2004, throws insight into individual differences in responses to a process of training and also their facilitation for certain types of training.

Dwelling upon "uniqueness" of the individual is impossible without incurring the wrath of many of our "scientific colleagues" who are 'oriented' towards abstracting and measuring the outcomes in terms of Quantity. Yoga is an experience, where the outcomes do not solely depend on the techniques, postures, but also on the relationship between different component within and outside the person. The quality and quantity of relationship one has between the body, breath, mind, teacher, environment and all other factors, has an impact not only on mind and body but also on the larger circle in which person exists.

A survey on a sample of practitioners (N = 216) of Yoga was conducted and their experiences with Yoga practice were recorded for a set of open-ended questions. The content analysis of the responses (Qualitative software) generated rich information on the subjective experiences of yoga practice such as feeling of calmness, energy, clarity, sense of peace, expansiveness, specific physical benefits etc. These descriptions are honest experiences, but are not quantifiable through any available questionnaires. Such types of responses were absent in the reports given by short-term yoga practitioners. Lastly, the psychological impact of yoga is maximally facilitated by not only the training aspect, but also the nature and personality of the practitioner, qualities of the teacher (the vital catalyst in healing process) and intelligent application of the tools.

Tools for Quantification of Yoga Experience

The issue of quantification is again a problem. Today, science has advanced so much that we are even talking in terms of quantifying "*Prana*"! But the sensitivity of measurement tools is another major issue. Tools used are not all encompassing, not sensitive enough to observe or record several factors.

Most tools are based on western psychometric principles. The reliability coefficient or its validity is in terms of 50% to 80%. Though they are good by themselves and useful to a certain extent, they are considered as important indicators of well-being, or health. There are many experiences related to the practice of yoga, which are not purely biomedical or psychological, but may address the deeper experience which cannot be measured or quantified through questionnaires or instruments. For example, how can we measure faith, *asthiratvam*, and *citta viskepam*, *santo'sam*...? These are the concepts relevant and leverages that transform the mind and cannot be measured. This is what I experienced when I was conducting a Yoga training and evaluating the psychological parameters using standardized questionnaires. There was a complete dichotomy between the objective measures and the subjective experience of the participants as elicited through interviews. The responses were so non-normative; it was not possible to quantify objectively the effect of yoga. But its impact in daily life of practitioners lives demonstrated the wide range of possibilities beyond body, mind in terms of quality of inter-personal relation.

Some of the assessment tools are oriented for clinical groups with a high loading on pathology (depression, anger, Anxiety or stress factors). The tendency of people to project themselves in a better frame can never be removed in the assessment or a tendency to be oversensitive or reactive is also there.

Tools need to be developed that are sensitive enough to measure the impact of yoga training. These need to be developed based on the experience of yoga practitioners, *e.g.*, awareness levels, confidence, motivation, expectancies, attitude towards life/self/teacher and all the subtle changes that may occur in the state of mind when one is practicing and after practice. I believe, quality measurements based on diary monitoring, sharing, and dialogues are best suited to evaluate outcome of yoga training. Sometimes, the questionnaires are too generic like feeling calm, contented, *etc.*, which are highly loaded on bias factor. Preferably using open-ended questions, specific to the individual can provide valuable information.

The slant towards qualitative research is inevitable because individual responses are as many as the variables involved. Sometimes responses may remain latent/dormant, some responses that may be expected may never surface, while certain outcomes reveal themselves in the most unexpected manner. Factors like faith, motivation, relationship with the teacher, *etc.*, continue to gain prominence. Mapping all this complexity and weaving them into the matrix of human experience continues to throw up new challenges in research.

This is what Dr. Robin Monro comments on "methodology of Science and Yoga,

> "... While modern scientists have looked "outward" for measurable observations for the basis of their knowledge, yogis have looked "inward" to their own bodies and minds. There is nothing unscientific about it. There is no reason from a scientific point of view why such internal information should not be utilized as an observational basis for scientific knowledge."

With more advancement in science, rigorous attempts are made to 'fit' yoga into a pure scientific model, and also substantiate such a stance using complex scientific procedures and measurements. But the bottom line is that ultimately human beings have to benefit. Scientists attempting research on yoga have forgotten, or perhaps wished away this basic purpose. Scientific procedures can help in creating standardized therapeutic modules that can perhaps replace "pills". But if individual differences are not taken into account, especially in an intervention where a person's physical, emotional, spiritual resources are harnessed to facilitate healing, such "yogic pills" may not only be ineffective, they can cause serious harm to the person at all levels. Yoga training is not only to build internal resource, but also utilize and apply the existing resource to enhance the quality of life.

Factors that Mediate Healing/change

Research in yoga intensely focuses on outcome variables, with little or no attention paid to other mediating factors that play a crucial role in compliance. Subjective factors such as individual attitudes and expectancies from therapy are more assumed than measured.

Yoga simply does not work if an individual does not assume responsibility and participate in the healing process. Yoga is self-empowering. Without faith and intense, appropriate effort, it simply does not work. It is not like swallowing a pill! Coming to the qualities of practice:

Sa tu deerga kala Nairantarya Satkara Adara Asevito Drdabhumihi *(Y.S.–I Ch)*

Practice/effort must be appropriate, consistent, for a long time, without interruption, with positive attitude and eagerness. These are very much part of a person's inherent personality.

How does one measure these personality traits or the student factor? According to the Health Belief model, belief in efficacy of treatment is one of the strong factors promoting high level of adherence. Faith (positive attitude) is a strong factor that determines compliance in an intervention. We are dealing with human beings here, and this factor varies in intensity.

As *Patanjali* states, *Mrdu—Madhya—Adhimatravatat tato Api Visheshaha...* (Y.S. 1.22)

How do we measure this?/How Yoga works? The teacher factor or the trainer factor. There is a need to distinguish between a yoga teacher/instructor and a yoga therapist. Yoga is essentially establishing a positive connection, which is constructive. The teacher is an important mediator in this process. *Yoga Rahasya (1.30)* talks about the qualities of a yoga teacher:

Jnani – one who knows.

*Maun*i- one who acts based on reflection.

Jitatmavan- one who is disciplined, patient and humble, learned and competent.

Experience of a teacher in terms of personal practice and attitude of care and compassion, intelligent application of tools *"yukti"* in a manner oriented to the needs and capacities of the individual *(Tasya Bhumisu Viniyogah YS 3. 6)* are essential qualities of a yoga therapist. The teacher must be a model of inspiration and Patanjali calls them as *"Nirmana citta."*

Humility to accept if something does not work! How much of importance is given to this aspect in yoga research? Or is it dismissed off as beyond the scope of scientific research? These are the ethical issues for somebody who is involved in authenticating yoga scientifically.

Finally, I would like to quote the statements of my yoga teacher, Shri. T. K. V. Desikachar who has been responsible for improving the quality of life of thousands of people through his wide teachings, he states (1987).

"Yoga is not a technology that can be generalized. It should respect and honor the individual, encourage and facilitate the individual to make use of the resources available to heal himself/herself. Consistent effort on part of the individual and the teacher are also important."

REFERENCES

Arpita (1990). Physiological and Psychological effects of Hata Yoga. *The Journal of International Association of Yoga Therapists* 1.

Berger, D.G., Owen, & B.G. (1992). Mood Alteration with Yoga and Swimming, Aerobic Exercises may not be necessary. *Perceptual and Motor Skills.* 75, 1331 – 1343.

Desikachar .T.K.V (1987). *Reflections On Yoga Sutras of Patanjali,* Krishnamacharya Yoga Mandiram, Chennai, India.

De Berry, S., Davis, S., & Reinhard, K.E. (1989). A Comparison of Meditation, Relaxation and Cognitive/Behavioral Techniques For Reducing Anxiety in A Geriatric Population. *Journal of Geriatric Psychiatry.* 22, 231 –247.

Latha (2003). Indian Approaches In Promotion Of Health UGC Major Project Report submitted to University Grants Commission.

Malathi, D. A., Shah, N., & Patil, N. S. (2000). Effects of Yogic Practices on Subjective Well Being. *Indian Journal of Physiological Pharmacology.* 44, 202 – 206.

Miller, J.J., Fletcher, K., Kabat, Z. (1995). Three Year Follow up and Clinical Implications of Mindfulness Meditations based on Stress reduction Intervention in the treatment of Anxiety Disorder. *General Hospital Psychiatry.* 17, 192 – 200.

Priyadarshini, N.D. (2001) *Yogasnas Training for Anthropometric and Psychological Changes among Adolescents.* Unpublished thesis submitted to University of Madras, Chennai.

Shrimathy. (2002). *Role of Yoga in Pain Management.* M.Sc. Dissertation submitted to University of Madras, unpublished.

Wood, C. (1993). Mood Change and Perceptions of Vitality. A Comparison of the effects of Relations Visualisation and Yoga. *Journal of Royal Society of Medicine, 86*, 254-258.

●●●

Part—III

Meditation Psychotherapy and Psychological Wellbeing

- Meditation: Concepts, Effects and Uses in Therapy
- Vipassana Meditation - A Positive Approach to Psychological Well-being
- Effect of Vipassana Meditation on Quality of Life, Subjective Well-being, and Criminal Propensity
- Occupational Stress Management – Through Meditation

18

Meditation: Concepts, Effects and Uses in Therapy

Alberto Perez-De-Albeniz and Jeremy Holmes

This article reviews 75 scientific selected articles in the field of meditation, including Transcendental Meditation among others. It summarizes definitions of meditation, psychological and physiological changes, and negative side-effects encountered by 62.9% of meditators studied. While the authors did not restrict their study to TM, the side-effects reported were similar to those found in the "German Study" of Transcendental Meditators: relaxation-induced anxiety and panic; paradoxical increases in tension; less motivation in life; boredom; pain; impaired reality testing; confusion and disorientation; feeling 'spaced out'; depression; increased negativity; being more judgmental; feeling addicted to meditation; uncomfortable kinaesthetic sensations; mild dissociation; feelings of guilt; psychosis-like symptoms; grandiosity; elation; destructive behavior; suicidal feelings; defenselessness; fear; anger; apprehension; and despair.

Meditation can be defined in a number of different ways, philosophical or operational. Webster's dictionary defines meditation as an 'act of spiritual contemplation'. It seems that in its wider modern usages, it denotes (Kokoszka, 1990): self-experience, self-realisation and, in some religious traditions, a specific practice to achieve the discovery of the ultimate truth.

From a psychophysiological perspective, meditation is the intentional self-regulation of attention, in the service of self-inquiry, in the here and now (Masion et al., 1995). Most descriptions of meditation expressed in behavioural terms (Craven, 1989), include the following components: (1) relaxation, (2) concentration, (3) altered state of awareness, (4) suspension of logical thought processes, and (5) maintenance of self-observing attitude.

There are many different techniques of meditation, which can be classified according to Shapiro (1982) as: those which focus on the field or background perception and experience, called 'mindfulness meditation; those which focus on a preselected specific object, or 'concentrative' meditation', and those which shift between the field and the object.

In mindfulness meditation, the subject sits comfortably, in silence, centring attention by focusing mental awareness an object or process (either the breathing process, a sound, a mantra koan or riddle evoking questions, a visualisation, or an exercise) and then consciously is encouraged to scan their thoughts in an open focus, shifting freely from one perception to the next (Kutz et al., 1985a, b). No thought, image or sensation is considered an intrusion. The meditator, with a 'no effort' attitude, is asked to remain in the here and now. Using the focus as an 'anchor' (Teasdale et al., 1995) brings the subject constantly back to the present, avoiding cognitive analysis or fantasy regarding the contents of awareness, and increasing tolerance and relaxation of secondary thought processes.

Meditation can also be practised walking or doing some simple exercises, where it aims to break down habitual automatic mental categories, thus regaining the primary nature of perceptions and events, focusing attention on the process while disregarding its purpose or final outcome. If based in a visualisation such as the Chinese Qi Gong meditation (Liu et al., 1990), the subject concentrates on a certain 'energy' (Qi) in his body, starting in his lower abdomen and then, through visualisation, circulating through various parts of the body, until the energy is eventually 'dispersed'. This is combined with repetitive, positive, reinforcing suggestions from the instructor and the subject himself, resulting in a strong belief in the subject that s/he can manipulate this 'energy' at will.

Meditation is claimed to enhance the sense of mastery through the mediator's self-observing cognitive attitude. The mediator realises his or her role as 'writer-director' in charge of inner dramas and discovers the element of choice in the 'cutting and editing' of perceptions of reality. It suspends habitual logical-verbal construing, and so frees the individual of his/her usual defensive constructions, allowing consciousness to move in new directions (Bogart, 1991). It is said to free the mediator from bodily and cognitive tensions.

Meditation is related but distinguishable from daydreaming, hypnosis (Fromm, 1975), praying, cardiovascular and neurovascular feedback, autogenic training and relaxation techniques (Kokoszka, 1994). Meditation differs from these other techniques or practices in its emphasis on maintaining alertness, and its philosophical/cognitive background aims at expanding self-awareness and an increased sense of integration and cohesiveness (Snaith, 1998).

Psychological Effects

Traditionally meditation has been practised within a religious context. Only in modern times have the techniques of meditation been extracted from their spiritual and philosophical context and applied to the promotion of individual well-being. Most literature in scientific journals and research about meditation has been based on this personal health-enhancing aspect (Epstein, 1990; Globus, 1980; Leuschitz & Harlman, 1996; Russell, 1986; Shapiro, 1994; Tyler, 1977; West, 1987). Atwood & Maltin (1991) described how meditation helps the patient to understand that there are no quick solutions. It develops patience: to be aware of the problem before attempting to solve it. It promotes a non-judgmental attitude, it helps the patient to come to terms with 'what is', rather than to fight hopelessly for 'what might be', or 'might have been'. It helps people to be comfortable with ambiguity, ignorance and uncertainty. Meditators learn to recognise and trust their inner nature and wisdom. Meditation fosters the recognition of personal responsibility. The meditator's feelings during and about meditation itself cannot be displaced or disowned.

Different components of the technique of meditation, such as physical posture, attentional focus, style and breathing, have been proposed as explanations for the positive effects of meditation (Colby, 1991; Levenstein, 1996). Kutz et al. (1985a, b) explained meditation as a repetitive dose of corrective emotional experience similar to an interpersonal therapeutic encounter which may have its counterpart in gradual interneuronal modulation. 'It's tempting to speculate that such neural plasticity can be enhanced by causing a functional shift in the state of the CNS. Such a psychobiological shift may be elicited by mental practices such as meditation'. Craven described the following effects: integration of subjective experiences, increased acceptance and tolerance of affect and increased self-awareness. Atwood & Maltin (1991) claim that meditation optimises the process of memory. Kutz et al. (1985a,b) reported an increase in vigor. Shapiro (1992) found that 88% of the subjects of her research subjects (n = 27) reported greater happiness and joy, positive thinking, increased self-confidence, effectiveness (getting things done), and better problem-solving skills. Other reported beneficial effects include enhanced acceptance, compassion and tolerance to self and others (Dua & Swinden, 1992), more relaxation, resilience, and better ability to control feelings (Scheler, 1992).

However, none of these findings were based on properly randomised and controlled trials, and a placebo comparison for meditation is even more problematic than it is for psychotherapy.

Physiological Effects

Meditation is claimed to produce an integrated response with peripheral circulatory and metabolic changes subserving central nervous activity. Jevning et al. (1992) called it an 'awakeful hypometabolic integrated response'.

The physiological effects include: increased cardiac output, slow heart rate (Dillbeck & Orme-Johnson, 1987), muscle relaxation (Narayu et al., 1990), apparent cessation of CO[sub 2] generation by muscle, decreased renal and hepatic blood flow, increased cerebral flow, decreased respiratory frequency (Kesterson & Clinch, 1989), significantly decreased sensitivity to ambient CO[sub 2], less O[sub 2] consumption (Wilson et al., 1987), increased skin galvanic resistance, decreased spontaneous electrodermal response, EEG synchrony with increased intensity of slow alpha in central and frontal regions, and increased theta waves in frontal areas of the brain (Telles & Desraju, 1993), enhancement of brain stem auditory evoked response (Liu et al., 1990), increased alpha and beta coherence (Sim & Tsol, 1992), and shift in hemispheral dominance with greater activation of the centres in the right hemisphere (to which non-verbal, intuitive, spatial, holistic, non-sequential qualities are attributed; Telles et al., 1994).

Metabolical effects include: increased blood pH during meditation but decreased arterial pH afterwards, resulting in a mild metabolic acidosis; decreased plasma lactate (probably due to changes in erythrocyte metabolism); changes of glucose metabolism pattern (Herzog et al., 1990); decreased adrenocortical activity just after 30 minutes of meditation and long-term decreased cortisol secretion (Sudsang et al, 1991); decreased TSH; increased concentration of arginine vasopresine (which is said to play an important part in learning and memory); increased levels of phenylalanine concentration (in 3-5 year meditators); increased 5 hydroxyindole-3 acetic acid urinary metabolite of serotonin after 30 minutes of meditation (Travis & Orme-John, 1989); and increased levels of melatonin (urinary 6 sulphatoxymelatonin) which is produced in the pineal gland (Masion et al., 1995). Through melatonin, there is an increased inhibitory effect of GABA, which has a benzodiazepine-like effect (analgesia, antistress, anti-insomnia; Elias & Wilson 1995; Harte et al., 1995).

Benson et al. (1990), in a descriptive study of three very experienced Tibetan monks, claimed that metabolic rate could be raised up to 61% or lowered to 64% at the meditator's will, and that EEG showed a marked asymmetry in alpha and beta activity between the hemispheres with increased beta activity. Lou et al. (1999), using 150 h20 PET measures of CBF (cerebral blood flow), found a differential activity noticeable mainly in the posterior sensory and associative cortices known to participate in imagery, in meditation, compared with the resting state of normal consciousness, although the mean global flow remained unchanged.

In summary, it seems that meditation has a bimodal biological impact along time. Initially there is a physiological relaxation response in the short term. This effect also corresponds with findings in the study of imagery on brain activity as described by Laine et al. (1997). More enduring hormonal and metabolic changes can later be detected in experienced meditations, some 12 to 18 months after starting meditation practice.

Side-effects

Not all effects of the practice of meditation are beneficial. Shapiro (1992) found that 62.9% of the subjects reported adverse effects during and after meditation and 7.4% experienced profoundly adverse effects. The length of practice (from 16 to 105 months) did not make any difference to the quality and frequency of adverse effects. These adverse effects were relaxation-induced anxiety and panic; paradoxical increases in tension; less motivation in life; boredom; pain; impaired reality testing; confusion and disorientation; feeling 'spaced out'; depression; increased negativity; being more judgmental; and, ironically, feeling addicted to meditation.

Other adverse effects described (Craven, 1989) are uncomfortable kinaesthetic sensations, mild dissociation, feelings of guilt and, via anxiety-provoking phenomena, psychosis-like symptoms, grandiosity, elation, destructive behaviour and suicidal feelings. Kutz et al. (1985a,b) described feelings of defencelessness, which in turn produce unpleasant affective experiences, such as fear, anger, apprehension and despair. Sobbing and hidden memories and themes from the past, such as incest, rejection, and abandonment appeared in intense, vivid forms and challenged the subject's previously constructed image of their past and themselves. On the other hand, it is not uncommon to encounter a meditator who claims that has found 'the answers' when in fact he has been actively engaged in a subtle manoeuvre of avoiding his basic questions.

Therefore, Shapiro (1992) recommended caution when the answer encountered to every dilemma was 'adverse effects are only part of the path. It takes years of practice'. This statement is reminiscent of the classical psychoanalytic dictum: 'insight causes cure; if you are not cured, by definition you need more insight'—and its misuse.

The side-effect profile summarised also resembles many of the neurotic/anxiety constellation of symptoms. None of the studies reviewed tried to disentangle the effects of meditation per se from the influence of the presenting problem or/and premorbid personality of the subjects. It is unclear whether certain personality types are more likely to try meditation or whether the effect of meditation increases the awareness of those feelings, symptoms and personality traits (Morse, 1984).

Meditation and Psychotherapy

Increased self-awareness is a common theme in most psychotherapies. It is often proposed as an initial step in freeing oneself from distressing symptoms, and forms the basis of behavioural monitoring and feedback, cognitive diaries and psychoanalytical analysis of transference, dreams and free association.

From a personal construct perspective (Kelly, 1955), meditative concentration techniques can be viewed as deliberately experimenting with 'constriction' in the Kellyan sense. In constriction the perceptual field is shrunk to a few elements in an attempt to reorganise and make manageable the construct system. Mindfulness techniques can be seen as 'dilation' in a Kellyan terms, whereby the person broadens his/her perceptual field to include more elements, with the aim of a more comprehensive organisation of his/her construct system (Del Monte, 1987).

Thus meditation allows its practitioner to step out of conceptual limitations, a process which is considered to be the hallmark of insight and creativity, and the converse of neuroticism (Craven, 1989; Greguire, 1990). The detachment from self experienced in meditation can be related to the split described by Freud (1930) between the experiencing ego and the observing ego. This capacity to rise above the self increases motivation, tolerance of guilt, and enhancing a sense of unity and centredness.

On the other hand, in order to reach this deeper stability, one has to become fundamentally destabilised, which may require preliminary strength and faith (Shapiro, 1992).

Freud, personally unfamiliar with meditation, interpreted the 'oceanic' meditative experience as a reaction formation, a defence of omnipotence against infantile helplessness. Even Jung (1936), who was better acquainted with both mystical philosophy and Eastern ways of thinking, was ambivalent about its use. He believed that Eastern methods and philosophical doctrines put Western attempts along these lines into the shade. On the other hand, he said; 'people will do anything, no matter how absurd, in order to avoid facing their own souls. They will practice yoga and all its exercises, observe a strict regime of diet, learn theosophy by heart, or mechanically repeat mystic texts from the literature of the whole world, all because they cannot get on with themselves and have not the slightest faith that anything useful could ever come out of their souls'.

Looked at more positively, meditation can be seen as an undifferentiated regressive state, which, like the mother-child bond, protects from fear of separation and desolation. It is a 'regression in the service of the ego' (Atwood & Maltin, 1991; Shaffii, 1973) where one's loneliness, even the problematic nature of one's existence, is threateningly close and all that matters is not being dead or disintegrating into non-existence. This very early 'narcissistic' feeling of injury, experienced as a loss of the safety provided by attachments to others, is temporarily counterbalanced by the meditation-induced enhanced sense of the tangible self (Bogart, 1991). Shaffii (1973) emphasised the importance of silence and conceptualises meditation as a temporary and controlled regression to the preverbal level or 'somatosymbiotic phase' of the mother-child relationship. This regression may rekindle unresolved themes from the developmental phase in which the individual develops a sense of basic trust.

In Buddhist terms, the ultimate aim, the realisation that the self-ego is illusory, seems entirely irreconcilable with the goals of psychotherapy, which is, rather, to facilitate the development of a coherent ego (Bradwejn et al., 1985). But both Buddhist thought and psychoanalytic object relations theory view human growth as a series of developmental stages (Engler, 1984). The ego is defined as an internalised image that is constructed out of experience with the object world and which appears to have the qualities of consistency, sameness and continuity. According to object relations theory, the major cause of psychopathology is the inability to establish a cohesive integrated self. In contrast Buddhist psychology states that the deepest psychopathological problem is the protagonist of a self, the 'clinging to personal existence'. But one has to be somebody before one can be nobody. Meditation may be most helpful to people who have achieved an adequate level of personality organisation. Meditation can help both with getting in touch with oneself, and with letting go of the self, where there is excessive investment in the self.

Perhaps meditation can offer the possibility of development beyond what most therapies can offer, but proceeds more effectively when certain fundamental ego-based issues, such as self-esteem, livelihood, intimacy and sexuality have been, at least to some extent, tackled (Finn, 1992).

Relevance to Clinical Practice

Research into meditation is mixed, and of poor quality. Most of the studies are methodologically flawed, with insufficient number of cases, lack of standardised diagnostic procedures and being limited to non-psychiatric populations (Atkinson et al., 1996).

Kutz et al., (1985a, b) studied the effect of a 10-week mindfulness meditation programme on 20 patients who were also undergoing long-term individual exploratory psychotherapy. The main outcome was improvement in measures of psychological well-being. Smith et al. (1995) studied 36 undergraduate volunteers, and found that meditation had a positive effect as part of a 'happiness enhancement program'. A three-year study with 22 subjects showed positive effects on people diagnosed with anxiety disorders, using a meditation-based stress reduction intervention (Miller et al., 1995).

Teasdale et al., (1995) found that mindfulness meditation used for stress reduction based on the skills of attentional control achieved positive effects for maintenance and relapse prevention of depression. This 'attentional control training' has also proven to be significantly beneficial in the treatment of chronic pain (Kabat-Zinn et al., 1992), psoriasis (Bernhard et al., 1988; Kabat-Zinn et al., 1998), epilepsy (Deepack et al., 1994; Persinger, 1993; Panjwani et al., 1995), substance misuse (Gelderloos et al., 1991), fibromyalgia (Kaplan et al., 1993), hypertension (Schneider et al., 1995), HIV patients (Taylor, 1995), anxiety-depression in old age (Deberry et al., 1989) and anxiety and panic disorders (Kabat-Zinn et al., 1992).

Kutz et al., (1985a, b) studied the effect of meditation on 20 patients diagnosed with narcissistic or borderline personality disorder (BPD), anxiety and obsessional neurosis: 50% of them showed improved tension reduction, and tolerance of stress; depression, anger, guilt, self-blame and self-esteem were all helped, and 65% greatly improved on therapists' estimate of insight and psychological mindedness.

Linehan (1993) based behaviour-dialectical therapy (DBT) on principles of Zen philosophy. In this approach, with its built-in paradox, the patient is encouraged to work towards self-acceptance of who s/he is, and promote change while avoiding rejection of who s/he is. Meditative techniques are adjunctive to individual and group therapy in a research package that proved beneficial in the treatment of borderline personality disorders with frequent parasuicidal behaviour.

Shapiro (1994) described contraindications for meditation in people suffering mental illness such as psychosis, schizoid and schizotypal personality, dissociative states, hypochondrial and somatization disorders, as there is a risk that the patient will be distressed and overwhelmed by the experience of the symptoms during meditation.

Bogart (1991) argued that Western therapy appears quicker and more successful than meditation in many areas such as grief, communication skills, maturation of relationships, sexuality and intimacy, career and work issues, fears and phobias, and early trauma—not surprising, given the lack of direct focus on symptoms or problems within meditation.

In a study with alcohol-dependent patients, using an 'attention placebo group' which consisted in a group practising bibliotherapy, Benson (1975) suggested that relaxation training, whether it was meditation, progressive relaxation, or attention placebo, had a positive effect compared with normal placebo, but there were no significant differences between the three different relaxation processes (Holmes, 1985; Lazarus & Mayne, 1990).

Some authors like Chang-Yong-Chung (1990) recommended meditation as advanced courses for training for psychotherapists as a way of improving rapport and empathy. But Pearl & Carlozzi (1994), in a study with 24 student volunteers compared with a control group of 26, in on 8-week trial found no significant effect on empathy, despite a positive effect on anxiety.

Meditation is an ancient technique that has recently been extracted from its spiritual framework, and applied to therapy for the enhancement of personal well-being.

Although we have limited ourselves to reviewing studies that refer only to meditation as a technique, there is abundant literature that relates meditation to a religious-philosophical framework. It could be argued that in extracting the technique from its theoretical and belief context, the meaning and effect of meditation is deprived of its essence—just as an interpretation, cognitive challenge, or a paradoxical injunction would not have the same impact/outcome when removed from its therapeutic context.

There are different types of meditation, but all seem to be fundamentally based on the concept of self-observation of the subject's psychic activity in the here and now, with an acceptance of process rather than content.

The practice of meditation has positive short- and long-term rewards, the main ones being a calm self-control, and what Benson called 'the relaxation response'. These effects include a wakeful hypometabolic physiological state and a balance of the parasympathetic or trophotropic and sympathetic or ergotrophic functions.

The evidence of meditative physical effects is consistent with increasing evidence of the biological impact of psychological interventions. It refutes convincingly the stereotypical criticism that talking therapies 'do nothing' or are 'just' placebo.

Meditation is not free from side-effects, even for long-term meditators or experienced teachers. Nor is it free of contraindications.

The common element with psychotherapy is the emphasis and goal of self-awareness, and the freeing of the individual from habitual patterns of thinking and feelings, paving the way for change. It differs from psychotherapy in that meditation is a completely private and silent exercise.

There is mixed research on the efficacy of meditation as therapy or an adjuvant to therapy. This study has not included anecdotal reports by therapists of the use of meditation as a personal aid and maintenance to their professional development. Most of the studies are based on small numbers, and lack standardised diagnostic procedures. The current evidence seems to indicate a value of meditation in the treatment of stress and anxiety related disorders, but there is a need for a rigorous meta-analysis in order to guarantee standards in evidence-based therapeutic practice.

REFERENCES

Atkinson, R.L., Atkinson, R.C., Smith, E.E., Ben, D.J. & Nolen-Noeksema, S. (1996). *Hilgard's introduction to psychology*, 12th edn.

Atwood, J.D. & Maltin, L. (1991). Putting eastern philosophies into western psychotherapies. *American Journal of Psychotherapy*, XLV, 368-382.

Benhard, J.D., Kristeller, J. & Kabat-Zinn, J. (1988). Effectiveness of relaxation and visualisation techniques as an adjunct to phototherapy and photochemotherapy of psoriasis, Journal *American Academy of Dermatology*, 19, 572-573.

Benson, H. (1975). The relaxation response. New York: Morrow.

Benson, H., Malhotra, M.S., Goldman, R.F., Jacobs, G.D. & Hopkins, P.J. (1990). Three case reports of the metabolic and electroencephalographic changes during advanced Buddhist meditation techniques, *Behavioural Medicine*, Summer, 90-95.

Bogart, G. (1991). The use of meditation in psychotherapy: a review of the literature, American Journal of Psychotherapy, XLV, 383-412.

Bradwejn, J. et al. (1985). Can East and West meet in psychoanalysis? *American Journal of Psychiatry*, 142(10), 1226-1228.

Cang-Yong Chung (1990). Psychotherapist and expansion of awareness. *Psychotherapy Psychosom*, 53, 28-32.

Cobly, F. (1991). An analogue study of the initial carryover effects of meditation, hypnosis and relaxation using native college students. *Biofeedback Self-Regulation*, 16(2), 157-165.

Craven, J.L. (1989). Meditation and psychotherapy. *Canadian Journal of Psychiatry*, 34, 648-653.

Deberry, S., Dams, S. & Reinhard, K.E. (1989). A comparison of meditation-relaxation and cognitive-behavioural techniques for reducing anxiety and depression in a geriatric population. *Journal of Geriatric Psychiatry*, 22(2), 231-247.

Deepack, K.K., Mnchanda, S.K. & Maheshwaril, M.C. (1994). Meditation improves clinicoelectroencephalographic measures in drug-resistant epileptics. *Biofeedback Self-Regulation*, 19(1), 25-40.

Delmonte, M.M. (1987). Constructivist view of meditation. *American Journal of Psychotherapy*, 41(2), 286-298.

Dillbeck, M.C. & Orme-Johnson, D.W. (1987). Psychological differences between transcendental meditation and rest. *American Psychology*, 42, 879-881.

Dua, J.K. & Swinden, M.L. (1992). Effectiveness of negative-thoughts-reduction, meditation and placebo training treatment in reducing anger, Scandinavian Journal of Psychology, 33(2), 135-146.

Elias, A.N. & Wilson, A.F. (1995). Serum hormonal concentrations following transcendental meditation: potential role of gamma aminobutyric acid, Med. Hypotheses, 44, 287-291.

Engler, J. (1984). Therapeutic aims in psychotherapy and meditation: developmental stages in the representation of self. Journal of Transpersonal Psychology, 16, 25-61.

Epstein, M. (1990). Psychodynamics of meditation: pitfalls of the spiritual path, Journal of Transpersonal Psychology, 22(1), 17-34.

Finn, M. (1992). Transitional space and Tibetan Buddhism: the object relations theory of meditation, in, Object relations theory and religion: clinical applications. Praeger.

Freud. S. (1930). Civilisation and its discontents, in Complete Psychological Works, Standard Edition, Vol. 21. London: Hogarth Press.

Fromm, E. (1975). Self-hypnosis: a new area of research, Psychotherapy: Theory, Research and Practice, 12, 295-301.

Gelderloos, P., Walton, K.G., Orme-Johnson, D.W. & Aexander, C.N. (1991). Effectiveness of the transcendental meditation in preventing and treating substance misuse: a review, International Journal of Addictions, 26(3), 293-325.

Globus, G.G. (1980). On 'I': the conceptual foundations of responsibility, American Journal of Psychiatry, 137, pp. 417-422. Golfman (1972). The Buddha on meditation and states of consciousness, Part 2: a topology of meditation techniques, Journal of Transpersonal Psychology, 4, 151-210.

Greguire, J. (1990). Therapy with the person who meditates diagnosis and treatment strategies, Transactional Analysis Journal, 20(11), 60-76.

Harte, J.L., Eifert, G.H. & Smith, R. (1995). The effects of running and meditation on beta-endorphin, corticotrophin-releasing hormone and cortisol in plasma and on mood, Biological Psychology, 40(3), 251-265.

Herzog, a. et al. (1990). Changes pattern of regional glucose metabolism during yoga meditative relaxation. *Neuropsychology*, 23(4); 182-187.

Holmes, D.S. (1985). To meditate or rest? The answer is rest, American Psychologist, 40(6), 725-731.

Jevning, R., Wallace, R.K. & Beidebach, M. (1992). The physiology of meditation: a review. Awakeful hypometabolic integrated response. *Neuroscience and Behavioural Reviews*, 16; 415-424.

Jung, C.G. (1936). 'Yoga and the West' and, 'The psychology of Eastern meditation', in Collected works, Vol. 11. Princeton, NJ: Princeton University Press.

Kabat-Zinn, J. et al. (1992). Effectiveness of a meditation-based stress reduction program in the treatment of anxiety disorders. *American Journal of Psychiatry*, 149(7); 936-943.

Kabat-Zinn, J. et al. (1998). Influence of a mindfulness meditation-based stress reduction intervention on rates of skin clearing in patients with moderate to severe psoriasis undergoing phototherapy (UVB) and photochemotherapy (PUVA), *Psychosom. Med*, 60(5); 625-632.

Kaplan, K.H., Goldenberg, D.L. & Galvin-Nadean, M. (1993). The impact of a meditation-based stress reduction program on fibromyalgia. *General Hospital Psychiatry*, 15(5), 284-289.

Kelly, G.A. (1955). *The psychology of personal constructs*. New York: Norton.

Kesterson, J. & Clinch, N.F. (1989). Metabolic rate, respiratory exchange ratio and apnoea during meditation. *American Journal Physiology*, R256, 632-638.

Kokoszka, A. (1990). Axiological aspects of comparing psychotherapy and meditation. *International Journal of Psychosomatics*, 37(1-4), 78-81.

Kokoszka, A. (1994). A rationale for a multilevel model of relaxation. *International Journal of Psychosomatics*, 41(1-4), 4-10.

Kutz, I., Burysenko, J.K. & Benson, H. (1985a). Meditation and psychotherapy: a rationale for the integration of dynamic psychotherapy, the relaxation response and mindfulness meditation. *American Journal of Psychiatry*, 142, 1-8.

Kutz, I., Leserman, J., Dorrington, C., Morrison, C.H., Borysenko, J. & BENSON, H. (1985b). Meditation as an adjunct to psychotherapy, an outcome study. *Psychotherapy Psychosomatics*, 43, 209-218.

Lane, R.D. et al., (1997). neuroanatomical correlates of happiness, sadness, and disgust. *American Journal of Psychiatry*, 154, 926-933.

Lazarus, A.A. & Mayne, T.J. (1990). Relaxation: some limitations, *side effects and proposed solutions, Psychotherapy*, 27, 261-266.

Leuschitz, J.K. & Hartman, V.L. (1996). Current psychology: developmental, learning, personality, social, 15(3), 215-222.

Levenstein, S. (1996). Is there health in wellness? (Editorial), *Journal of Clinical Gastroenterology*, 23, 94-96.

Linehan, M. (1993). *Cognitive-behavioural treatment of borderline personality disorder*. New York: Guilford Press.

Liu G.L., Rong-Quing Cui, Guo-Zhang Li & Chi-Mang Huang (1990). Changes in brainstem and cortical auditory potentials during Qi-Gong meditation. *American Journal of Chinese Medicine*, 18, 95-103.

Lou, H.C., Kjaer, T.W., Friberg, L., Wildschiodtz, G., HOLM, S. & NOWAK, M. (1999). A 150-H20 PET study of meditation and the resting state of normal consciousness. *Hum. Brain Map*, 7, 98-105.

Masion, A.O., TEAS, J., HERBERT, J.R., Werheimer, M.D. & Kabat-Zinn, J. (1995). *Meditation, melatonin and breast/prostate cancer: hypothesis and preliminary data, Medical Hypotheses*, 44, 39-46.

Miller, J.J., Fletcher, K. & Kabat-Zinn, J. (1995). Three years follow-up and clinical implications of a mindfulness meditation-based stress reduction intervention in the treatment of anxiety disorders. *General Hospital Psychiatry*, 17(3), 192-200.

Morse, D.R. (1984). Who benefits from meditation? *International Journal of Psychosomatics*, 31(2), 2.

Narayan, R. et al. (1990). Quantitative evaluation of muscle relaxation induced by kundalini yoga with the help of E.M.G. integrator. *Indian Journal Physiological Pharmacology*, 34(4), 279-281.

Panjwani, U. et al. (1995). Effect of Sahaja yoga practice on stress management in-patients of epilepsy. *Indian Journal Physiological Pharmacology*, 39(2), 111-116.

Pearl, J.H. & CarlozziI. A.F. (1994). Effect of meditation on empathy and anxiety. *Percept. Motor Skills*, 78(1), 297-298.

Persinger, M.A. (1993). Transcendental meditation and general meditation are associated with enhanced complex partial epileptic-like signs: evidence for 'cognitive kindling'? *Percept Motor Skills*, 76(1), 80-82.

Russell, E.W. (1986). Consciousness and the unconscious: Eastern meditative and Western psychotherapeutic approaches. *Journal of Transpersonal Psychology*, 18, 51-72.

Scheler, M.F. (1992). Effects of optimism on psychological and physical wellbeing: theoretical and empirical update. *Cognitive Therapy and Research*, 16, 201-228.

Schneider, R.H. et al. (1995). A randomised controlled trial of stress reduction for hypertension in older African Americans, *Hypertension*, 26(5), 820-827.

Shaffu, M. (1973). Silence in the service of ego: psychology of meditation. *International Journal of Psychoanalysis*, 54, 431-443.

Shapiro, D.H. (1982). Overview: clinical and physiological comparison of meditation with other self-control strategies. *American Journal of Psychiatry*, 139, 267-274.

Shapiro, D.H. (1992). Adverse effects of meditation: a preliminary investigation of long-term meditators. *International Journal of Psychosomatics*, 39, 62-67.

Shapiro, D.H. (1994). Examining the content and context of meditation: a challenge for psychology in the areas of stress management. *Psychotherapy and Religion Values*, 34(4), 101-135.

Sim, M.K. & Tsol, W.F. (1992). The effects of centrally acting drugs on the EEG correlates of meditation. *Biofeedback Self-Regulation*, 17(3), 215-220.

Smith, W.P., Compton, W.C. & West, W.B. (1995). Meditation as an adjunct to a happiness enhancement program. *Journal of Clinical Psychology*, 51, 269-273.

Snaith, P. (1998). Meditation and psychotherapy. *British Journal of Psychiatry*, 173, pp. 193-195.

Sudsuang, R., Chentanez, V. & Veluvan, K. (1991). Effect of Buddhist meditation on serum cortisol and total protein levels, blood pressure, pulse rate, lung volume and reaction time. *Physiology Behaviour*, 50(3), 543-548.

Taylor, D.N. (1995). Effects of a behavioural stress-management program on anxiety, mood, self-esteem and T-cell count in HIV positive men, *Psychol Rep*, 76(2), 451-457.

Teasdale, J.D., Segal, Z. & Williams, M.G. (1995). How does cognitive therapy prevent depressive relapse and why should attentional control (mindfulness) training help? *Behaviour Research Therapy*, 33, 25-39.

Telles, S. & Desraju, T. (1993). Autonomic changes in Brahmakumaris Raja yoga meditation. *International Journal of Psychophysiology*, 15(2), 147-152.

Telles, S. et al. (1994). Plasticity of motor control systems demonstrated by yoga training. *Indian Journal of Physiology & Pharmacology*, 38(2), 143-144.

Travis, F.T. & Orme-John, D.W. (1989). Field model of consciousness: EEG coherence changes as indicators of field effects. *International Journal of Neuroscience*, 49, 203-211.

Tyler Carpenter, J. (1977). Meditation, esoteric traditions: contributions to psychotherapy. *American Journal of Psychotherapy*, 394-404.

West, M.A. (1987). *The psychology of meditation*. Oxford: Clarendon Press/Oxford University Press.

Wilson, A.F., Jevning, R. & Gulch, S. (1987). Marked reduction of forearm carbon dioxide production during states of decreased metabolism. *Physiology and Behavior*, 41, 347-352.

●●●

19

Vipassana Meditation - A Positive Approach to Psychological Well -being

Ritu Modi and Abha Singh

Vipassana meditation is a scientific technique of self-exploration: a system of self- transformation by self-observation. It means to see things as they are, to see things in their true perspective and in their true nature. The objective of Vipassana meditation is to purify the mind, and free it from misery by gradually eradicating the negativities within. It is believed that sustained practice of Vipassana brings about total transformation of the human personality. From the psychological point of view, Vipassana meditation can be described as a technique of non-verbal, self-administered psychoanalysis. Its theoretical basis, mechanism and psychological effects are discussed and reviewed in this paper.

Health as defined by the World Health Organization is a state of complete physical, mental, and social well-being and not merely an absence of disease or infirmity. Health is a dynamic concept and can be defined as a multi-dimensional process involving the well-being of an individual in the context of his/her environment.

This paper shall deal primarily the mental aspect of health since it is the 'mind' which is the central directing force of one's entire life and activity and also because every health related disorder is affected directly or indirectly by psychological factors. Hence it is rightly said that mind matters most.

Vipassana meditation is a unique technique for obtaining peace and harmony with in an individual at the experiential level. The great sage of India, *Gautama the Buddha*, discovered this technique through his deep meditation. He attained enlightenment through this technique and was liberated from all the defilements of the mind. He taught Vipassana- a way to purify the mind of its negativities of carving and aversion. The practical, results-oriented nature of Vipassana is what appealed to S. N. Goenka. In 1955, he undertook a course and found that it was indeed a life-transforming experience.

Vipassana Meditation

Vipassana is a Pali word meaning "insight". It is a system of self-transformation by self-observation; the objective is to eventually reach a state of inner and outer calmness and balance of mind (Thray Sithu Sayagyi U Ba Khin, 1983). Vipassana means to see things as they are, to see things in their true perspective and in their true nature. It is in essence, a technique of self-observation and self-exploration.

Objectives of Vipassana

- To purify the mind.
- To bring about the total transformation of the human personality.

Vipassana meditation can be described as a technique of purifying the mind of its baser Instincts so that one begins to manifest the truly human qualities of universal goodwill, kindness, tolerance, sympathy, humility, equanimity, etc., and simultaneously gains an insight into the true nature and purpose of human existence. This is achieved in a very scientific manner through a systematic cultivation of right mindfulness coupled with non-reactivity; that is to say, development of the habit of paying penetrating attention to whatever is happening in our total organism-the body with its five senses and the mind which operates in and through it-without any admixture of subjective judgments or reactions.

Steps of Vipassana

To begin with, one has to take a vow of observing certain rules of moral conduct (sila). These are: abstention from *killing, stealing, sexual misconduct, lying and taking any intoxicant*. This first step itself is likely to bring about positive changes in a person's life style.

The second component of this training is called Anapana, *i.e., awareness of respiration.* This involves continuous "observation" of the natural flow of incoming and outgoing breath. Gradually the mind gets concentrated on this natural activity and the person can exercise greater control over his mind. It promotes awareness of the present moment, equanimity and tranquility of mind, since the act of breathing is free from any craving or aversion.

The third step called development of 'panna' or wisdom-involves *purification of mind through enhanced awareness.* The person engages himself in choice less and effortless observation of body sensations and tries to develop an attitude of non-judgmental and non-reactionary. This practice has a corrective influence on psychic disturbances. Whatever arises in the mind, anger, insecurity, fear, passion or sadness, is associated with certain internal body sensations. Observing these sensations in a detached manner helps the individual handle these emotions.

Mechanism and Psychological Effects

Vipassana meditation trains the concentrated attention to follow the mechanics of mental processing in a detached manner. In this the practioner allows the controlled release of mental contents like craving and aversion, past and future in a seemingly endless stream of memories. (Fleischman P.R., 1986). Since the meditator is deeply relaxed, the whole contents of his mind can be seen as composing a "Desensitization hierarchy"; in this sense, Vipassana meditation may be natural global self-desensitization (Goleman D., 1977).

Through the practice of Vipassana meditation, one learns that the territory of the mind is far more extensive than Freud X., (yr) realized. Brain researchers too have identified the enormous capacity of the human nervous system. This untapped potential can be identified through Vipassana meditation. It helps in the release of stress and in the maximization of psychological growth and integration (Doshi.,J. yr). As one gets more and more established in the practice of meditation, there are fewer mental problems, and even psychosomatic disorders like hypertension, peptic ulcer, irritable bowel syndrome, asthma, and eczema get ameliorated. Vipassana meditation, therefore, leads to better health and a happy, blissful mind. There is less mental tension and confusion, and with such a clear and calm mind, one is able to deal easily with one's problems, thus living a merry and joyful life (Nichani., J. N., yr).

Researchers have observed that Vipasana meditation is effective in reducing tension headache (Sharma Mahendra. P., Kumariah, V., Mishra, H., & Baroohi J. P., 1990). Vipassana meditation emphasizes both conscious life style changes in the area of morality and deeper psychological analysis which alters the contents and the processes of the mind in fundamental ways (Chandiramani et al., 1995). Detailed scientific research studies carried out to assess the impact of Vipassana meditation on the prisoner's mental health and criminal propensity proves that Vipassana is capable of transforming criminals into better human beings. In their study they found that the Vipassana course had a significant and positive effect on the subjective well-being of female prisoners (Khurana yr, Amulya yr, and Dhar. P. L., 2000).

A study indicates that majority business management student get psychological benefits out of the Vipassana Meditation Process. Among the Psychological benefits 36.2% of students reported that they obtained peace and stability of mind, strong will power, become quite, calm and relaxed. They could be able to understand the strength and weaknesses, and become more composed, compassionate, determined, vigorous and developed the feeling equanimity. Their ability to concentrate in day to day classes increased (24.1%) and gained better control over anger, agitation, frustration, reaction formation and hyper activeness (22.6%)(Kumar M.D.,2005). A study conducted on migraine patients in which participants completed training of intensive meditation and continued frequent practice of Vipasana meditation for one year experienced reduced frequency, duration, and severity of headaches along with improved awareness of the triggers of their symptoms, improved quality of life and mental health, improved heart rate variability, and reduced inflammation (Kerrie, 2008).

Now we want to mention a few cases of individual with mental disorder to emphasize the changes in these individual due to the impact of Vipassana meditation (Khosla. R., 1994). Psychological parameters studied before Vipassana and one year after Vipassana are presented as follows:

Test	***Case Study of Depression***		***Case Study of Anxiety Panic Disorder***		***Case study of Obsessive Compulsive Disorder***	
	Pre-Vipassana	*1yr After*	*Pre-Vipassana*	*1yr After*	*Pre-Vipassana*	*1yr After*
Personality hardiness	74	52	62	40	102	64
Symptom checklist	226	60	110	53	144	58
Depression scale	20	04	06	02	12	02
Coping scale	92	44	80	54	124	86

This is evident from the above case studies that regular practice of Vipassana meditation will help in alleviating mental disorders. However, a lot of patience and diligence are needed on the part of meditator. Additionally, professional psychiatric advice and proper guidance by a qualified Vippassana teacher are required to achieve goals.

Vipassana meditation is a technique to purify mind to free oneself from misery by gradually eradicating the negativities within. It teaches one how to become a detached observer while keep appreciating the impermanence of feeling and sensation, happiness or unhappiness. With the help of Vipassana meditation we can change human turbulence into calmness with vitality and make it a psychological well-being measure of an excellent method to develop potential of human mind.

REFERENCES

Chandiramani, K., Verma, S. K., & Dhar, P. L. (1995). Psychological effects of Vipassana on Tihar Jail inmates. Research Report, Vipassana Research Institute.

Doshi, J., Vipassana and Psychotherapy. http://www.vridhamma.org/Vipassana-and-Psychotherapy.aspx

Fleischman P.R. (1986). The Therapeutic Action of Vipassana and Why I Sit, Buddhist Publication Society, Kandy, Sri Lanka.

Goleman D. (1977). Meditation and Consciousness: An Asian Approach to Mental Health, *American Journal of Psychotherapy,* 30, 41-54.

Kerrie, (2008). Vipassana Meditation for Chronic Daily Headache (Migraine): Clinical Trial Recruiting Participants. .http://www.thedailyheadache.com/2008/04/vipassana-meditation-for-chronic-daily-headache-migraine-clinical-trial-recruiting-participants.html

Khosla., R. (1994). Before and after : Six case studies of improvement in Mental health, Vipassana Research Institute; An International Seminar on Vipassana and its relevance on the present world, IIT, Delhi.

Khurana, Amulya and Dhar., P. L. (2000). Research Paper on Inmates of Tihar Jail, Delhi: presented by Dr Amulya Khurana and Prof. P. L. Dhar, Indian Institute of Technology, New Delhi.

Kumar M.D. (2005). Advantages of Vipassana Meditation on Psychosomatic, Professional and Managerial development of Business Graduates A qualitative Research. Sinhgad Business School, Sinhgad Technical and Educational Society Kusgaon, Lonavla-410 401, E-mail: dilmail@rediffmail.com

Nichani., J.N. Vipassana Meditation and Health http://www.vridhamma.org/Vipassana-Meditation-and-Health.aspx

Sharma Mahendra. P., Kumariah, V., Mishra, H., & Baroohi J. P. (1990). Therapeutic effects of Vipassana meditation in tension headache. *Journal of Psychology and Clinical Studies*, 6(2), 201-206.

●●●

20

Effect of Vipassana Meditation on Quality of Life, Subjective Well-being, and Criminal Propensity

Amulya Khurana

Crimes are acts that are forbidden and punished by law; these acts may threaten the well-being of the society, or injure any of its members. People are most likely to commit a criminal act between the age of fifteen and twenty five years. Imprisonment is a method of dealing with people who commit crimes by confining them to a fortified boundary with certain strict rules for all - that is, the prison. Crime, like any other action of the body, is a manifestation of thoughts in the mind.

Crime has come to be regarded as essentially a social problem, and retribution as the object of improvement is discarded. Detention as an objective of imprisonment is also very limited in scope. Reformation of the offender is being regarded as an ultimate aim of the prison sentence. Rehabilitation of the criminals has become one of the most important objectives of the jail authorities. Apart from the criminal aspect, many inmates manifest mental disorders in prison as a result of stresses of incarceration. The stresses behind the bars include separation from their family members, over crowding, sensory deprivation, exposure to a high-density of hard-core offenders and a variety of uncertainties, fear, and frustrations. The period of trial is of great stress to the individual. Loss of social status, uncertainty of outcome of the trial, fear of punishment, staying in an unusual place like police station or jail and the financial upsets harass the individual. If the trial period is prolonged for months or years which is very common, then the undertrial's mental condition becomes bad. The hard life in the prison further aggravates the situation. The undertrial's quality of life and subjective well-being are seriously affected by aforesaid conditions in the prison.

Psychological factors such as frustration, hostility, and feelings of helplessness might be the cause or the consequence of criminal behaviour and in some cases, both. Prison reform measures should lead to some reduction in inmate's feelings of hostility, helplessness and other negative emotions. Vipassana is being practiced in Tihar jail as a prison reform measure with the ultimate goal of prevention of crime and reintegration of prisoners into mainstream society following their discharge from prison. An unfavourable attitude towards law may be responsible for criminal behaviour and needs to be corrected in the course of reforms. On many occasions it is the feeling of alienation from the mainstream life which results from a misfit of individual goals with cultural norms and it might result in criminal activities.

Since Vipassana (VM) is believed to be a technique that facilitates deeper psychological introspection and to bring about lasting behavioural changes, it was considered worth while to assess some of these changes in a scientific manner. The main aim of the present study was to investigate the effect of Vipassana meditation on Subjective Well-Being and Criminal Propensity of Tihar Jail inmates. The study has been conducted on both male (adolescent) and female inmates. Also one of the goals was to see the overall psychological bearing of Vipassana meditation on prison inmates.

Vipassana is a genuine non-sectarian methodology for mind control and purification. The question arises what for Vipassana be practised in prison. Prison life is a cursed life. In traditional sense, it is the worst life in every sense. It blocks the overall unfolding of personality. It takes away freedom from the individual. For the inmates life inside prison is bizarre, torturous, painful, unhealthy, suffocating and slave like. The purpose is to make prison life better, to add a humanistic dimension to it, to help the inmates introspect and examine themselves and possibly understand the purpose of life better. Vipassana as a meditational technique is dedicated to fulfill these higher goals of life. It is believed that Vipassana has a great role to play in transforming prison life.

The positive impact of Vipassana on various aspects of mental health and personality has been reported in a number of studies and it was therefore expected that similar results would come in the case of inmates.

The technique of Vipassana is basically a path leading to freedom from all sufferings: it uproots craving, aversion and ignorance, which are the basic cause for all our miseries. Those who practise it remove, little by little, the root causes of their sufferings and steadily emerge from the darkness of former tensions to lead happy, healthy, productive lives. There are many examples bearing testimony to this fact. Several experiments have been conducted at prisons in India. In 1975, Goenkaji conducted a course for 120 inmates at the Central Jail in Jaipur, the first such experiment in Indian penal history. This course was followed in 1976 by a course for senior police officers at the Government Police Academy in Jaipur. In 1977, a second course was held at the Jaipur Central Jail. These courses were the subject of several sociological studies conducted by the University of Rajasthan. In 1990, another course was organised in Jaipur Central Jail in which forty life-term convicts and ten jail officials participated with positive results. In 1991, a course for life-sentence prisoners was held at the Savaramati Central Jail, Ahmedabad, and was the subject of a research project by the Dept. of Education, Gujrat Vidyapeeth. The Rajasthan and Gujrat studies indicated definite positive changes in the attitude and behaviour of the participants, and showed that Vipassana is a positive reform measure enabling criminals to become wholesome members of society.

Vipassana was introduced in Tihar Jail in November 1993 when the first course was organized in Central Jail No. 2, where 96 convicts and 20 staff/officers of jail participated. Its success led to a succession of courses, including the largest ever Vipassana course of over 1000 prisoners in April 1994. This was followed by setting up of a regular Vipassana centre inside

Central Jail No. 4, where two courses are held every month till date. A detailed investigation into effect of Vipassana on inmates was undertaken under the aegis of department of Psychiatry, AIIMS in 1994 and its results were very encouraging. Two studies were carried out in 1994. The first study was carried out on 120 subjects in January 1994.

The dimensions studied were well being, hostility, hope, helplessness, personality, psychopathy and in the case of psychiatric disorders, anxiety and depression. It was followed by another study which was carried out in April 1994 on 150 subjects. The sample consisted of two groups: one group of 85 subjects who attended a 10 day Vipassana course and the other group of 65 who did not. The dimensions studied were anomie, attitude to law, personality and psychiatric illness.

Immediately after the course, the subjects were found to be less hostile towards their environment and felt less helpless. The psychiatric patients, constituting about 23% of the total sample, reported good improvement in their anxiety and depressive symptoms. Subjects without any psychological symptoms also reported improvement in the form of enhanced well being and a sense of hope for the future. Their sense of alienation from the mainstream life, though unchanged immediately after the course, was found to be lower after three months. The follow-up evaluations at three and six month intervals revealed further improvement on many of these dimensions. The Vipassana Research Institute has documented other examples of the positive impact of Vipassana in such fields as health, education, drug addiction, and business management.

Review of Literature

A number of studies have been carried out to investigate prison life. A brief description of these studies is given below. Krishna

(1993) reports the presence of neuroticism, anxiety, extraversion, and morality guilt among adolescents who are high on delinquent behaviour. She says that there are positive relationships between delinquent behaviour and these personality factors. Osofsky (1996) reveals the presence of certain psychological or personality factors exhibited by prisoners and the importance of these in creating more stress within the prisons. These factors are neuroticism, anxiety, aggression, hostility, and guilt. It has been found that severe psychopathological emotion is higher in adolescents exhibiting higher degree of offences. Ahmad (1988) has also reported that meditators show overall better adjustment and personality organization than non-meditators.

According to Aminabhai (1996) Yoga training leads to highly significant improvement in subject's mental health. Deepak, Manchanda, and Maheswari (1994) have reported that continuous meditation can substantially improve the clinico-electroencephalographic measures in drug resistant epileptics. Jhansi, and Rao (1996) have investigated the role of practicing

Transcendental Meditation (TM) in improving the attention regulation capacity of its practitioners. Their study reveals greater attention regulation capacity among TM practitioners compared to their counterparts, due to the regular cognitive exercises involved in meditation practice. Jin (1992) has observed the efficacy of Tai chi, a moving meditation, in reducing mood disturbance caused by mental/emotional stressors. Yoga is claimed to endow perfect physical, mental and social well being of an individual. A series of research investigations have revealed that there are many beneficial effects of yoga, which would help in the stress management (Selvamurthy, 1993). Yoga and meditation can contribute positively to various cognitive processes, including perception and in turn, on Subjective Well-being, Quality of Life and Criminal Propensity. Vipassana is a particular technique of self-examination, a scientific method of self-observation that results in the total purification of the mind and the highest happiness of full liberation (Vipassana Research Institute, 1990).

Chandiramani, Verma, Dhar, and Aggarwal (1994) have studied the psychological effects of Vipassana meditation (VM) on Tihar jail inmates. They report that VM brought significant improvement in psychological parameters like sense of hope and well-being. There has been considerable reduction in the neurotic predisposition, hostility and feelings of helplessness reported by the prisoners. Mahendram, Kumariah, Mishra, and Baroohi (1998) have observed that VM is effective in reducing tension headache. Venkantesh, Pal, Negi, Verma, Sapru, and Verma (1994) have observed that yoga practitioners, both males and females, have more positive attitude towards yoga than control group males and females. Control group showed higher neurotic trend, and yoga group showed significantly higher scores on social desirability. The authors have also found that Life event scores (past one year) were significantly less in yoga practitioners. Khurana (1996, 1999) conducted field experiments using 'before and after' design to find out the effect of VM on Quality of Life (QOL) and Subjective Well-being (SWB) of undertrials, in Tihar jail. She found positive effect on VM on QOL and SWB of undertrials, though not significant. Therefore, she recommended that control group design should be used in further study. Chaudhary (1999) investigated the effectiveness of Vipassana meditation, as a technique of stress management and reformation among adolescent prisoners. In her study, Chaudhary reported that both state anxiety and trait anxiety reduced significantly among adolescents who had done the Vipassana course. She also reported that there was a decrease in aggression among undertrial prisoners who had undergone Vipassana course. There was an increase in the feelings of positive emotions such as, hopefulness, self control, conformity, and compassion, was more after practicing Vipassana, as compared to non-practitioners of Vipassana.

According to Chandiramani et al (1995), Vipassana meditation emphasizes both conscious life style changes in the area of morality and deeper psychological analysis, which alters the contents and the processes of the mind in fundamental ways. Vipassana meditation courses have been found to bring out many positive changes in the behaviour of jail inmates (Shah, 1976; Unnithan & Ahuja, 1977;

Hammersley & Creganj, 1986). On the basis of clinical experience, Chandiramani et al (1995) have stated that mild to moderately severe neurotic cases of anxiety, depression and adjustment problems show complete recovery as a result of Vipassana. They also reported that there was considerable reduction in the neurotic predisposition, hostility and feelings of helplessness reported by the prisoners; while the sense of hope and well being were enhanced, following Vipassana courses. On the basis of the above review of research, it is assumed that Vipassana will have a significant positive effect on the Quality of Life, Subjective Well-being, and Criminal Propensity of undertrials.

Vipassana Meditation: An Introduction

Vipassana is an ancient meditation technique rediscovered by Gautama the Buddha, about 2500 years ago. It is currently being taught in India and several other countries under the guidance of Shri S. N. Goenka, the principal teacher of Vipassana. It promotes conscious lifestyle changes, enhances concentration of mind and facilitates deeper psychological introspection to bring about lasting behavioural changes.

Vipassana means "insight" - seeing things as they really are. To learn this technique one is required to take a ten day residential course under a qualified teacher. To begin with, one has to take a vow of observing certain rules of moral conduct (sila). These are: abstention from killing any sentient being, stealing, sexual misconduct, lying, and taking any intoxicant. This first step itself is likely to initiate positive changes in prisoners. The second component of this training is called Anapana, *i.e.*, awareness of respiration. This involves continuous "observation" of the natural flow of incoming and outgoing breath. Gradually the mind gets concentrated on this natural activity and the person can exercise greater control over his mind. It promotes awareness of the present moment, equanimity and tranquillity of mind, since the act of breathing is free from any craving or aversion.

The third step called development of pañña or wisdom - involves purification of mind through enhanced awareness. The individual engages himself in choiceless and effortless observation of body sensations and tries to develop and attitude of non-judgement and non- reaction. This practice has a corrective influence on deep-rooted habits. Whatever arises in the mind, be it anger, fear, insecurity, passion or sadness, is associated with certain internal body sensations. Observing these sensations in a detached/impersonal manner helps the individual handle these emotions.

People from different backgrounds have undergone residential courses of Vipassana and found it of practical value in everyday life. For the duration of the retreat, students remain within the course site, having no contact with the outside world. They refrain from reading and writing, and suspend any religious practices or other disciplines. They follow a rigorous daily schedule which includes about ten hours of sitting meditation. They also observe silence, not communicating with fellow students: however, they are free to discuss issues concerning meditation with the teacher and any material problems with the management.

The observation of rules of moral conduct allows the mind to calm down sufficiently to proceed with the task at hand. Secondly, for the first three-and-a-half days, students practise Anapana meditation, focusing attention on the breath. This practise helps to develop control over the unruly mind. These first two steps of living a wholesome life and developing control of the mind are necessary and beneficial, but are incomplete unless the third step is taken: purifying the mind of underlying negativities. This third step, undertaken for the last six-and-a-half days, is the practise of Vipassana: one penetrates one's entire physical and mental structure with the clarity of insight.

Students receive systematic meditation instructions several times a day, and each day's progress is explained during a video taped evening discourse by Shri Goenka. Complete silence is observed for the first nine days. On the tenth day, students resume speaking, making the transition back to a more extroverted way of life. The course concludes on the morning of the eleventh day.

Vipassana enables one to experience peace and harmony: it purifies the mind, freeing it from suffering and the deep-seated causes of suffering. The practice leads step-by-step to the highest spiritual goal of full liberation from all mental defilement.

About the Study

The study aimed at finding out the effect of Vipassana meditation (VM) on Quality of Life (QOL), Subjective Well-being (SWB), and Criminal Proponsity (CP) among Tihar jail inmates. A brief description of each of these concepts/variables is given below.

According to Goldenson (1984), mental health is a state of mind, characterized by emotional well-being, relative freedom from anxiety and disabling symptoms and a capacity to establish constructive relationship with ordinary demands and stresses of life. Ryff et al (1995), have proposed a theoretical model of well-being, which encompasses six distinct dimensions of wellness: 'autonomy', 'environment', 'mastery', 'personal growth', 'positive relation with others', 'purpose in life', and 'self-acceptance'. Earlier, Sahoo and Bidyadhar (1988) stated that at least four dominant dimensions influence the way people evaluate their own subjective mental health: 'evaluation of positive affective experience', 'evaluation of negative affective experience', 'feeling of personal competence on handling negative experience' and 'feeling of personal competence in driving positive experience'.

Subjective well-being is an important aspect of one's total health status. It is a mental state, which helps a person to maintain equilibrium, anchored by hope and optimism, even in adversity. A human being in a prison, particularly an undertrial, is normally under high anxiety and stress. It is evident from research that yoga, meditation and religious practices have a positive impact to reduce stress and enhance mental health. Although, a few studies have been conducted on jail inmates (Eber, 1975; Khuruna, 1996), little has, however, been reported regarding the effect of Vipassana meditation on subjective well being of undertrials.

Quality of Life is defined as the degree of excellence of one's life that contributes to satisfaction and happiness and benefits mental health. Quality of Life of an individual would be affected by a number of factors, particularly by the significant positive and negative life events. As stated by Milbrath (1979) 'Subjective studies of Quality of Life typically have shown that most people derive their greatest sense of Quality of Life from their home and family life and from the close supportive relationships they have with friends and colleagues'. Criminal Propensity is the notion of an underlying, or latent characteristic of all individuals - aggression, impulsiveness, self-control, or conditionality - that has a direct effect on a person's likelihood of committing criminal acts. Research findings suggest that people with Criminal Propensity score high on Neuroticism, Extroversion, Psychoticism and Lie tests.

Objectives

The objectives of this study are:

1. To find out the effect of Vipassana Meditation (VM) on Subjective Well-being of Tihar Jail inmates.
2. To investigate the effect of VM on QOL of Tihar Jail inmates.
3. To examine the effect of VM on Criminal Propensity of inmates.
4. To assess the overall experience of inmates who regularly practice Vipassana.
5. To find out the difference, if any, in the effect of VM on SWB and CP of male and female inmates.

Hypotheses

Based on the review of literature the following hypotheses were formulated:

1. There will be a significant positive effect of VM on the QOL of inmates of Tihar Jail.
2. VM will have a significant positive effect on the SWB of inmates.
3. Criminal Propensity of inmates will decrease significantly after attending the course of VM.

4. There will be significant difference in SWB and CP of experimental (Vipassana) group and control (non-Vipassana) group.
5. Male and female inmates will differ significantly in SWB and CP, as a result of VM. Rationale behind the formulation of the hypotheses:

The training in Vipassana involves awareness of respiration which involves continuous observation of the natural flow of incoming and outgoing breath. This enables the mind to become concentrated and tranquil. Such a person can exercise greater control over his/her mind. Vipassana involves purification of mind through enhanced awareness which in turn helps an individual inculcate and attitude of non-reactive observation. Thus when feelings of negative emotions, *i.e.* anger, aggression, fear, insecurity etc. arise, the individual can handle them better. The hypotheses are supported by a few researches done using the technique of Vipassana and other forms of meditation on the levels of anxiety, aggression, hopelessness etc. (Kannapann & Kalliappan, 1983; Jin, 1992; Chandiramani, Verma, Dhar and Aggarwal, 1994).

Method of Study

Research design:

The research design, sample characteristics, tools of measurement and statistical analysis for the study are given below.

Both control group and 'before and after' experimental designs were used to find out the effect of VM on QOL, SWB, and Criminal Propensity (CP) of Tihar Jail inmates. The Experimental group was exposed to VM where as the control group had no exposure to VM. The participants of the VM (experimental group) were also tested on the above variables before and after they were exposed to VM. The scores of the experimental and the control groups as well as before and after their (experimental group) exposure to VM were compared to find out the effect of VM. This study was carried out in five sub-groups (study 1, study 2, study 3, study 4, and study 5).

The first study (study 1) was carried out on male adolescents randomly selected from Ward 7, and 3 of Jail No. 5. The sample consists of 45 participants each from Vipassana and Non-Vipassana group. The experimental group was the Vipassana group. The participants were tested on Quality of Life, Subjective Well-being and Criminal Propensity.

As the researchers found certain anomalies in the first study, they decided to conduct the study again. They decided to drop the Life Satisfaction Questionnaire (LSQ) in later studies, as the participants had faced difficulties in understanding it. Also the other two questionnaires (Subjective Well-being and Criminal Propensity) were made simple through translation. In the study, the number of participants in experimental group (Vipassana group) was 49, and the number of participants in the control group (Non-Vipassana group) was 39.

Study 2 was conducted on female inmates in Jail No. 1. Thirty participants were taken in both the experimental group and the control group each. The experimental group participated in a 10-day Vipassana course. They were tested before and after the Vipassana course, and their scores on Subjective Well-being and Criminal Propensity were compared. These scores of the experimental group were also compared with that of the control group.

Study 3 was conducted on a group of adolescents who volunteered to undergo VM course. A pre-post comparison of their scores on the selected variables was made.

Study 4 and 5 were similar to the study 3. Both were before-after tests on selected variables on adolescent inmates.

Sample

For study 1, the experimental group was selected from among adolescent inmates who had undergone Vipassana meditation earlier. They are termed the Vipassana group (N = 45). The control group (N = 45) was selected randomly from inmates who did not attend Vipassana. Both the groups belonged to same age groups (18-25 years) and similar level of educational background. They were compared on their scores in the relevant scales *i.e.*, Subjective Well-being and Criminal Propensity.

For study 2, the experimental group consisted of 30 female inmates who had attended Vipassana course. They were tested on the scales just before and again after the Vipassana course. A control group (N = 30) was also randomly selected from among those who did not participate in Vipassana Meditation course. Their scores were compared to those of experimental group's pre and post meditation scores.

For study 3, the experimental group (Vipassana) consisted of 49 participants and the Control group (non-Vipassana) consisted of 39 participants. Both the groups were male Adolescents.

For study 4, the sample size was 26 (male adolescents). This was a before-and-after Study.

In study 5, there were 28 adolescent male participants. This was also a before-and-after Study.

Data collection was done in a very disciplined manner with the help of volunteers - mostly old Vipassana meditators including a few inmates.

Tools

1. The Subjective Well -being Scale (Nagpal and Sell, 1985) was used to measure Subjective Well-being. It has 40 items (Appendix 1-a). This scale has high inter-rater reliability, inter-scores reliability, and test-retest reliability. The scale has been found to be highly significant and satisfactory in validity. Subjective Well-being has been reported as a composite measure of independent feelings about a variety of life concerns, in addition to an overall feeling about life in positive and negative terms, *i.e.*, general well-being and ill-being. Not surprisingly, general well-being in its positive affect and, to a somewhat lesser degree, its negative affect appear to be stable over time to an extent that they can probably be called personality traits. The Subjective Well-being Inventory (SUBI) is designed to

measure feelings of well-being or ill-being as experienced by an individual, or a group of individuals in various day-to-day life concerns. The Inventory measures 11 factorial dimensions, viz. (1) General well-being-positive affect (2) Expectation-achievement Congruence (3) Confidence in coping (4) Transcendence (5) Family group support (6) Social support (7) Primary group concern (8) Inadequate mental mastery (9) Perceived ill-health (10) Deficiency in social contacts (11) General well-being-negative affect. The sample for this study consists of prisoners. Few items (questions) from the original scale are not applicable to prisoners. Through proper analysis those questions which are not suitable to prison life are selectively removed from the original list. The new questionnaire contains 30 items (see Appendix 1-b).

2. Quality of Life: The term 'Quality of Life (QOL)' is a new name for the earlier terms such as 'general welfare' and 'social well-being'. QOL is defined as the degree of excellence of one's life that contributes to satisfaction and happiness and benefits mental health. The concept of QOL is subjective. QOL of an individual would be affected by a number of factors, particularly by the significant positive and negative life events. These life events may be related either to his family or society or community where he lives or his own personal life (Verma, 1996). In this study Life Satisfaction Scale (PGI, Chandigarh, 1986) has been used to measure QOL. The concept of Life Satisfaction (LS) is very similar in meaning to QOL. LS measures the same psychological functions as that of QOL. (PGI, Chandigarh 1986) Life Satisfaction Scale is a reliable and valid scale (Appendix-2).

3. Criminal Propensity Scale (C): The Criminal Propensity Scale (C) (Appendix-3b) has been prepared by Sanyal and Kathpalia (1999), on the basis of Eysenckian theory (Appendix-3a). It is a 40-item scale. Studies based on

Eysenck Personality Questionnaire have revealed that criminals score significantly high on psychoticism and neuroticism score and low on the lie score, unlike that of control group of non-criminals. Eysenck (1976) described the criminals to be on Psychopathic gradient *i.e.*, they showed high Neuroticism, Extroversion and Psychoticism and low on Social Desirability (L). 'C' Scale has been developed for the sole purpose of Indian setting, and is hypothesized to predict the criminal prone behaviour in individuals. It is claimed that the 'C' Scale is the first of its type adapted and applied in the Indian setting. Subdimensions of 'C' are given below:

- **Psychoticism:** A factor developed by Eysenck for distinguishing the three groups of normal, schizophrenic, and manic depressive individuals from each other. Two terms that are closely identified with psychosis are insanity and dementia.
- **Neuroticism:** A functional mental disorder characterized by a high level of anxiety and other distressing emotional symptoms, such as morbid fears, obsessive thoughts, compulsive acts, somatic reactions, dissociative states, and depressive reactions. The symptoms do not involve gross personality disorganization, total lack of insight, or loss of contact with reality, and are generally viewed as exaggerated, unconscious methods of coping with internal conflicts and the anxiety they produce. Neuroticism implies proneness to neurosis; also, a mild condition of neurosis. Neuroticism is one of two major dimensions in Eysenck's factor theory of personality, the other being introversion-extroversion.
- **Lie:** It is a dimension in Eysenck's factor theory of personality. Lying means making false statements with conscious intent to deceive. Nonpathological lying is often found in children or adults seeking to avoid punishment or to save others from distress ('white lies'). Pathological

lying is a major characteristic of the antisocial personality. When lying behaviour reaches excess then it is considered to be an abnormal behaviour.

- **Extraversion:** Noting that some people live within themselves and others only in their converse with other people, Jung postulated two great types characterized by the inward or the outward turning of the libido, by preoccupation with the world of the self or by preoccupation with social reality. This outward turning of the "libido", or "preoccupation with social reality" or in broader sense "love for others" is known as extroversion. This personality characteristic, when present in an excess in a person results in same form of abnormality.

The Criminal Propensity Scale has been designed for the Indian setting, which may be useful in contributing to predict the criminal prone behaviour in individuals. Researchers observed that the inmates had some difficulty in understanding the meaning of some of the questions. Thus the scale was further simplified through change in language and two items from the original scale (Appendix-3b) were dropped. This modified scale (Appendix- 3c) was finally used in the present study.

Statistical Analysis

The statistical analysis was carried out in data in order to test all the hypotheses framed. In the present study various univariate statistical techniques such as mean, standard deviation and 't' tests were used to analyze the data.

RESULTS AND DISCUSSION

The first study was conducted on the adolescent prisoners on 19th of June 1999. The purpose of this particular study was to see the difference in scores on Subjective Well-being, Criminal Propensity and Life Satisfaction, between inmates, who had prior practice of Vipassana meditation (experimental group), and inmates who did not attend Vipassana. The analysis and results of the scores of these two groups are given below:

Study 1

Table 1: Significance of difference between mean scores on Life Satisfaction between Vipassana (N = 45) and Non-Vipassana (N = 45) groups in Tihar jail.

Vipassana- XA	Non-Vipassana- XB	-XD	T
58.57	56.51	2.06	0.79

to btained = 0.79

Degrees of Freedom (DF) = 88

Examining the one-tailed tcriticals at 88 degrees of freedom: tcriticals .01 level 2.37 > 0.79

Degrees of freedom (df) = 88

Examining the one-tailed t at 88 degrees of freedom: t .01 level 2.37>0.79. It is concluded that though the sample which practised Vipassana had a larger score on LS scale than Non-Vipassana group, the difference was not statistically significant.

The results did not come as expected. The scores on this scale by the two groups did not differ significantly. It was later known through analysis that both the groups faced problems in understanding and comprehending the meaning and implication of the items in the Scale. As pointed out by volunteers who helped fill the questionnaires, most of the participants were illiterate, and they could not do the fine distinction on 5-point scale needed in this questionnaire. Due to this reason this questionnaire was dropped in the later studies.

Table 2: Significance of difference between mean scores on Subjective Well-being between Vipassana group (N = 45) and Non-Vipassana group (N = 45).

Vipassana	Non-Vipassana		
-	-	-	t
X1	X2	X1-X2	
68.35	62.84	5.51	3.47

to btained = 3.47

Degrees of Freedom (DF) = 88

Examining the one-tailed tcriticals at 88 degrees of freedom: tcriticals.01 level 2.37 < 3.47

It is concluded that the sample which practised Vipassana scored significantly higher on subjective well being than the control group which did not practice Vipassana. The two groups differ significantly at P<.01 The hypothesis No. 1 stands validated. It appears that practice of Vipassana brings mental balance, calm, proper self-analysis, positive thinking and responsibility to the Vipassana practitioners.

Table 3: Significance of difference between mean scores on Criminal Propensity between Vipassana (N = 45) and Non-Vipassana (N = 45) group

A)

Criminal Propensity	*Vipassana -XA*	*Non-Vipassana -XB*	*Mean Difference -XA - XB*
Lie	6.90	6.90	0
Psychoticism	3.13	2.70	0.43
Extroversion	5.73	5.40	0.33
Neuroticism	4.60	6.29	-1.69
Total	20.36	21.29	-0.93

(B)

-XA	-XB	SXA	SXB	t
20.36	21.29	4.76	2.98	0.63

to btained = 0.63

Degrees of Freedom (DF) = 88

Examining the one-tailed t criticals at 88 degrees of freedom: t criticals .01 level 2.37 > 0.63.

It is concluded that the group which practised Vipassana, though scored lower in Criminal Propensity than Non-Vipassana group, the difference was not significant. It was hypothesized that Vipassana group will score less on Criminal Propensity than the Non-Vipassana group. But result did not come as was expected. Scores of both the groups did not differ significantly. Several causes were identified for this result. First, the Hindi version was translated from Eysenck Personality Questionnaire. Participants could not understand the meaning of many of the questions. Almost fifty percent of the participants were either illiterate or very lowly qualified. It was felt that many items should be made very simple, so that the participants will fully understand the questions. Accordingly questions were made simpler after thorough analysis. Three of the questions which were not suitable for the prison life were dropped and the new simplified questionnaire contained 37 items instead of 40 in the original one.

Study 2

The second study was conducted among female inmates of Tihar Jail to evaluate the effect of Vipassana meditation on their Subjective Well-being and Criminal Propensity. An experimental group was selected, which had prior familiarity with Vipassana. A control group was also selected, which did not have any prior familiarity with Vipassana. Both were administered Subjective Well-being and Criminal Propensity Questionnaires. The experimental group was again tested after undergoing a 10-day Vipassana course. The results are given below:

Table 4: Significance of difference between mean scores on Subjective Well-being Scale, before and after attending the Vipassana course.

N = 30

-X1	-X2	-XD(Ê D/N)	SDD	-S x D	t
59.13	64.47	5.33	10.43	1.94	2.75

to btained = 2.75

Degrees of Freedom (DF) = 29

Examining the one-tailed t criticals at 29 degrees of freedom: t criticals .01 level 2.46 < 2.75

It is concluded that the group which attended the Vipassana meditation showed significant improvement in their scores on

Subjective Well-being Scale. The post Vipassana score marked a significant increase over the pre Vipassana score on Subjective Well-being. This implies that the Vipassana course had a significant and positive effect on the Subjective Well-being of female prisoners.

Table 5: Significance of difference between mean scores on Criminal Propensity, before and after attending Vipassana course.

N = 30

Criminal Propensity	*-XA (Pre)*	*-XB (Post)*	*- -XA - XB(Ê D/N)*
Lie	7.10	6.37	0.73
Psychoticism	2.07	2.40	-0.33
Extroversion	5.70	5.37	0.33
Neuroticism	6.80	5.63	1.17
Total	21.67	19.77	1.90

B)

N = 30

-XA (Pre)	-XB (Post)	-XB(Ê D/N)	SDD	-S x D	t
21.67	19.77	1.9	4.03	0.75	2.54

t obtained = 2.54

Degrees of Freedom (DF) = 29

Examining the one-tailed t criticals at 29 degrees of freedom: t criticals .01 level 2.46 < 2.54

With 29 degrees of freedom t = 2.46 for P = .01 (one-tailed). The calculated value of t, *i.e.* 2.54 exceeds this and is therefore significant. The means of the two conditions differ significantly.

The pre and post scores of experimental group on Criminal Propensity was found to differ significantly at P < .01 level. After attending the VM course the Criminal Propensity of inmates decreased. This implies that VM can help in checking the tendency to commit crime. One particular observation was that Vipassana course brought down scores on all the subdimensions of 'C' Scale except one *i.e.*, psychoticism.

Table 6: Difference between mean scores in Criminal Propensity between Vipassana (post) Group (N =30) and Non-Vipassana group (N =30)

N = 30

Criminal Propensity	*-XB*	*-XC*	*- -XB - XC*
Lie	6.37	8.15	-1.78
Psychoticism	2.40	2.13	0.27
Extroversion	5.37	3.47	1.90
Neuroticism	5.63	7.32	-1.69
Total	19.77	21.07	-1.30

7: Significance of difference between mean scores on Criminal Propensity between Vipassana group and Non-Vipassana group

N = 30

-XB	-XC	SXB	SXC	t
19.77	21.07	3.23	2.79	-2.207

to btained = -2.207

Degrees of Freedom (DF) = 60

Examining the one-tailed t criticals at 60 degrees of freedom: t criticals .01 level 2.39 > 2.21 The calculated value of t is slightly less than the required value (2.39) and is therefore not significant at this level. The calculated value of 't' exceeds this and is therefore significant at this level. The means of the two groups differ significantly. This implies that Vipassana group showed less tendency to commit crime than their counterparts in Non-Vipassana group, though the confidence level of this assertion is a bit lower.

The two conditions differ at mean level but the difference is not significant. It was expected that since the experimental group would score less on Criminal Propensity than the control group. But the results showed that the control group scored lower than the experimental group, though the difference was not significant. The experimental group has scored less in three subdimensions of 'C' *i.e.*, Lie, Psychoticism, Neuroticism, but scored substantially more on Extraversion than that of control group. This one big difference brought the total score against the hypothesis that the experimental group would score less on 'C' than control group.

Table 8: Difference between mean scores on criminal propensity of experimental (pre) and control group.

N=30

Criminal Propensity	*-XA*	*-XC*	*- -XA - Xc(Ê D/N)*
Lie	7.10	8.15	-1.05
Psychoticism	2.07	2.13	-0.06
Extroversion	5.70	3.47	2.23
Neuroticism	6.80	7.32	-0.52
Total	21.67	21.07	0.60

This could be attributed to the fact that the experimental group, though familiar with Vipassana, has a large number of people who are not able to maintain the continuity of their practice. Consequently the salutary effects of VM practice wane. This is corroborated by the results of the comparison between Non-Vipassana group and the experimental group just after they had done a course (Tables 6a, 6b), where the difference is statistically significant.

Table 9: Significance of difference between mean scores on a Subjective Well-Being Scale between the Vipassana group (post)(experimental group - XB) and the control group (XC).

nXB=30

nXC=32

N=62

-XB)	-XB	-XD	S2B	S2C	t
64.47	57.66	6.81	92.45	-74.99	11.15

to btained = 11.15

Degrees of Freedom (DF) = 60

At .01 level, t criticals (DF = 60) = 2.39 < 11.15

It is evident from table 8 that the mean difference in the scores of Subjective Well-being between experimental group and control group is significant at 0.01 level. This suggests that VM has a positive effect on the SWB of inmates.

Table 10: Significance of the mean scores on a Subjective Well-Being Scale between the Vipassana group (pre) (XA) and the control group (XC).

N = 62

-XA	-XC	-XD	S2A	S2C	t
59.13	57.66	1.47	112.18	-74.99	1.497

to btained = 1.497

At .01 level, t criticals (DF = 60) = 2.39 > 1.497

(Two-tailed) P < .01

At .05 level, t criticals (DF = 60) = 2.00 > 1.497

It is concluded that the two conditions do not differ significantly.

The result shows that though the experimental group which had prior familiarity with Vipassana meditation has scored little more than the control group, the mean difference between these two groups is not significant. Here again the results have the same pattern as with Criminal Propensity and the reasons given above are applicable here too.

Study 3

This was the repeat study done in October, 1999 using the questionnaires made simple through retranslation. The Life Satisfaction Scale was dropped from the study. Here special care was taken to ensure that the participants fully understood the questions, before giving answers to them. Sufficient number of volunteers were employed to take care of illiterate participants. The results are given below.

Table 11: Significance of mean score difference on Criminal Propensity between Vipassana and Non-Vipassana groups.

Criminal Propensity	*Non-Vipassana*	*Vipassana*	*-XD*
Lie	6.95	6.31	0.64
Psychoticism	2.38	2.12	0.26
Extroversion	6.18	4.94	1.24
Neuroticism	6.18	4.94	1.24
Total	21.69	19.31	2.38

10b:

nXa = 39

nXb = 49

-XA	-XB	-XD	S2A	S2B	t
21.69	19.31	2.38	5.44	20.54	2.83

At .01 level, t criticals (DF = 86) = 2.37 < 2.83

P < .01

It is concluded that subjects who have done Vipassana meditation have scored less on Criminal Propensity than the control group, who have not done Vipassana. Vipassana group has scored significantly lower than the Non-Vipassana groups on this scale. It was hypothesized that Vipassana group will show less Criminal Propensity than the Non- Vipassana group. The result confirmed this hypothesis. 'C' Scale has four subdimensions *i.e.*, Psychoticism, Extroversion and Neuroticism. The Vipassana group has scored less than the Non- Vipassana group on all these subdimentions. This result suggests that Vipassana has lowering effect on Criminal Propensity.

It is concluded that subjects who have undergone VM course have scored more on Subjective Well-being than the control group, which have not undergone Vipassana course. And this difference is statistically significant. Vipassana has brought a better sense of Subjective Well- being to its practitioners. The result came as was expected.

Table 12: Significance of mean difference on Subjective Well-being between Vipassana and Control (Non-Vipassana) groups

(Non-Vipassana) nXa = 39

(Non-Vipassana) nXb = 49

-XA	-XB	-XD	S2A	S2B	t
60.44	66.55	6.11	127.58	77.27	2.704

At .01 level, (one-tailed) t criticals (DF = 86) = 2.37 < 2.704

Study 4

Study 4 was conducted in the month of December 1999. It was a before-and-after test. The adolescent group was administered Subjective Well-being (SWB) and Criminal Propensity (CP) questionnaires both before and after the Vipassana course. Effort was made to make the data collection procedure more disciplined. The results are shown below.

Table 13: Significance of difference between mean scores on Criminal Propensity Scale before and after attending the Vipassana course.

Participants	*Conditions*	*Mean*	*Mean Difference*	*'t' Value*
N=26	Before	18.19	-0.43	0.29
	After	18.62	tobtained = 0.29	

Degrees of Freedom (DF) = 25

t criticals 0.01 level (one-tailed) = 2.48 < 0.29

Table 14: Significance of difference between mean scores on Subjective Well-being before and after attending the Vipassana course

Pre	Post	Difference	't' Value
66.26	66.46	0.20	0.44

to btained = 0.44

Degrees of Freedom (DF) = 25

t criticals 0.01 level (one-tailed) = 2.48 < 0.44

As seen from Tables 12 & 13, the results are not as expected. In fact there is an increase in CP score. Though there is a slight increase in the SWB score, it is far too small to be significant. In order to identify the possible reasons, detailed discussions were held with the course management and it was discovered that there had been severe intra-camp disturbances during the VM and some participants had to be expelled. These disturbances may not have allowed the remaining participants to practice seriously, and so they could not benefit to the extent possible.

Study 5

Study 5 was conducted in the month of March 2000. It was a before-and-after test. Participants were adolescents. The group was administered Subjective Well-being and Criminal Propensity (CP) questionnaires, both before and after the meditation course. Data collection was conducted in a disciplined manner. Scores are given below:

Table 15: Significance of difference between mean scores on Criminal Propensity before and after attending Vipassana (N=28)

Participants	*Conditions*	*Mean*	*Mean Difference*	*Variance*	*'t' Value*
N=26	Before	18.19	-0.43	27.71	0.29
	After	18.62		22.88	

tobtained = 1.689

Degrees of Freedom (DF) = 27

Examining the one-tailed tcriticals at 27 degrees of freedom: tcriticals .01 level 2.47 > 1.69 It is concluded that the group which attended the Vipassana course did score less (mean) on Criminal Propensity but the difference was not statistically significant.

Examining the one-tailed tcriticals at 27 degrees of freedom: tcriticals .01 level 2.47 > 1.16 It is observed that there is slight increase in the SWB score of participants after they were exposed to VM, though the difference was not significant. It implies that though sustained practise of VM even better result could be achieved.

Table 16: Significance of difference between mean scores on Subjective Well-being Scale, Before and after attending the course.

N=28

Before	After	Mean Difference	Variance Before/After	't' Value
63.89	65.53	1.65	100.39/81.66	1.16

tobtained = 1.16

Degrees of Freedom (DF) = 27

The following conclusions represent the findings of the study.

1. The first and second hypotheses were accepted since level of Criminal Propensity came down and that of Subjective Well-being went up after practicing Vipassana, among female inmates.
2. The second hypothesis that Vipassana group (who have done Vipassana course earlier) would score less on Criminal Propensity and more on Subjective Well-being than Non-Vipassana group have come significant only in case of male inmates. Male inmates of Vipassana group scored less on Criminal Propensity and more on Subjective Well-being than Non-Vipassana group. The difference was statistically significant. The same did not hold for female inmates. Though the Vipassana group (female) scored more on Subjective Well-being than control group (Non-Vipassana), the difference was not statistically significant. Surprisingly the Vipassana group (female) scored more on Criminal Propensity than that of control group, when it was expected that Vipassana group would score significantly less on Criminal Propensity than the control group. It implies that female inmates benefited less from doing Vipassana course. It might be the case that they could not comprehend the core meaning and philosophy of Vipassana meditation. Some of the participants of the

Vipassana group complained that during the Vipassana session they felt shortage of space. They were confined to a small place for which they could not keep proper distance from each other and instinctively communicated with each other. The female group reported and increase in the feelings of positive emotions such as, hopefulness, self control, conformity, compassion, and mental peace after doing Vipassana course.

It was also decided to study a select group of inmates (N = 18 male) who had done several Vipassana courses during the span of last few years, and had been selected to undergo a 20-day meditation course, which is one of the more advanced meditation courses in Vipassana. The researchers talked to this group of senior Vipassana practitioners (seniority not in the sense of age, but in the sense of number of courses attended), and asked them several important questions about their experience with Vipassana regarding feelings, attitude, friendship, health, and mental peace. As a trial, these students were also requested to fill the SWB scale before the beginning of the 20-day camp. The mean value was extremely high (78 in a maximum possible score of 90) clearly showing that their sustained practise had benefited them immensely.

This was all before they attended the 20-day Vipassana course. After they underwent this course, the researchers again went to them and discussed several matters concerning life, emotion, society, family, responsibility, health, and mental peace. They were also requested to share their thoughts with other inmates and jail officials. It was felt by the researchers that the 20- day Vipassana course had brought further positive change in their over all personality and attitude towards life. The 20-day course consolidated well, what they had already gained from practicing Vipassana for several years. Such was the impact of their presentation that The Additional D.G (prisons) who was present during this feed back session remarked that to him it seemed as if he was sitting in a temple and listening to some saintly people, rather than sitting in a prison. And the Principal Investigator of this Project was also motivated so much that she sat in a VM course soon thereafter. In short, Vipassana meditation has been found to be effective not only in reducing Criminal Propensity, and increasing Subjective Well-being but also in bringing deeper level overall positive change in personality and attitude towards life and society. The benefits of Vipassana are many. But the same can be achieved only through sustained practice.

Limitations of the Study

1. Ideally, the researchers should have full control over the physical and social environment of the participants, with no one interfering or doing anything to modify the impact of corrective efforts. Unfortunately, this could not be ensured fully, although the authorities did their best to cooperate in this regard. Too much physical proximity among meditators proved to be detrimental to maintenance of silence in case of females.
2. Since many (more than 50%) of the participants in both experimental and control groups were illiterate, they faced serious difficulties in comprehending the real meaning and implication of the individual questions in the questionnaire, even if the researchers made translational simplification of the questions twice during the study.
3. Observations about the regular practice/non-practice of Vipassana could not be regularly made. Participants' overall behaviour patterns were also not recorded in the present study.

REFERENCES

Ahmad Safia., Ahmjad Hanon., & Sumboo S.S.(1988) Personality study of individuals regularly practicing transcendental meditation technique. *Journal of Personality and Clinical Studies*, 4(1), 89-92.

Aminabhavi Vijayalaxmi A. (1996). Effect of yogic practice on attitudes toward yoga and menta health of adults. Praachi *Journal of Psycho-Cultural Dimentions*, 12(2), 117-120.

Chandiramani, K., Verma, S. K., & Dhar, P. L. (1995). Psychological effects of Vipassana on Tihar Jail inmates. Research Report, Vipassana Research Institute.

Chaudhary, L. (1999). Effectiveness of Vipassana meditation as a technique of stress management and reformation among adolescent prisoners. Unpublished dissertation.

Deepak, K. K., Manchanda, S. K., & Maheshwari, M. C. (1994). Meditation improves clinico- electroencephalographic measures in drug resistant epileptics. *Biofeedback and Self Regulation*, 19(1), 25-40.

Eber, H. W. (1975). *Some psychometric correlates of inmates behaviour*. Georgia Department of Corrections, Atlanta.

Eysenck, S. B., & Sysenck, H. J. (1975). Manual of the EPQ (Personality Questionnaire). London: Hodder and Stoughton Educational; San Diego: Educational and Industrial Testing Service.

Goldenson, R. M. (1984). *Longman Dictionary of Psychology and Psychiatry*. Longman Publishing Co., New York.

Hammersle, R., & Cregan (1986). *Drug addiction and Vipassana Meditation*. 'A Reader': International Seminar, Vipassana Research Institute, 211-214.

Jhansi, Rani N., & Krishna Rao, P. V. (1996). Meditation and attention regulation. *Journal of Indian Psychology*, 14(1&2), 26-30.

Jin, Putia. (1992). Efficacy of Tai Chi, brisk walking, meditation, and reading in reducing mental and emotional stress. *Journal of Psychosomatic Research*, 36(4), 361-370.

Khurana, A. (1996). Effect of Vipassana Meditation on Quality of Life of Undertrials, in Vimla Veeraraghavan (Ed.) *Certain Perspectives of Quality of Life*. Krishna publishers, Delhi.

Khurana, A. (1999). Vipassana Meditation and Subjective Well-being of undertrials. *Indian Journal of Criminology*, 20-25.

Kisker, G.W. (1972). Disorganized Personality. 3 ed., McGraw Hill, Inc, Japan.

Kishore Chandirimani, S. K. Verma, P. L. Dhar and N. Aggarwal. (1994). Psychological effects of Vipassana on Tihar Jail inmates: A preliminary report on Vipassana - Its relevance to the present world - An International Seminar, April, 1994.

Krishna, Usha. (1993). Adolescent's delinquent behaviour and personality. *Indian Journal of Criminology*, 21(3), 90-94.

Mehrabian, A., & O' Reilly, E. (1990). Analysis of personality measures in terms of basic dimension of temperament. *Journal of personality of board psychology*, 38, 492-503.

Milbrath, L. (1979). Policy relevant quality of life research, Annals, *AAPSS*, 444, 32-45.

Moudgil, A. C., Verma, S.K.& Kaur, Kuldip (1986) P.G.I. Quality of Life Scale (Revised Form). *Indian J. Clinical Psychology*, 13: 175-184

Nagpal, R., & Sell, H. (1985). Subjective Well-being, SEARO Regional Health Paper No. 7. *World Health Organization*, New Delhi.

Osofsky HJ. (1996). Psychiatry behind the walls: mental health services in jails and prisons. *Bull Menninger Clin*, 60(4), 464-479.

Phares, E. J. (1968). Differential utilization of information as a function of internal-external control. *Journal of Personality*, 36, 649-662.

Ryff, C. D., Keyes, C. L., & Corey, L. M. (1995). The structure of psychology well-being Revisited. *Journal of Personality and Social Psychology*, 69(4), 719-727.

Sahoo, F. M., & Bidyadhars (1988). The subjective components of psychological well-being in Indian professions. An idiographic investigation using the lens model. Unpublished Dissertation, Utkal University, Bhubaneswar, India.

Sanyal, S. & Kathapalia, V. (1999). *Development of the 'C' Scale on the basis of Eyesenckian theory* (Criminal Propensity Scale).

Selvamurthy, W. (1993). Yoga and stress management: Physiological perspectives. Proceedings of the Indian Science Congress, Part IV, 169.

Shah, (1976). *Impact of Vipassana Meditation on prisoners.* College of Social Work, Mumbai (A Report).

Sharma Mahendra. P., Kumariah, V., Mishra, H., & Baroohi J. P. (1990). Therapeutic effects of Vipassana meditation in tension headache. *Journal of Psychology and Clinical Studies*, 6(2), 201-206.

Unnithan T. K. N., & Ahuja, R. (1977). Prisoners' meditation camp: A sociological analysis. *The Maha Bodhi Journal*, 85, 303-309.

●●●

21

Occupational Stress Management – Through Meditation

M.A. Bhardwaj

We are living in an era of growing complexities and pressures where human constitution and capacities are being taxed severely. 'Stress' is the most frequently used concept in today's management lexicon. Stress at work place means raising tempers, lowering productivity and having an insider's impact on both morale and lines. Margolis and Kores (1974) defined job stress as a condition worth interacting with worker's characteristics to disrupt psychological and physiological homeostatis . Research studies by Bond, Galivsky & Swanbeing 1998, Kemp 1994, Pestonjee & Muncherij 1999, Yoko *et. al.,* 1997 have revealed that when employees experience stress, it leads to many physical and mental health problems and ultimately leads to affect negatively job performance. There are various coping strategies of stress which focus either organizational factors, or individual factors. Individual focused coping strategies try to change an individual attitudes and attributes. Today many people are engaged in traditional Indian therapies such as Yoga & meditation in order to cope up with stress. Alongwith this rational emotive therapy, personal skills awareness biofeedback, interpersonal awareness, time management are also effective ways and techniques of stress management. Studies by Higgirs & Nancy 1986, Kagav & Kagav 1995 support this.

- Meditation is a very effective method of relaxation. Meditation is basically focusing thoughts on one relaxing thing for a sustained period of time. It makes your mind diverted and relaxed and at the same time gives your body time to relax and recuperate and clear away toxins that may have built up through stress.

Meditation is particularly useful when-

(1) You have been under long term stress.

(2) You have been worrying about problems.

When mediation is used it can:

(1) Slow breathing.

(2) reduce blood pressure.

(3) reduce anxiety.

(4) eliminate stressful thoughts.

(5) help in clear thinking.

(6) reduce irritability.

Various meditation techniques are:

(a) *Breathing:* focusing your attention on breathing by counting on breaths in and out.

(b) *Focusing on an Object*: Here the attention is completely focused on an object such as a flower, candle flames, flowing designs.

(c) *Focusing on a Sound:* The classic example is the Sanskrit word 'Om' meaning perfection.

(d) *Imagery:* Creating a mental image of a pleasant and relaxing place in your mind. Involving all your senses in imagery.

In all these methods it is important to keep your attention focused.

Objective

The present study examined the effectiveness of meditation in managing occupational stress of industrial employees (executives).

METHOD

Sample

The sample consisted of 50 executives working in corporate sectors (IT & marketing sectors) in Mumbai, Maharashtra. The age range was 30 to 40. All the participants were experiencing high level of occupational stress. The sample was divided randomly in to two groups: - Meditation group (N=25) and Control group (N-25). Two subjects from the meditation group left the study.

Tools

For the present research study, Occupational Stress Index (OSI) by Shrivastava and Singh (1981) was used. The reliability of the test is .90 & the validity is .59.

Method of Meditation

Meditation is an active process, which seeks to exclude outside thoughts by concentrating on all mental faculties on the subject of meditation. In the training /intervention programme, the selected sample was given training in meditation (20-30 min.) for four months.

Procedure

Initially before starting meditation training, the participants in the mediation group were oriented towards job stress and consequences. Then the experts in the meditation gave them training of meditation twice in week for one month and then fortnightly in the remaining three months. After the training, the stress level was measured. The control group was not given any such training.

RESULTS

For the present research study before and after design was used. The level of stress were compared before training and after training of meditation group. Similarly comparisons were made between control and meditation groups. The mean SD and't' values were calculated to measure the significance of difference between the groups.

TABLE 1

Showing the Extent Occupational Stress before and after Training of Meditation Groups N=23.

	Occupational Stressors	*Before training Mean*	*After training Mean*	*'t' Value*
1	Role overload	22.76	21.86	1.59
2	Role ambiguity	14.26	14.42	1.21
3	Role conflict	21.06	18.32	2.59 **
4	Group pressures	18.40	14.00	4.18**
5	Responsibility	10.80	11.34	1.03
6	Under participation	17.17	12.86	0.97
7	Powerlessness	15.80	10.44	3.57**
8	Poor Peer relations	19.56	16.32	2.01*
9	Intrinsic Impoverishment	10.66	10.98	1.85
10	Low status	16.70	8.13	1.06
11	Strenuous work conducting	12.34	11.66	0.46
12	Unprofitability	8.20	7.24	0.91
13	Overall Occupation Stress	148.30	141.27	3.91**

* P<0.05, ** P<0.1

TABLE 2

Showing the Level of Occupational Stress of Control Group N=25. Before and after 4 Months.

	Occupational Stressors	*Before training Mean*	*After training Mean*	*'t' Value*
1	Role overload	21.59	20.49	0.39
2	Role ambiguity	13.29	14.29	0.57
3	Role conflict	21.53	22.08	0.84
4	Group pressures	17.87	16.35	1.04
5	Responsibility	10.89	9.37	0.62
6	Under participation	13.40	12.39	0.54
7	Powerlessness	14.30	13.34	0.07
8	Poor Peer relations	12.46	10.08	1.21
9	Intrinsic Impoverishment	12.64	14.61	1.98*
10	Low status	8.18	9.13	0.04
11	Strenuous work conducting	10.40	10.46	0.02
12	Unprofitability	7.31	7.38	0.01
13	Overall Occupation Stress	147.97	146.83	0.48

* P<0.05

TABLE 3

Showing Comparison Between Control and Meditation Group Before and After 4 Months.

Sl. No.	*Occupational Stress*	*Before*		*“t” value*	*After*		*“t” value*
		Meditation	*Control group N=23*		*Meditation group*	*Control group N=25*	
1	Role overload	22.76	21.59	0.56	21.86	20.49	0.89
2	Role ambiguity	14.26	13.29	0.03	14.42	14.29	0.03
3	Role conflict	21.06	21.53	0.02	18.32	22.08	2.68**
4	Group pressures	18.40	17.87	1.11	14.00	14.35	1.98*
5	Responsibility	10.80	10.89	0.02	11.34	9.37	2.08
6	Under participation	17.17	13.40	2.07*	12.86	12.39	0.02
7	Powerlessness	15.80	14.30	1.12	10.44	13.34	1.97*
8	Poor Peer relations	19.56	12.46	14.28*	16.32	10.08	4.34**
9	Intrinsic Impoverishment	10.66	12.64	1.98*	11.98	14.61	2.02*
10	Low status	6.70	8.18	1.78	8.13	9.13	0.10
11	Strenuous work conducting	12.34	10.40	1.41	11.66	10.46	0.30
12	Unprofitability	8.20	7.31	0.98	7.24	7.38	0.04
13	Overall Occupation Stress		148.30	147.97	1.01	147.2	146.83
2.76**							

*P<0.05, ** P<0.01

From the above results, it can be said that for the meditation group, after the training of meditation there was significant difference with respect to role conflict. (t=2.59 p<0.01), group pressures (t =3.57 p<0.01), poor peer relations (t=2.01 p<0.05) and overall occupational stress (t=3.91 p<0.01). The impact of meditation was significant when the executives were reassessed immediately after training.

On the basis of table no.3, it is apparent that before the meditation training, there were already significant differences between meditation group and control group for the stressors under participation, poor peer relations and intrinsic impoverishment. After the meditation training, the intervention group significantly differed than control group with respect to role conflict group pressure, powerlessness, poor peer relations intrinsic impoverishment and overall occupational stress ($t=2.76$ $p<0.01$). This medicates that there is a noticeable moderating effect of meditation techniques on the level of stress. Practicing meditation made the executives relaxed, more focused, helped in improved concentration. Overall, it can be suggestsed that meditation when practiced regularly and consistently can make desirable modification in the coping style of the employees and so can charge the level of stress experienced.

Industries/ corporate sectors or at any employment setting if such type of individual coping strategies are practiced regularly, they can reduce, prevent or atleast help in moderating the physiological impact of stress, anxiety and frustration of job and life in general.

REFERENCES

Dennis, A. and Gallenag, D. (1993), Job satisfaction and job related stress. *Journal of Behavioral Assessment, 3,* 11-23.

Dhillon, S. (1989), Perceived Organizational Stress and Job Satisfaction. *Journal of Community and Research, 16,* 61-67.

Invancevich, J.M., & Matteson, M.T. (1980). Stress and Work: A managerial Perspective Glenview It. Scott Foresman.

Koteswari, V.B. & Allam, Z. (2005). Job Stress among manager Pracchi Journal of Pschocultural dimensions *21* (1), 13-18.

Pestonje, D.M. & Mukherjee, N. (1999). Stress and coping lesson and suggestsions. *Studies in stress and its management*, New Delhi: Oxford and IBH publishing Co. Pvt. Ltd.

Shrivastava, A.K. & Singh K. (2003). Stress management: A cognitive intervention approach. *Journal of IAAP*, *29*, 31-36.

Yoko, S. and Shigenous, M. (1997). Employees stress status during the 1st decade (1982-92). *Industrial Health, 35,* 441-450.

●●●

Index

●●●